THE ITALIAN COMMUNIST PARTY

The Italian Communist Party

THE CRISIS OF THE POPULAR FRONT STRATEGY

GRANT AMYOT

ST. MARTINS PRESS   NEW YORK

Library of Congress Cataloging in Publication Data

Amyot, Grant.
    The Italian Communist Party.

    Bibliography: p. 232
    Includes index.
    1. Partito communista italiano.   2. Italy—
Politics and government — 1945-   I. Title.

JN5657.C63A788   1981   342.245075   80-26959
ISBN 0-312-43920-2

CONTENTS

PREFACE

Eurocommunism was born in Italy. This is a study of its formulation and development in the Italian context, and the different interpretations it has been given within the Italian Communist Party. But, though it elucidates the meaning of Eurocommunism and its background, and points out how it is an original strategy for the working class of Western Europe (see Chapter 2), it is not primarily a history of political thought; it seeks to explain why the more reformist, right-wing version of Eurocommunism is dominant within the PCI. In order to do so, it concentrates on the challenge offered to the conservative strategy of the PCI leadership by the leftist tendency symbolised by Pietro Ingrao. This group developed a more radical interpretation of the same Euro-communist strategy. They too wished to break with the view of revolution, traditional in the working-class movement, as an assault on the Winter Palace: the seizure of state power by a politicised vanguard which exploits the inevitable crisis of capitalism. But they wished to do so in the name, not of a policy of alliances with the middle classes, but of a revolutionary strategy suited to the conditions of advanced capitalism. While both the Leninist and the social-democratic traditions recognise a radical distinction between economic and political struggles, the Ingrao left sought to eliminate this barrier and give day-to-day economic and social conflicts political content and political objectives (see Chapter 3).

The conservative Eurocommunist ideology which so many cadres had absorbed and the operation of the 'iron law of oligarchy' in the PCI stood in the way of the Ingrao left (see Chapter 1). Nevertheless, it has been able to challenge the leadership on several occasions. Though it has by no means disappeared today, it was closest to gaining a decisive influence within the Party in the early 1960s. For this reason the more detailed empirical section of this study (Chapters 4 to 10) concentrates on this period and the background to it.

I decided to explain the rise and failure of the Ingrao left by means of a study of its support at the level of the cadres of the provincial federations. These are the most active and influential group of Party members, the functionaries and local militants (from 1 to 3 per cent of the membership) who are the backbone of the organisation. This level of the party is also more accessible to investigation, through interviews (see Appendix) and documentary sources, than the rank and file. Furthermore, much evidence about the attitudes of the mass membership can be uncovered through an enquiry focusing on the provincial cadres.

Five provincial federations were selected for detailed research in the light of my hypotheses concerning the causes of the rise of the Ingrao left (outlined in Chapter 4). Thus two provinces that underwent very rapid socio-economic change in the period 1950-66 (Turin and Perugia), one which experienced little transformation (Naples) and two intermediate cases (Modena and Bari) were chosen. And one federation with a large concentration of intellectuals in the PCI (Naples) and one with quite a small number (Modena) were selected, along with three that had a moderate number of them. One 'red' province where the Party was firmly entrenched in local power (Modena) and one where its position was less secure (Perugia) were also chosen. The five federations were sufficiently differentiated along the left-right spectrum, and reasonably well distributed between the north, south and centre of Italy.

Even after the Ingrao left's defeat at the XI Congress of the PCI in 1966, events in Italy and abroad continued to demonstrate the relevance of its analyses and proposals. Chapters 11 to 13 deal with the further development of Eurocommunism by the PCI up to 1979, and the reasons why the right-wing interpretation of that strategy, now embodied in the policy of 'historic compromise', has continued to prevail.

This book is based on a PhD thesis submitted to the University of Reading; the major part of the research was carried out from 1970 to 1973 with the generous assistance of a Canada Council doctoral fellowship. It could not have been written without the comradely co-operation of many officials and members of the PCI, whom I wish to thank most sincerely. A large number of other friends and teachers have helped me at various stages in the work. I am especially grateful to Percy Allum, my doctoral supervisor, for his invaluable guidance and friendship. I should also like to thank in particular Philip Williams, who first directed me towards the study of the PCI, Steve Hellman, for his comments on an earlier draft of this work, and Jock Gunn, for his encouragement and prodding at a crucial moment. Finally, to D.B., who helped and supported me throughout the writing of this book, my debt is unbounded.

Rome

1 THE PARTY AND THE FAILURE OF REVOLUTION IN THE WEST

1. Explanations of the Deradicalisation of Working-class Parties

For the past sixty years socialist militants and theorists have attempted to explain why no revolution has occurred in the advanced capitalist countries. Marx had clearly indicated that the development of capitalism and the sharpening contradiction between capital and labour which accompanied it would create the most propitious conditions for a socialist revolution. He also identified the industrial working class as the principal revolutionary agent, because it was educated and organised by life in the capitalist factory. Most socialists of the II International believed that the economic collapse of capitalism was inevitable (see Chapter 2, Section 1). They expected this economic crisis would provoke a workers' revolution.

The events of the twentieth century seem to have so far disappointed such sanguine hopes. The working class of Europe, with its impressive organisational strength, its social-democratic parties, trade unions and co-operatives, acquiesced in the great capitulation of August 1914 and allowed itself to be led into the First World War. When a socialist revolution did break out, in 1917, it was in backward Russia; and the series of revolutionary uprisings in Europe which followed the war were all eventually crushed. Since that time, all subsequent revolutions have occurred in less developed states – China, Vietnam, Cuba – while the working-class movement of the major capitalist countries has not been able to seize power anywhere. The world economic crisis which began in 1929 did not lead to the expected socialist revolution. Possible opportunities, such as the Popular Front's electoral victories in France and Spain in the 1930s or the anti-fascist Resistance movement in the 1940s, were not exploited. The problem of the socialist revolution in the West is still as relevant as it was when Antonio Gramsci, the Italian Communist leader, posed it in the 1920s. Not only has revolution not taken place, but the prospect of it has even apparently receded, as most mass working-class parties have tended to drift to the right, abandoning a revolutionary position, if they had one, for an accommodation with the capitalist system.

The Leninist tradition offers one explanation of this situation; the working class lacked revolutionary leadership. In the Leninist schema, an economic crisis of itself is not sufficient to generate a socialist revolution – a revolutionary party must also exist, ready to lead the working class when the moment of crisis arrives. If this leadership is lacking, it is because the working-class party has been corrupted in some way: it is dominated by the working-class aristocracy, as Lenin suggested was the case with the socialist parties which supported the war effort in 1914, or it includes non-working-class elements. Another somewhat different explanation of the deradicalisation of working-class parties, which, however, remains within the same problematic, is offered by writers who, noting the growing material affluence of the proletariat and the absence of major economic crises since the Depression, maintain that the working class itself is no longer a revolutionary agent because it has become *embourgeoisé*. More convincing attempts to explain deradicalisation go beyond such largely economic considerations, introducing ideological and political factors as well. Such are, among others, the theories based on the work of Gramsci and Roberto Michels's 'iron law of oligarchy'.

Class Structure

The first group of explanations concentrates on the class structure of capitalist states, and in particular on their working classes and their socialist parties. Lenin's theory of the working-class aristocracy is one such explanation. Up to 1914 he had regarded the centrist groups in European social democracy (e.g. Kautsky in Germany) as genuine revolutionaries; the failure of most socialist parties to oppose the war forced him to radically alter his position. He found the chief cause of reformism in the European working-class movement in imperialism:

> Imperialism, which means the partition of the world, . . . which means high monopoly profits for a handful of very rich countries, creates the economic possibility of bribing the upper strata of the proletariat, and thereby fosters, gives form to, and strengthens opportunism.[1]

The model for this theory was England; Lenin was able to take his cue from some analyses of Marx and Engels, such as that contained *in nuce* in Engels's letter to Marx of 7 October 1858:

> The English proletariat is becoming more and more bourgeois, so that this most bourgeois of all nations is apparently aiming

ultimately at the possession of a bourgeois aristocracy and a bourgeois proletariat *as well as* a bourgeoisie. For a nation which exploits the whole world this is, of course, to a certain extent justifiable.[2]

The consequences were reformism and opportunism in the working-class movement:

This clearly shows the causes and effects. The causes are: (1) exploitation of the whole world by this country; (2) its monopolistic position in the world market; (3) its colonial monopoly. The effects are: (1) a section of the British proletariat becomes bourgeois; (2) a section of the proletariat permits itself to be led by men bought by, or at least paid by, the bourgeoisie.[3]

Lenin here identified two separate, but related, effects of imperialism on the working class of the imperialist countries. First, an 'upper stratum' of the proletariat, which, he is careful to point out, constitutes a minority of the class as a whole, detaches itself from the rest of the class and adopts a bourgeois ideology. In Great Britain this upper stratum 'furnishes the bulk of the membership of cooperatives, of trade unions, of sporting clubs, and of numerous religious sects', and it was enfranchised (1916) while the lower stratum was not. Thus imperialism 'has the tendency to create privileged sections also among the workers, and to detach them from the broad masses of the proletariat'.[4] Second, another section of the working class, while not members of this working-class aristocracy themselves, are led by parties whose leaders are 'bought' by the bourgeoisie. This often involved political privileges, such as peerages, for such leaders.[5] He refers to two letters by Engels, in which he first laments the absence of a workers' party in England and the tendency of the workers to follow the Conservatives and Liberal Radicals, and second castigates 'the worst type of English trade unions which allow themselves to be led by men bought by, or at least paid by, the bourgeoisie'.[6] The non-'aristocratic' elements of the proletariat still have some share, real or imagined, in the profits of imperialism, 'a temporary share now and then', wrote Engels,[7] but above all are often followers of parties or unions whose leaders have been 'bought'.

The theme of the betrayal or 'sell-out' of the social-democratic leadership was popular among Communists because of its polemical value, but cannot be taken seriously as a general explanation of the rightward drift of all social-democratic parties. While many social-democratic leaders (but by no means all) have indeed been 'bought' with peerages, governmental patronage or even personal bribes, the direction of an entire party or movement does not, and cannot, depend on the actions of a few individuals. As for the first effect mentioned by Lenin, that the working-class aristocracy constitutes a mass base of the social-democratic parties, comparative studies of the membership of Communist and social-democratic parties have generally found that the better paid, more highly skilled workers and the worse paid and less skilled were divided roughly evenly between the two.[8] It may be, however, that in some parties the mass of cadres and activists (not simply a few leaders) are members of the 'working-class aristocracy' and exert decisive influence within the party.

Others have explained the rightward movement of socialist parties by the presence within them of *non*-working-class elements. It was, indeed, a standard charge, used by both the left and the right against each other in the disputes within the socialist movement before 1914, to say that the other faction was the representative of bourgeois elements within the party. In general both factions had a considerable number of bourgeois or petty bourgeois in their leadership, while their mass membership remained largely working class.[9] The presence of bourgeois intellectuals as leaders has been so common in the working-class movement that it cannot be associated with either the left or the right. However, the presence of a *mass* of non-working-class members or voters has, on occasion, had some influence on the policies of socialist parties. A classic example was the SPD of Baden and Württemburg in the 1890s and early 1900s. It was driven to the right partly by its peasant and urban petty-bourgeois followers. In considering the Communist parties, which have so assiduously courted the 'middle strata' since 1935, this hypothesis will have to be carefully considered.

Another explanation of reformism based on the class structure of the advanced capitalist states suggests that the working class *as a whole* rather than simply a minority of it, has become *embourgeoisé*. There is a danger of circularity in this argument, but this integration is usually demonstrated by reference to workers' income levels, consumption patterns or political and social attitudes.[10] For some writers this *embourgeoisement* is the result of material prosperity, usually held to be the effect of technical progress rather than of imperialist super-profits, *tout court*; many others, however, cite the pervasive influence of bourgeois ideology and consumerism, amplified by the modern mass media which make the diffusion of these messages technically possible.[11] Such theories, based principally upon observation of the American working class, suggest that the working class is no longer revolutionary and that the same is true of its parties and trade unions. They have been absorbed by the capitalist system, and if there are any revolutionary agents, they must be sought elsewhere. Herbert Marcuse in his later writings suggested that students, the urban sub-proletariat and racial minorities are the revolutionary agents in advanced capitalism — i.e. the most marginalised and 'alienated' from the system.[12] Others have formulated the argument somewhat differently and proposed that the most 'alienated' and oppressed elements *within* the working class, the 'massified' workers, the unskilled, assembly-line proletariat, are the potentially revolutionary elements; this amounts in practice to something similar to Lenin's 'working-class aristocracy' explanation, though it is founded on different grounds.

Another attempt to transfer this analysis based on the theory of alienation into the working class itself can lead, however, to diametrically opposite conclusions. The most alienated, in this interpretation, are those who have the greatest capacities but are frustrated because they cannot use them fully. Therefore a 'new working class', with more technical training and formal education, is the truly revolutionary element because of its understanding of the production process and its desire to control it and direct it to less irrational purposes. The 'new working class' are the 'intellectuals' of the class. One of the most articulate and persuasive exponents of this point of view is the late Serge Mallet.[13] He attributes the bureaucratisation and loss of revolutionary *élan* of the working-class movement to changes in the organisation of work under capitalism, in particular Taylorism and assembly-line production, which produced changes in the structure of the working class. The new 'mass' worker created by this process lost his sense of control over and involvement in the productive process and began to concentrate on improving his lot as a consumer; hence the growth of reformism in both the social-democratic and Communist components of the working-class movement: 'The worker of the era of the mechanization of labour not only, as Marx foresaw, ceases to feel himself an individual producer, but finally ceases to consider himself as a producer at all.'[14]

Mallet sees the revolutionary vanguard of the working class in the technically trained workforce of the most advanced industries: 'The modern working class has an immediate interest in uninterrupted technical development and in its consequences: a substantial reduction in working time, professional re-qualification, the possibility of change, or more varied activity, within the sphere of production.'[15] He also rebuts the objection that this 'new working class' is in fact a working-class aristocracy: they do not reap the surplus profits of colonialism, in fact they appeared at the same time as the colonial empires were disappearing and the capitalism of the metropoles was having to meet more intense competition on world markets.[16] (Lenin often predicted that, with the end of Britain's colonial monopoly and increasing inter-imperialist rivalry, the working-class aristocracy would disappear.) Using these hypotheses, Alain Touraine was able to interpret the events of May-June 1968 in France as a revolt by the professionalised workers and by students who were, to a large degree, future professionalised workers, against the ruling 'techno-bureaucracy'.[17] In conclusion, the evidence for these theories that all or part of the working class has become *embourgeoisé* is inconclusive, and the actions of the French proletariat in 1968 and the Italian in 1969-70 and after tend to undermine them. (We shall return to the Italian case below.)

Ideology

A second group of explanations of the failure of socialist revolution in the West concentrates on the role of ideology. Some theorists, like Marcuse, consider that the all-pervasive dominant ideology has caused the definitive *embourgeoisement* of the working class; many others, however, view the intellectual hegemony of the bourgeoisie over the proletariat as a temporary phenomenon which can be overcome by the working-class movement. In any case, there can be little doubt that it has played an extremely important role in moderating the revolutionary thrust of many socialist parties. For instance, militarism and nationalism influenced many German workers in the pre-1914 period, and no doubt this was one of the reasons for the SPD's 'great betrayal' of 4 August 1914. In Great Britain the ideology of imperialism and chauvinism had a powerful influence on all classes. Its hegemony was all the stronger because the fusion of aristocracy and bourgeoisie had created what was virtually a united ruling class without deep-seated conflicts of interest or major ideological divisions. Faced with a single dominant ideology, incorporating nationalism and an interpretation of British history in which the Crown, the Constitution and parliamentary government were justified and glorified, the working class fell under its sway: hence many of the peculiarities of British Labourism.[18] Similarly, the French workers' movement in the Third Republic was powerfully influenced by bourgeois radicalism, with its Jacobin, nationalist and anti-clerical elements.

The working class, in its infancy at any rate, was obliged to adopt the ideology of the bourgeoisie. For Nicos Poulantzas, this influence may persist for a long time, and affect the working class even in its maturity: '. . . the working class often cannot avoid living after the mode imposed by the dominant ideology, even in its revolt against the existing system'.[19] Gramsci, however, makes this ideological hegemony of the ruling class one of the central features of the 'historic bloc' which allows it to maintain itself. Ideology is the cement of the historic bloc, the group of classes or fractions of classes that support the ruling class. Along with political parties and other institutions of civil society, it holds it together, binding the subordinate classes to the ruling class and ensuring the stability of the whole.

Gramsci uses the term 'ideology' in a very wide sense: 'a conception of the world that is implicitly manifest in art, in law, in economic activity, in all manifestations of individual and collective life'.[20] For him, 'All men are philosophers' because they have a spontaneous philosophy, but he distinguishes between different levels of ideology. Philosophy, the highest, alone aims at a completeness and coherence. It is the most dynamic, and reflects the specific exigencies of ideology. The lower levels – religion, common sense and folklore – are progressively less coherent and sophisticated. Common sense, for instance, is a 'chaotic aggregate of disparate conceptions, and one can find there anything one likes'.[21] All the lower levels contain a great admixture of elements of previous philosophies and religions, which have left 'stratified deposits in popular philosophy'. It is easy to see how the working class could be prevented from reaching a revolutionary consciousness by bourgeois ideology in this wide sense.

In Gramsci's view the working class, as a potentially revolutionary class, goes through several stages of consciousness before reaching the final stage of 'integral autonomy' (revolutionary consciousness). The first is the 'economic-corporative' stage, in which members of the same trade or profession develop a sense of solidarity among themselves, but not with members of other trades. The second is that of class solidarity in the purely economic realm:

Already at this juncture the problem of the State is posed – but only in terms of winning politico-juridical equality with the ruling groups: the right is claimed to participate in legislation and administration, even to reform these — but within the existing fundamental structures.[22]

Gramsci also polemicises with 'theoretical syndicalism', which he considers a product of the trade-unionist mentality. In the third and last stage, revolutionary consciousness, a class not only achieves complete ideological autonomy from the dominant class, but displays an ability to hegemonise other classes by transcending its own narrow, economic interests and taking account of theirs as well.[23] In the first two stages, particularly the second, the working class is not totally subject to the dominant ideology, but embraces a subordinate ideology which allows it to press its demands within the framework of the system.

This subordinate ideology, however, is as effective a barrier to revolution as that of the ruling class. When the workers adopt an 'economistic' ideology of this type,

> The transformation of the subordinate group into a dominant one is excluded, either because the problem is not even considered (Fabianism, De Man, an important part of the Labour Party), or because it is posed in an inappropriate and ineffective form (social-democratic tendencies in general) . . .[24]

This ideology of class solidarity within the existing system is analogous to what Parkin calls the 'subordinate value system' of individuals, 'a moral framework which promotes *accommodative* responses to the facts of inequality and low status'.[25] Trade unionism is a typical expression of this ideology; Parkin calls it a form of 'instrumental collectivism'.

An important element in the transition from an ideology of subordinate class solidarity to a revolutionary world-view is the revolutionary intellectual. For Gramsci the new ideology could be propagated in the working class only by a proletarian party whose 'general staff' was recruited from the traditional intelligentsia. These alone have the innovative capacity to formulate a totally new explanation of society and history, to provide a framework into which the particular experiences of the working class can be fitted.[26] But just as intellectuals can give rise to an autonomous, alternative *Weltanschauung* in the working class and its party, so can they also, as Parkin suggests, replace this ideology with a reformist one, in which case the working class reverts to the state of subordinate class solidarity.[27]

Therefore there can be two explanations of the prevalence of reformist ideology in a working-class party, one relating it to the as yet undeveloped consciousness of the class, the other attributing it to the active role of the party and its intellectuals in introducing a non-revolutionary ideology. The lack of ideological homogeneity of the working class and its party, and the coexistence of several levels of ideology (philosophy, religion, common sense and folklore), make each concrete situation complex.

Organisation

A third group of explanations for deradicalisation is associated with the 'iron law of oligarchy'. In his *Political Parties* Roberto Michels argues that every large organisation, such as a party, inevitably falls under the control of a small minority of its members.[28] In political parties these are the permanent officials and deputies who develop a greater familiarity with party business and to whom the mass membership is in any case usually glad to delegate control. The leaders consolidate their power, using the monopoly of political resources which leadership puts at their disposal. This dominance of the bureaucrats and elected representatives has a powerful conservatising influence on the party. First, it becomes interested in increasing its organisational strength — i.e. in gaining more voters and members — and therefore must moderate its policies in order to appeal to sympathisers or more moderate, hesitating electors. In the same way it often begins to appeal to non-proletarian classes in an effort to improve its electoral position or to reach a majority. (It would be wrong to think that it is a natural tendency of *all* working-class parties to seek a majority in parliament, and to appeal to middle strata or elements of the bourgeoisie on the basis of their own material interests in order to do this[29] — they do so only when other conditions have already driven them towards a reformist position. A salient counter-example is the electoral strategy of the parties of the III International in the period 1919-34.) Secondly, the party, when it has become bureaucratised, becomes much more timid and fearful of the repressive action of the state. The organisation becomes an end in itself, to be protected at all costs.[30]

Michels's thesis has had great influence on all subsequent studies of European socialist parties. It is one of the most persuasive explanations of the deradicalisation of working-class parties yet advanced. But it ignores or discounts the counter-tendencies, the forces which push working-class parties back towards a radical course,

which have their roots in the socio-economic changes and relations
of force between classes in the society in which the party operates.
Michels himself recognised this when he wrote, 'The democratic
currents in history resemble successive waves. They break ever on
the same shoal. They are ever renewed.'[31] But the prevailing tone
of his work is pessimistic, and he does not pay much attention to
the sources of the 'successive waves' of democracy. Not only domestic
changes, but also international influences and events, may give rise
to counter-tendencies. The Russian revolution, whatever its consequences for the internal organisation of the workers' parties, reversed
the drift to the right that was Michels's main preoccupation; whereas
one would expect his thesis to apply *a fortiori* to Communist parties,
where the rules of democratic centralism, including the formal ban
on factions, make the position of the leadership far stronger *vis-à-vis*
the mass membership than in the social-democratic parties which he
studied. Michels's theory is, in the end, probably most persuasive when
used in conjunction with one or more other factors; without them,
the 'iron law of oligarchy' will not hold.

2. The Deradicalisation of the PCI

One of the most successful, and most genuinely radical, of the Western
working-class parties is the Italian Communist Party. In electoral terms
its record is unparalleled: it reached an unprecedented 34.4 per cent of
the popular vote in 1976, falling back to 30.4 per cent in 1979.
Nevertheless, it had by that date substantially abandoned the hopes of
imminent revolution it held in 1921, in favour of another strategy
which envisaged the attainment of socialism through a more gradual
modification of the capitalist system, to be achieved by working
within some of its major institutions. Since 1972 the PCI has explicitly
pursued the objective of a government coalition including itself and
the Christian Democratic Party, the major party of the centre-right.
This was not a radical innovation, but the logical outcome of a strategy
the Party had adopted over thirty years before. Clearly this strategy
could lead to the PCI's integration into the system. That such a danger
is real has been demonstrated by the events since the general election
of 20 June 1976. By its abstention in Parliament the PCI kept the
Christian Democratic cabinet headed by Giulio Andreotti in office.
In return, it extracted few concrete concessions beyond the speakership of the Chamber of Deputies and the chairmanships of some

parliamentary committees. The PCI's abstention in the vote of confidence in the Andreotti government symbolised its moderation (see Chapter 13). But the timing and the causes of this shift to the right are still to be elucidated. We shall examine first these causes, and second the most important attempt to reverse this trend: the movement within the Party in the period 1960-6 in support of a more aggressive, radical policy.

This left-wing tendency is generally known by the name of its most prominent leader, Pietro Ingrao, though it was made up of several groups and currents, which, in part, chose Ingrao as their figurehead. The Ingrao left wanted the PCI to make its immediate objective socialism, rather than an intermediate phase such as 'progressive democracy'. They wanted the Party to assign more importance to the working class and its struggles, and to see these struggles as an integral part of its strategy for socialism. They also called for more internal party democracy and an independent stance in the Sino-Soviet dispute, rather than alignment with the USSR (see Chapter 3). In the rest of this chapter we shall set out our major hypotheses about the de-radicalisation of the PCI; these shall be developed further in Chapter 2. We shall then consider the reasons for the appearance of the Ingrao left and the causes of its ultimate defeat. These shall be further elaborated in Chapter 4.

In the first place, the theory of the working-class aristocracy does not seem to have any significant role in explaining the moderation of the PCI. Lenin did not include Italy among the Great Powers which derived huge super-profits from imperialism; the Italian colonial empire never yielded great returns. Gramsci, it is true, attributed the reformism and corporatism of some groups of northern workers (e.g. those of Reggio Emilia) to the semi-colonial exploitation of the south.[32] But the 'crumbs' received by the working class from this exploitation were meagre and the PSI turned left in 1911-12, in spite of Liberal Prime Minister Antonio Giolitti's attempt to gain its backing. It opposed the Libyan War and refused to support Italian participation in the First World War. There is even less evidence that the PCI has represented a 'labour aristocracy' in the past thirty years. Almost every survey and study has shown that the PCI receives more support from the lower strata of the working class than from the higher, or at least equal support from the two groups.[33] The best-paid members of the working class have tended to support more strongly the Christian Democrats, the Social Democrats or the Socialists, though many of the worst-paid workers, freshly recruited from the countryside, workers in

small factories, irregularly employed, and sub-proletarians have
continued to support the DC as well. While the question is clearly
complex, there is no prima facie evidence to support this version of the
'working-class aristocracy' thesis in the case of the PCI. The tendency
for the worst-paid, least skilled workers in some northern factories
to occasionally support the groups of the extraparliamentary left or the
actions which they organise does not prove that only the upper layer
support the PCI; nor has it been shown that the militancy of this lower
stratum of workers is permanent, or will be converted into a lasting
commitment to groups to the left of the PCI.[34]

As for the possibility that the leaders of the PCI might have been
'bought', this could be true in one sense only: they have been allowed,
even in the context of a state system extremely hostile to them, to
occupy some offices and positions of political influence — e.g. in
municipal government and in parliamentary bargaining over legislation.[35] If this form of participation in political power has had a
conservatising effect on some of the Party's cadres — or on the Party
as a whole — this is because it has created in some an 'administrative'
mentality. It has made them very much aware of the limits and
constraints imposed by the capitalist system on the Party's action and
it has allowed the Party to finance and expand its operations (e.g. by
appointing Party members to jobs in 'red' communes, by receiving
percentages from holders of municipal contracts). The conservatism
of some Communist local administrators or managers of co-operatives
(particularly noticeable where the Party controls local government,
and especially in Emilia-Romagna) is akin to the organisational
conservatism described by Michels. After 1969 there was an increase
in the number of positions available to the PCI: trade-union representatives on boards of social security administrations (*mutue*); regional
government officials; officials in local governments won by the PCI
in 1975. Furthermore, in 1974 Parliament voted a law providing for
very generous public financing of political parties: the PCI receives
approximately 10 billion lire (US $12,500,000) annually in this way.
This expansion of the 'patronage' available to the Party may have
modified its social nature and its attitude to the system, but it is too
early to draw conclusions on this point.

Nor does a theory relying on the supposed *embourgeoisement* of
the whole Italian working class seem very plausible as an explanation
of the PCI's movement towards reformism. The material standard of
living of the working class has improved considerably over the past
three decades, but there does not seem to be any connection between

these improvements and the movement of the Party to the right; at first glance, it would seem that the contrary is true. The increase in the industrial militancy of the key sectors of the working class from the low point of the mid-1950s to the major strike wave of the 'hot autumn' of 1969-70 would be the best proof that Italian workers have not become domesticated and have not come to accept the system. Wage increases seem to have stimulated 'leftism' within the Party (e.g. after 1962). The political tenor of many of the recent strikes demonstrates that an anti-capitalist consciousness has spread within the working class, though it is not unmixed with elements of corporatism. In the 1970s, it is true, a clear differentiation between the stably employed, well-paid workforce (both white- and blue-collar) and the unemployed and 'marginal', non-unionised workers, often employed clandestinely to avoid social security payments and taxes, has appeared. This development has taken place in concomitance with the gradual entry of the PCI into the governmental area; it is a result of the improved position of the working class since the trade-union struggles of the late 1960s and early 1970s. Again, it does not represent a consolidated situation.

At the same time, bourgeois ideology has not hegemonised the working class, though it has of course been subjected to the appeals of consumerism and capitalist values at the common-sense level. New groups of the proletariat have been won over to the working-class parties, and the influence of Marxism within Italian culture as a whole and within the bourgeoisie itself has been growing. In Italy the bourgeoisie was not as united ideologically as in Britain or Germany; it found its ideological expression in part in Catholicism and in part in classical liberalism. It was therefore less able to exercise hegemony over other classes. In the post-war period both Catholicism and liberalism have been in decline, though they received temporary reinforcement during the Cold War from the pro-American, anti-Communist climate of opinion. Just as in the liberal era, the Italian bourgeoisie after 1945 failed to establish a solid intellectual and moral hegemony over the subordinate classes. Not only did a large part of the working class remain in opposition, but much of the south was prevented from revolting only by the liberal use of corruption and fraud (the *Cassa per il Mezzogiorno* and similar projects).

While none of the above hypotheses seems, prima facie, to explain the PCI's movement towards reformism, the effects of the presence of bourgeois elements within the Party deserve more attention. Their numbers, among electors, members and leaders of the PCI, are considerable. For instance, in 1972 an estimated 27·8 per cent of the PCI's voters were bourgeois or petty bourgeois.[36] In the same year 31.6 per cent of the Party's economically active members belonged to the same classes.[37] Many of these, however, were substantially proletarianised in spite of their formal class position — e.g. share-croppers, poor peasants or lower white-collar workers. Among the Party leadership the number of non-workers is much greater. For instance, in the period of 1946-58 only 31.6 per cent of PCI parliamentarians were children of manual workers.[38] Similarly, the majority of members of PCI federal committees (67 per cent in 1972[39]) are of non-working-class origin. Nevertheless, it would be difficult to demonstrate that these bourgeois groups directly influenced the PCI's line in the direction of their own class interests, except perhaps in some fields of secondary importance (e.g. small industrialists in the 'red' regions). The vast majority of the Party remained proletarian, and the members of other classes that joined it, other than those substantially proletarianised, generally did so because of a commitment to the ideals of socialism, rather than out of a desire to further their own material interests. No particular interest group seemed to have strong enough representation within the PCI to secure, on the basis of its own strength, special consideration for its point of view. The Party's many policies in favour of the material interests of particular middle-class groups are better explained as products of the Popular Front strategy adopted by the Comintern in 1935 (see below). Many of the leaders had broken with their class years before, often suffering prison or exile for their choice. Indeed, the members of the middle classes in the PCI seem in many cases to have behaved more like the 'general staff' which Gramsci considered necessary in any revolutionary party, supplying it with fresh ideas and ideological direction.

On the other hand, the increase in the number of posts available to Party members since 1969, and the movement of the more revolutionary younger people into groups and parties to the left of the PCI since 1968, have led to an increase in the numbers of middle-class youth who have joined the Party and entered its *apparat* or assumed other important positions. Many of these new recruits have no clear commitment to revolution, and some, certainly, seem to have been attracted to the Party in part because of their desire for gainful employment; most of them come from the intellectual petty bourgeoisie. These changes in the class character of the Party (particularly its functionaries and middle-level cadres) seem to be both cause and effect of some aspects of the PCI's policy since 1969, in particular the adoption of the policy of the 'historic compromise' and the agreements concluded with the DC in 1976-7. For the first time, the interests and attitudes of this group may be coming to have a weight in the determination of Party policy. (From 1972 to 1975 the percentage of workers in the federal committees fell further, from 33 per cent to 24.9 per cent.[40])

A more promising hypothesis attributes the rightward movement of the PCI to the presence of a subordinate, non-revolutionary ideology in the working class and the party. The ideological weakness of the bourgeoisie has prevented it from exercising hegemony over the working class as a whole (as distinct from some segments of it); rather, another, distinctively working-class ideology has kept the proletariat within the bounds of reformism. This ideology is not the simple result of the relative immaturity of the class — it is not a backward working class still in an economic-corporative or class solidarity phase of consciousness. Rather, it has been actively introduced by the mass party of the working class. This Popular Front ideology, also known as 'frontism', is an expression of the post-war strategy of the PCI. This strategy is quite complex, and has a revolutionary as well as a reformist aspect. It will be discussed in detail in Chapter 2; here only the latter is important. Its central feature is the belief that an alliance between the working class and elements of the petty bourgeoisie and the bourgeoisie proper, leading to an intermediate stage of 'progressive democracy' or democratic, anti-monopoly government, is necessary as a first step towards the attainment of socialism. It was laid down as a policy for all Communist parties, then engaged in the anti-fascist struggle, in 1935 by the VII Congress of the Comintern, and has remained the central axis of their practice in one form or another ever since. Togliatti, Secretary-General of the PCI, had been one of its originators. He promoted it enthusiastically within his own party, but it was not accepted by all or at once.

The Communist Party itself contains within its ranks different ideologies and different levels of ideology. Similarly, the Popular Front ideology developed at different levels. The Gramscian framework is very useful in elucidating this complex structure. Frontism did not follow exactly the pattern outlined by Gramsci in that it was first introduced not as a philosophy but rather as a practical political line. Nevertheless, it did evolve its own expression at the philosophical level, known as 'Marxist historicism'. This was an attempt to develop the thought of Gramsci himself in an idealist direction, with a double objective: first, to facilitate the passage of intellectuals of Crocean

and Hegelian background to Marxism — the winning over of these
intellectuals was an important aspect of the Party's policy of alliances,
especially in the south;[41] second, to justify the theory that a non-
insurrectionary, almost gradual route to socialism was possible, through
the conquest in the first place of 'hegemony' in civil society, particularly higher culture, after which the state and the economy would fall
almost automatically into the hands of the workers' movement. This
second aim also was functional to the policy of alliances. 'Marxist historicism' was accompanied by a cultural policy based on the encouragement
of 'national-popular' as opposed to 'cosmopolitan' literature and art.
This position, again, claimed to be based on the views of Gramsci;
it saw as its aim the bridging of the gulf separating the intellectuals,
especially the writers, from the people. Such a policy, with its stress
on national and generically popular rather than class themes, could
also serve the policy of alliances, while it also bore a similarity to
'socialist realism', the official cultural line in the USSR.[42]

At the level of religion, where it was perhaps strongest, the
Popular Front ideology involved an interpretation of Italian history,
coupled with the cult of the Constitution and the Resistance. The
historical component was again, it was claimed, based on Gramsci,
though here also certain liberties were taken with his thought. His
explanation of the weakness of the post-Risorgimento Italian state,
brilliantly synthesised in the Lyons Theses, was the basis of this version
of a century of Italian history, but his ideas were reinterpreted in the
light of the strategy of the Popular Front. Gramsci's stress on the
importance of the bourgeoisie's failure to carry out an agrarian reform
in the 1860s was used to buttress the thesis that Italy had still not
completed her bourgeois-democratic revolution, and that an inter-class
alliance was necessary to achieve this before the advance to socialism
could be undertaken. Gramsci's concept of the failed agrarian revolution was also made to bear the burden of explaining the relative
slowness of Italy's economic growth, although Gramsci himself had
been interested in elucidating political history only.[43] The rise of
fascism was attributed to this backwardness of Italian capitalism,
and, of course, to the maximalism and sectarianism of the PSI, which
failed to recognise the necessity of pursuing a policy of alliances with
the petty bourgeoisie. The culminating point of this historical account
was the Resistance, in which the Communist Party and the working
class took up the banner of the national interest. The cult of the
Resistance, in which the *unity* achieved by all the anti-fascist forces
is constantly stressed, has been assiduously cultivated by the PCI.

An extensive round of commemorative activities associated with the Resistance provide many opportunities for returning to the theme; the Party attempts to make these events as 'unitary' as possible, with the participation of Christian Democrats, Republicans and even Liberals. It also tries to recreate the unity of the armed Resistance in the present, by urging unity of the anti-fascist forces against the threat to democracy represented by the MSI, other neo-fascist organisations and their terrorist arms. Anti-fascism has an important function in the PCI's relations with other parties, but it is a crucial element of the frontist ideology within the Party as well.

The Constitution was seen as the embodiment of the inter-class unity around progressive goals that had been achieved during the Resistance; the subsequent extrusion of the PCI and PSI from the government was explained by American interference in Italian affairs.[44] The aims of the PCI, in this perspective, were clear: a constant effort to form alliances with non-proletarian groups, particularly the middle strata, for the completion of the democratic revolution and the implementation of the Constitution.

The 'common sense' level of the frontist strategy is simply the reduction of the broad design to a series of practical maxims for conduct, such as the need to seek 'unity of all the democratic forces' in any concrete situation, or to have 'unitary' meetings, e.g. to commemorate the Resistance. The level of 'folklore' in the PCI is, however, much more complex; it contains many elements from previous periods in the Party's history, and, at the present time, much of the folklore is still the deposit of the Stalinist era. The new line, which the leadership attempted to bring to the mass membership since the war, and especially since 1956, has not yet had time to fully take hold. Therefore, much Party folklore still refers to the future 'X hour', the moment of the revolutionary seizure of power. There are even stories about the Party's supposed arms caches that circulate among the least informed members and supporters. Another part of Party folklore consists of stories and recollections about Stalin, about the USSR as a model socialist state etc., though these are less and less frequent today. A strong sense of internationalism and of the duty of international solidarity is another element which could be placed in the levels of common sense and folklore, because it is to a large extent a residue of the previous era of the history of the Communist movement.

Thus, in spite of its incomplete penetration of the Party, especially at the level of folklore, the Popular Front ideology has been a major

cause of the moderation of the PCI's positions. It was consciously
adopted and promoted by Togliatti when the PCI was still a small
clandestine organisation. Its impact, however, has been greatly
reinforced by the rules of democratic centralism and the operation of
the 'iron law of oligarchy'. These, acting jointly, have effectively
prevented any revision of the fundamentals of the Popular Front
strategy; they have, so to speak, frozen aspects of the Party's
fundamental position at the situation of 1935. At that time, it was
no doubt a realistic and appropriate course for a revolutionary party
in Italy; but reality has changed dramatically since then.

The 'iron law of oligarchy' has certainly made its effect felt
within the PCI. The advantages of the leadership over the mass
membership of the Party are multiplied by the large size of the Party
apparat, which includes some 3,000 full-time officials working for the
Party itself (some generous estimates, which include functionaries of
mass organisations, local governments etc., place the figure at over
10,000[45]), by the power of the Party press and by the large number of
jobs in local government, trade unions and other organisations which
are in the Party's appointment. (This vast network controlled by the
Party also offers resources for oppositional factions, however.) The
fact that the majority of functionaries are recruited from the middle
classes and have superior educational backgrounds, more political
experience and greater resources than the ordinary members increases
their power. Since the PCI, in keeping with Togliatti's conception of
the *partito nuovo* (see Chapter 2, Section 2), has become a mass party
rather than a cadre party, the differences in political knowledge and
skills are much greater than in the Leninist party of the classic type,
and the need of guarantees of internal democracy is all the greater.
Other phenomena associated by Michels with oligarchy within parties,
such as the veneration of leaders, have certainly appeared in the PCI.
(This was especially true of Togliatti, but many other leaders, not
excluding Enrico Berlinguer, have been the object of it in a lesser
degree.)

At the same time, the framework of democratic centralism, based
on the usage of the III International, though relaxed somewhat in
practice for modern Italian conditions, has further strengthened the
leaders' hand.[46] In the words of one former member of the Central
Committee:

There are, if we keep to the essential, two fundamental rules. First
of all, the existence of a leading group (*gruppo dirigente*), which,

historically, is formed by the method of co-optation and functions
as the mediator between the immediate experience of the class
and the revolutionary tradition. In the second place, the taking of
collective decisions through a debate which is real and free, but is
carried on principally within the various [Party] organs and leads
to the achievement of unity successively from the higher organs
to the lower.[47]

This practice is a far cry from Leninist principles of democratic
centralism. Furthermore, the prohibition of factions introduced as a
temporary measure by the X Congress of the Russian Communist
Party in 1921 has been preserved, and even strengthened, in the parties
which owe their origins to the III International. In the PCI the tradition
of unanimous voting in every deliberative organ had been established;
this was finally called into question after 1956, and especially after
1961, when Amendola and other leaders maintained that majorities
and minorities could form on particular questions, so long as they did
not 'degenerate' into factions. Furthermore, the preoccupation with
unity had led to another practice, not contemplated by Lenin, the
'solidarity' of the higher organs, the effective decision-making bodies,
vis-à-vis the lower: for instance, the Executive (*Direzione*), Politburo
and Secretariat present a united front to the Central Committee
whatever discussions they may have had among themselves over a
particular proposal. As we shall see, it was for breaking this unwritten
rule that Ingrao incurred the wrath of some of his colleagues in the
Politburo.

Once the united leadership has launched a proposal — for instance,
the theses for a Congress of the Party — a fairly broad and open debate
is allowed within the lower organs. However, this debate is unlikely to
fundamentally alter the line pursued by the Party; its real purpose, in
the eyes of the leadership, is to make the rank and file aware of the
Party's line, to convince them of its correctness and to rebut any
possible objections to it by encouraging their expression during the
discussion. While the leadership must and often does take into
consideration the opinions and humours of the mass membership,
and these debates are a useful way of sounding out these opinions,
the rank and file has no way of substantially correcting the main lines
of Party strategy, which have already been decided. Several practices
discourage this. First, the report or motion or theses which form the
basis for discussion in Party assemblies are always furnished by the
higher organs, be they the national leadership or the local secretariat.

Motions or amendments from the rank and file are rare, though not unheard of, but in any case the main lines of discussion are laid down from above. Secondly, these motions and reports are usually omnibus documents covering everything from the current international situation to the organisational problems of the Party in the locality; they are also vague and imprecise on certain key points. Therefore the debate is often not focused on particular issues and it is thus all the more difficult for dissent to crystallise.

Since open disagreement with the motion or theses is frowned upon as contrary to Party custom and democratic centralism (though of course it is sometimes expressed), dissent is usually made manifest in more roundabout ways. A speaker, for instance, may lay stress on one part of the motion and ignore other parts; he may quote with approval one or more previous speakers and disregard the remarks of others; he may introduce new points, without bringing out the fact that they may be in contrast with some aspect of the official line. This subtle interplay of *distinguos* and references is typical of *public* assemblies and published reports of meetings; in the closed sessions of the Central Committee, for instance, debate can often be very frank and even heated, and this has become clearer in the published summaries in *l'Unità* in recent years. But these practices make it very difficult for any but Party officials and intellectuals to understand and participate in debates on the Party's policy. The form of Party documents also tends to create a gap between discussion of the Party's line and the Party's day-to-day practice; often the former, because of its intellectualistic and somewhat vague character, has little real effect on the latter.

Furthermore, more direct control from above is exercised by the practice of sending functionaries from the higher body to 'hold' (and supervise) the congresses (and occasionally other meetings) of the organisations immediately below. Indeed, in some federations it is common to explain every major change in line or significant political development to the base of the Party by organising a *tournée* in which the federal functionaries cover all the sections in a matter of a few days. In the case of a congress, the delegate of the higher body participates in the choice of the new leaders of the section of federation in question, and makes the concluding speech in which he evaluates the congress from the point of view of the centre, praises or reprimands the section or federation for its recent work, and deals with objections to the Party's line that have been raised. Furthermore, the higher organs intervene often in the selection of the leadership of the organisations under them; and, above all, the selection of functionaries is not subject to even a formal process of election — they are co-opted by the secretariats.

This centralised and in practice less than democratic internal regime is mitigated by a relatively tolerant application of the rules. First, the leading organs, at each level, function in a genuinely collegial fashion. There is real debate within them, and these differences of opinion are sometimes communicated to the rank and file. Furthermore, Party members are allowed a large margin of freedom for theoretical discussion and research, and this work in turn fertilises the political practice of the Party. Different tendencies of thought and interpretations of the Party's line are tolerated. But their proponents do not have the means to alter the basic elements of the general line. Hence, the internal structure of the Party has helped to preserve the Popular Front strategy from major revision for over forty years.

That the Ingrao left failed to exert a significant influence on the policies of the Party, and was decisively defeated, though not totally eliminated, at the XI Congress in 1966, attests to the strength of the ideology of the Popular Front and the 'iron law of oligarchy'. Its lack of success would seem to indicate that the trend to de-radicalisation in the Western working-class parties is general and ineluctable. Yet a closer analysis of the causes both of its rise and of its fall will demonstrate the specificity of these causes, the products of a particular conjuncture in the history of the Italian working-class movement.

Notes

1. V.I. Lenin, *Imperialism, the Highest Stage of Capitalism* (Peking, 1970), p. 125.
2. Quoted in ibid., p. 129.
3. Ibid., pp. 129-30.
4. Ibid., pp. 127-8.
5. V.I. Lenin, 'Imperialism and the Split in the Socialist Movement' in his *British Labour and British Imperialism* (London, 1969), p. 147.
6. Quoted in Lenin, *Imperialism*, p. 129.
7. Preface to the 2nd edn of F. Engels, *The Condition of the Working Class in England*, quoted in Lenin, *British Labour*, p. 144. On this subject cf. the acute observations of E. Hobsbawm in *Revolutionaries* (London, 1973).
8. N. Poulantzas, 'On Social Classes', *New Left Review*, 78 (Mar.-Apr. 1973), p. 36; cf. O.K. Flechtheim, *Die KPD in der Weimarer Republik* (Frankfurt/Main, 1969), pp. 311-25, and F. Borkenau, *International Communism* (London, 1938), pp. 364-6.
9. See R. Michels, *Political Parties* (New York, 1959), pp. 316-17; also his

Il proletariato e la borghesia nel movimento socialista italiano (Turin, 1908), esp. pp. 357 ff.

10. See D. Lockwood, 'The New Working Class', *Archives Européennes de Sociologie*, vol. 1, no. 2 (1960).

11. See H. Marcuse, *One-Dimensional Man* (Boston, 1965), and C.W. Mills, *The Power Elite* (New York, 1956), esp. Ch. 13.

12. See H. Marcuse, 'Repressive Tolerance' in H. Marcuse, B. Moore Jr and R.P. Wolff, *A Critique of Pure Tolerance* (Boston, 1965).

13. S. Mallet, *La nouvelle classe ouvrière* (Paris, 1969).

14. Ibid., p. 35.

15. Ibid., p. 43.

16. Ibid., pp. 94-8.

17. A. Touraine, *Le mouvement de mai ou le Communisme utopique* (Paris, 1968).

18. See P. Anderson, 'Origins of the Present Crisis', *New Left Review*, 23 and 25 (Jan.-Feb. and May-June 1964), and T. Nairn, 'The English Working Class', *New Left Review*, 24 (Mar.-Apr. 1964).

19. N. Poulantzas, *Pouvoir politique et classes sociales* (Paris, 1968), p. 198.

20. A. Gramsci, *Selections from the Prison Notebooks*, eds. Q. Hoare and G. Nowell Smith (London, 1971), p. 328.

21. Ibid., p. 422-3.

22. Ibid., p. 181.

23. Ibid., pp. 181-2; see also A. Gramsci, *Quaderni del carcere*, ed. Valentino Gerratana (4 vols., Turin, 1975), vol. III, pp. 2283-4, 2287-9, where a list of six stages is given.

24. Gramsci, *Prison Notebooks*, pp. 160-1.

25. F. Parkin, *Class Inequality and Political Order* (London, 1972), p. 81; see also pp. 88-96 for a discussion of the subordinate value system.

26. Gramsci, *Prison Notebooks*, pp. 152-3.

27. Parkin, *Class Inequality*, pp. 98-101; cf. also pp. 128-36, where the deradicalisation of working-class parties is treated.

28. Michels, *Political Parties*, *passim*.

29. See e.g. A. Przeworski and J. Sprague, 'A History of Western European Socialism', paper presented at the Annual Meetings of the American Political Science Association, Washington DC, Sept. 1977, pp. 13-22.

30. Michels, *Political Parties*, see esp. Part 6, Ch. 1: 'The Conservative Basis of Organization'.

31. Ibid., p. 408.

32. A. Gramsci, 'Alcuni temi della quistione meridionale', *La costruzione del Partito comunista 1923-1926* (Opere, vol. 12, Turin, 1971), pp. 141-2, 149-50.

33. See e.g. S. Tarrow, *Peasant Communism in Southern Italy* (New Haven and London, 1967), p. 136; cf. D. De Masi and G. Fevola, *I lavoratori nell' industria italiana* (Milan, 1974), vol. II, p. 414: in this survey of over 7,000 workers, 40 per cent of the unskilled manual workers indicating a party preference chose the PCI, compared to 42 per cent of the skilled manual workers.

34. See the series of studies, *Lotte operaie e sindacato in Italia: 1968-1972*, directed by A. Pizzorno, Bologna, 1974-8.

35. See P. Ferrari and H. Maisl, *Les groupes communistes aux assemblées parlementaires italiennes (1958-1963) et françaises (1962-1967)* (Paris, 1969).

36. My own elaboration of Demoskopea data reported in P.A. Allum, *Italy – Republic without Government?* (London, 1973), p. 81; cf. P. Sylos Labini, *Saggio sulle classi sociali* (Bari, 1975), pp. 189-92, who gives a much higher estimate of 39.4 per cent for PCI and PSIUP.

37. Elaborated from data in *Classe, consigli, partito* (*Il Manifesto*, quaderno no. 2, Rome, 1974), p. 212.

38. G. Sartori, *Il Parlamento italiano* (Naples, 1963), p. 89.

39. *Corriere della Sera*, 14 Dec. 1976.

40. Ibid.

41. See R. Luperini, *Gli intellettuali di sinistra e l'ideologia della ricostruzione nel dopoguerra* (Rome, 1971). One example of this approach is N. Badaloni, *Il marxismo come storicismo* (Milan, 1962); cf. F. Cassano (ed.), *Marxismo e filosofia in Italia 1958-1971* (Bari, 1973).

42. The literature on the cultural policy of the PCI is extensive. See Luperini, *Gli intellettuali di sinistra*, for a good, though polemical, survey. See also A. Asor Rosa, *Scrittori e popolo* (Rome, 1964).

43. J. Cammett, 'Two Recent Polemics on the Character of the Italian Risorgimento', *Science and Society*, vol. XXVII, no. 3 (Fall 1963).

44. This judgement has recently been revised by some PCI scholars.

45. See F. Lanchester, 'La dirigenza di Partito: Il caso del PCI', *Il Politico*, vol. XLI, no. 4 (Dec. 1976); for other estimates, see S. Passigli, 'Political Finance: Italy', *Journal of Politics*, vol. 25, no. 4 (Nov. 1963), and J. Meynaud, *Rapport sur la classe dirigeante italienne* (Lausanne, 1964), p. 29.

46. See S. Sechi, 'L'austero fascino del centralismo democratico', in M. Barbagli, P. Corbetta and S. Sechi, *Dentro il PCI* (Bologna, 1979).

47. L. Magri and F. Maone, 'Problemi di organizzazione nell'esperienza del PCI' in *Classe, consigli, partito*, p. 188. The following discussion is based in part on this article.

2 THE ORIGINS OF EUROCOMMUNISM: THE PARTY'S STRATEGY FROM 1926 TO 1956

1. The Comintern and Revolution

The major factor explaining the deradicalisation of the PCI is the ideology which has dominated it for 45 years, its own version of Eurocommunism which its leaders developed on the basis of the Popular Front policy of the Comintern. This ideology is complex, however, and has not only a reformist aspect, which has predominated in the PCI, but also a revolutionary potential.

The Eurocommunist strategy, which the PCI pioneered, is sharply different from the Leninist perspective which the Communist parties adopted at their foundation. The Leninist conception of revolution involves a revolutionary *crisis* which will galvanise the masses into action. Until 1935 the parties of the Comintern expected that revolution would break out in Western Europe as a result of a catastrophic crisis of capitalism, manifesting itself in economic collapse or, more likely, war. This belief was similar to the 'breakdown theory' current in the II International (1889-1914): the theory that the collapse of the capitalist economy was inevitable because of a necessary tendency to overproduction and/or a falling rate of profit. A further guarantee of ultimate success was the Marxian prediction that capitalist development was leading inexorably to the polarisation of society into a proletarian majority on the one hand and a small minority of capitalists on the other. The petty bourgeoisie, the leaders of the II International believed, was destined to disappear.

The breakdown theory, while it promised the socialist parties ultimate, inevitable victory, not only predisposed them to await passively the great moment, but also implied that revolution would break out as a result of very sharp *defensive* struggles waged by the workers for their immediate basic needs in the face of the consequences of the crisis: unemployment, wage cuts and misery. No offensive demands, such as greater control on the shop floor, had to be put forward by the working-class party. The theory also implied a distinction between economic and political struggles. Day-to-day actions over wages and hours were not integrated with political activity, which consisted of election campaigns, May Day demonstrations and perhaps the occasional purely demonstrative political strike.[1] The two types of action, political and trade-union, proceeded in relative independence until the moment of the crisis, although the party might hope to gain new recruits through its support for union struggles.[2]

The momentous experience of the October Revolution paradoxically led to no fundamental revision of this breakdown theory. The Bolshevik leaders had themselves been schooled in the Marxism of the II International, and, furthermore, the theory could be stretched to fit the Russian Revolution: the masses had been galvanised into action by a catastrophic crisis, the war. They had engaged in extremely sharp struggles for immediate basic needs and such bourgeois-democratic goals as land reform ('peace, bread and land') rather than for directly socialist objectives. The war was a result of imperialist rivalry, but inter-imperialist competition in its turn sprang from the contradictions of capitalism. Stalin predicted in 1924 that further inter-imperialist wars were inevitable, and would spark further revolutions.[3] The Bolsheviks added only one element to the schema: the vanguard party, whose leadership was necessary to direct the masses in the moment of crisis, harnessing their defensive struggles to the fight for the control of state power. While Lenin had originally theorised the necessity of a vanguard as a response to specifically Russian conditions, where the immediate economic struggles of the working class were inevitably isolated from the major political issues of an overwhelmingly peasant country,[4] the Comintern presented the Russian experience as a model for the Western European Communist parties as well, in the simplified form: crisis plus vanguard party equals revolution.

The attempt to repeat the Russian experience in Western Europe, embodied in the strategy of the Communist parties from 1919 to 1935, was singularly unsuccessful. However, it was largely because of the exigencies of Soviet foreign policy that the Comintern abandoned this line in 1934-5 in favour of the strategy of the Popular Front. Stalin, fearful that Nazi Germany might attack the USSR, became eager to form alliances with the Western European democracies, particularly Britain and France. Therefore the Western Communist parties were encouraged to press for governments of anti-fascist unity and to cease frightening their local bourgeoisies with the revolutionary rhetoric of 'class against class' which had prevailed during the so-called 'third period' (1928-34). While some of the Western parties were eager to accept the new strategy, the timing and circumstances of its adoption make it clear that the decisive initiative came from Moscow, from the Comintern leadership if not from Stalin himself.[5]

The new policy was sanctioned by the VII Congress of the Comintern in August 1935. Georgi Dimitrov, Secretary-General of the International, in his report first proposed the abandonment of the sectarian attitude towards social democracy summed up in the epithet 'social fascism' in favour of a United Front of the working-class parties. Then he advanced the idea of an even broader Popular Front:

> The success of the whole struggle of the proletariat is closely related to the fighting alliance of the proletariat with the working peasants and the fundamental masses of the urban petty-bourgeoisie, who constitute the majority of the population even in the most industrially developed countries.[6]

As practice was soon to make clear, this anti-fascist Popular Front was also to include members of the bourgeoisie proper, with the exception of monopolists and representatives of finance capital, who were held to be the principal social basis of fascism.[7] The policy of unity with the petty bourgeoisie and elements of the bourgeoisie was to be implemented on two levels, the social and the political. The Communists were to address themselves to these strata both directly, by supporting their demands and attempting to recruit them as members or sympathisers, and indirectly, by allying with the parties that represented them.

The aim of these alliances was not socialist revolution, but the constitution of a democratic and anti-fascist, but not anti-capitalist, government. Thus, both in the scope of the proposed alliances and in their objectives, the Popular Front strategy represented a departure from the Leninist model of revolution. However, it was not founded on any new theoretical analysis of the nature of capitalism or imperialism, other than the very schematic formula defining fascism as the dictatorship of finance capital, so that the theory of the previous period (breakdown plus vanguard party equals revolution) survived in the minds of Communists long after 1935; it was in fact canonised in Stalin's essay 'Dialectical and Historical Materialism' which first appeared in 1938 and remained the basic primer in Marxism-Leninism for Communist militants until his death.[8] The Popular Front strategy appeared as a new tactic, rather than a fundamental change of perspective. Hence to some it seemed simply a ruse or a temporary expedient. This is one of the reasons for the accusation of duplicity (*doppiezza*) levelled at the Italian and other Western Communist parties ever since 1935. And, in fact, many militants did remain attached to the previous conceptions of a catastrophic crisis, armed insurrection and the dictatorship of the proletariat, which had a more solid theoretical foundation than the Popular Front strategy.

The Comintern attempted to join these two basically inconsistent perspectives together by means of a two-stage theory of revolution. In the first phase, a democratic, anti-fascist coalition government, the Popular Front, would come to power. This stage was later named 'progressive democracy'. This government would control or nationalise only the large monopolies, while non-monopolistic capital would be protected and even encouraged. This progressive democratic government would somehow lay the basis for the second stage, the socialist revolution and the dictatorship of the proletariat. Dimitrov only hinted at such a two-stage theory in his report to the VII Congress, in which he said: 'It may be that the *United Front government* will in some countries prove to be *one* of the most important forms of transition to the proletarian revolution.'[9] At the same time, he denied that this form of transition constituted an 'intermediate democratic stage', and the measures he suggested Communists should demand from a United Front government, such as control of production and of the banks and the dissolution of the police and its replacement by a workers' militia, indicate that he had in mind a rather rapid transition. However, the progressive democracy advocated by the Communist parties since 1935, and particularly during and after the Second World War, is precisely a type of 'intermediate democratic stage', intended to reconcile the policy of broad anti-fascist alliances with the ultimate goal of socialist revolution.

The adoption of the Popular Front strategy was an international decision imposed on all parties of the International whether they themselves welcomed it or not. The Comintern was dissolved in 1943, but so far not one Communist party in a capitalist state has departed from the policy of broad alliances between the working class, the petty bourgeoisie and elements of the bourgeoisie, usually identified as the 'anti-monopolistic' forces. Since 1945 the enemy has no longer been fascism (except in countries such as Spain and Portugal), but rather the monopolies; however, the potential allies and the goals of the strategy have remained the same. The following quotations from party programmes demonstrate the continuing fidelity of even the pro-Soviet Communist parties to the line of the Popular Front:

Wage- and salary-earners, farmers, professionals, intellectuals, small businessmen and non-monopoly capitalists have in common their

opposition to the reactionary policies of monopoly capital . . .
The defeat of monopoly capitalism requires unity of the working
class and other democratic forces in a new political alliance. The
Communist Party works for such a new political alliance, a
democratic, anti-monopoly, anti-imperialist alliance, based on the
working class, the national and democratic forces in French Canada,
the farmers, the middle strata, the non-monopolist bourgeoisie,
all those affected by monopoly policies.[10]

(Communist Party of Canada, 1971)

As our Party foresaw . . . the conditions are rapidly ripening for
a common action by all the strata stricken or threatened by the
monopolies.
More and more French society is characterised by the concentration
of an enormous power in the hands of a small group of monopolists,
at one pole, and by the deterioration of the living and working
conditions of the vast majority of the population, at the other
pole.[11]

(French Communist Party, 1969)

The main contradiction today is the contradiction between the
domestic financial oligarchy and imperialism, primarily U.S.
imperialism, on the one hand, and all other social classes, strata,
and groups, the overwhelming majority of the people, on the other.
Greece will arrive at socialism after passing through a revolutionary
continuous process [sic] which will consist of two stages of
revolutionary change: the democratic, anti-monopoly and anti-
imperialist stage, and the socialist stage . . .
The establishment of the new democracy [the first stage] will not
be the result of political combinations from above . . . but an act of
the people engaged in revolutionary struggle, an act of the working
class — the vanguard force of society — of the peasants, urban
middle strata, democratic intellectuals, youth, the people's sons
in the armed forces, democratic-minded officers and NCOs, popular
clergymen and, to a degree, small and medium employers pressed
by the greedy monopolies.[12]

(Communist Party of Greece, 'Exterior', 1973)

The Canadian and the Greek parties are among the most faithful to
Moscow, while the French party had not yet embraced a Eurocommunist position in 1969.

The same basic strategy, with minor national variants, has been adopted in such diverse countries as Italy, France, Great Britain, Chile and Greece. But the different parties have attempted to resolve the contradiction between the Popular Front strategy and the long-term goal of a socialist revolution on Leninist lines in different ways. The parties that have remained loyal to Moscow have been the least successful in this task. While their real day-to-day activity is aimed at the formation of an anti-monopoly alliance, they have not recognised the need to revise the pre-1935 theoretical and strategic perspective. They no longer hold that a catastrophic economic crisis or a war is necessary for socialist revolution, but they occasionally agree that the monopolies' control of the economy leads to economic crisis, because they restrict production, and hence to an attack on the people's standard of living, giving rise to a strong impulse towards the formation of a Popular Front and its victory at the polls. These formulations are often theoretically confused, but they demonstrate that the expectation that capitalism will break down under the weight of its economic contradictions is still very much alive. Furthermore, they have not completely eliminated from their programmes references to the possible need for armed revolution, especially in the event of resistance by the bourgeoisie to a democratic government, or to the dictatorship of the proletariat as an essential phase of the transition to the second stage of socialism. Their statements on this question too are often confused: on the one hand, Khrushchev, in keeping with the policy of broad alliances, had admitted that different roads to socialism were possible as early in 1956 (and Dimitrov had suggested the dictatorship of the proletariat might not be a necessary phase in 1946); on the other, these parties do not wish to explicitly reject the concept, thus seeming to side with the Eurocommunist parties in this ideological dispute. Moreover, they continue to present the USSR and the other Eastern European states as models of socialism. These features of their policies alienate the middle strata and non-monopoly capitalists, whose alliance is essential for the first stage, the democratic, anti-monopoly government. These groups are unlikely to ally with a Communist party whose programme envisages that the democratic, anti-monopoly government will be followed by the dictatorship of the proletariat and the elimination of most private business.

The Eurocommunist parties, on the other hand, have accepted the spirit of the Popular Front fully and carried it to its logical conclusions. They have stressed the first stage, the anti-monopoly alliance, at the expense of the second, the transition to socialism. In practice, and in spite of references to the eventual socialist goal and to the need to introduce 'elements of socialism' in some of their leaders' speeches,[13] they have relegated the transition to socialism to an unspecified future time. This has been necessary in order to reassure the potential allies, the petty bourgeoisie and the anti-monopolistic elements of the bourgeoisie proper. For the same reason, the Eurocommunist parties have accepted bourgeois democracy as their terrain of operation for the foreseeable future. They have been more willing than the pro-Soviet parties to enter into alliances and coalitions with other parties with the objective of reaching the stage of progressive democracy. They have explicitly stated that socialism will be achieved by parliamentary means, without passing through the dictatorship of the proletariat. They have also affirmed their independence from the USSR and made clear that the type of socialism they wish to build in Western Europe will be very different from that already existing in the socialist countries. (Only Santiago Carrillo of the Spanish Communist Party has gone so far as to deny that the USSR and the People's Democracies are socialist states.) Furthermore, the Eurocommunist parties have offered specific guarantees that the economic position of the petty bourgeoisie and non-monopoly bourgeoisie would not be undermined in the first stage of progressive democracy; the PCI even went so far as to promise that the transition to socialism would occur only when these allies agreed to it.[14]

The Eurocommunist parties have not, however, simply reduced the two-stage approach that characterises the orthodox version of the Popular Front to a reformist strategy in which only the first stage remains. For, in spite of its emphasis on the first stage and on alliances, the Popular Front strategy contained the germ of a new model of revolution, radically different from that handed down by the II International and from that suggested by the October Revolution. While the Popular Front strategy certainly led the Communist parties to wage many defensive struggles, for the preservation of bourgeois democracy from fascism and for the protection of interests threatened by the monopolies, it nevertheless could be developed in an offensive direction as well. The coming to power of the Popular Front was to be essentially the product of a *political* conjuncture and a *political* alliance; an economic crisis did not play a necessary role in its victory. The Communist parties were therefore stimulated to think politically, rather than await economic developments. Only later was it possible to revise the Marxian prediction that capitalism would collapse under its economic contradictions. Thinking politically led some Communist leaders, notably Palmiro Togliatti, PCI Secretary-General from 1926 to 1964, to think in terms of a positive programme and an offensive strategy, rather than simply defensive struggles. And once the economic breakdown of capitalism could no longer be predicted with confidence, such a positive, offensive strategy became a necessity. Togliatti's concept of 'structural reforms' was a first step towards such a strategy. While the defensive, reformist side of the Popular Front line prevailed in the practice of the Eurocommunist parties, some groups within them perceived and developed its offensive possibilities.

2. Togliatti and the Italian Road to Socialism

The unique Italian version of the Popular Front strategy, known as the *via italiana al socialismo* (Italian road to socialism), was elaborated largely by Togliatti. The position adopted by the Comintern, rather than any independent reflection by the Italian leadership, determined the post-war line of the PCI. But it coincided with Togliatti's own interpretation of the Italian situation, which was the product of his analysis of the events of 1918-22, when the sanguine revolutionary hopes of the immediate post-war period were frustrated and, instead, fascism rose to power. A crisis had led not to revolution, but to a reactionary victory, and Togliatti was not content to attribute this failure to the absence of a vanguard party; he sought to investigate the specific errors of political leadership which had led to the left's defeat and to re-examine the relationship between crisis and revolution.

In his 1928 article 'A proposito del fascismo' (On Fascism),[15] Togliatti, following Marx, noted that the petty bourgeoisie was incapable of organising itself as a class and hence was always politically subordinate to some other class. The outcome of the class struggle between the proletariat and the bourgeoisie, he went on, depended on which of the two contending classes secured an alliance with this intermediate stratum. Togliatti further developed his theory in his *Lectures on Fascism*, given in early 1935 at the party school of the PCI in Moscow.[16] While accepting, formally at any rate, the official Comintern definition of fascism as 'the open, terroristic dictatorship of the most reactionary, most chauvinist, and most imperialist elements of finance capital', he implied that the real distinguishing feature of the fascist regimes was their mass base among the petty bourgeoisie, both urban and rural. He attributed the rise of Italian fascism in large part

to the failure of the Socialist Party to secure an alliance with the middle
strata in the post-war period. Specifically, he criticised the PSI's agrarian
policy, which held out to the intermediate strata of the countryside, the
small renters and sharecroppers, only the prospect of 'proletarianisation',
of absorption into the mass of miserable and underemployed *braccianti*
(day-labourers). This line, which reflected the fatalistic expectation of
class polarisation typical of the II International, drove the bulk of the
rural petty bourgeoisie of the Po Valley into the arms of the fascists,
whose agrarian programme promised landownership to all. Togliatti
argued that the Socialists should have offered all classes in the countryside
the possibility of owning their own land, thus eliminating the 'feudal
residues' constituted by sharecropping (*mezzadria*) and similar agrarian
contracts which sanctioned the dependence of the peasant on the landlord:

> In Italy two things have always been said: on the one hand Italian
> agriculture had very important residues of feudal economic
> structures, and on the other hand it has always been said that in the
> Italian countryside the situation was such that the fundamental
> impulse was towards the ownership of the land. Because of this
> situation there existed in the countryside elements of a bourgeois-
> democratic revolutionary movement. (The proletarian revolution
> will have to solve the problem of giving land to the peasants, in so
> far as this is what the Italian peasants demand, their fundamental
> aspiration.)[17]

From this analysis, he argued that a 'policy of alliances' with the
middle classes was essential for the Communist Party in order to
ward off the fascist danger.

But the disastrous results of the Italian crisis of 1918-22 also
led Togliatti to question the relationship between crisis and revolution.
The Socialist Party's policy in this period had combined propaganda
for the revolution, often couched in bombastic rhetoric, with a
concrete policy of support for the economic demands of many
categories of workers.[18] The victories of the latter in many branches
of industry served only to aggravate the economic situation of the
country; some socialists openly defended a *politique du pire* as a means
of hastening the moment of revolutionary crisis. Instead, economic
crisis and working-class agitation only strengthened the right and drove
many of the middle strata into the fascist camp. Togliatti concluded
from this that a revolutionary party must offer positive solutions in
the near and medium term to the problems facing the country, short

of the solution of socialist revolution, and that it must never, on the other hand, aggravate a crisis with a policy of 'the worse, the better'. In arguing that a catastrophic crisis would lead to a victory of the right, he was preparing the ground for an alternative to the breakdown theory. On the basis of this analysis, Togliatti never ceased to criticise the notion that a revolutionary party should limit itself to denunciation of the existing order and propaganda (and support for trade-unionistic struggles without regard for their consequences for the national economy):

> In the past we have often been faced with dangerous situations, created by the policy of the ruling classes. For the most part, however, we and the other parties which represented the working masses were content to denounce the consequences of this policy and to say to the people: look, learn, see the faults of your rulers and of the regime under which you live. It was, in substance, the position of an association of propagandists for a different and better regime. But today can we limit ourselves to a position of this sort?
> . . . If we limited ourselves to taking such a position, we would be making a great mistake.[19]

Instead of waiting for the economic breakdown of capitalism, or, worse, accelerating it, the party had to advance positive political proposals that would offer a solution to the country's problems and consolidate a broad alliance, including the petty bourgeoisie and part of the bourgeoisie, around the working class. The agrarian reform proposed in *Lectures on Fascism* was one such positive proposal. It was repeated at the V Congress of the PCI (1945-6), where the Party's objective for the immediate future, after the defeat of the Nazis and Fascists, was stated to be the elimination of the roots of fascism, the monopolies and the large landed estates. The agrarian reform was to be accompanied by an industrial reform, which was to include the nationalisation of the large monopolies, banks and insurance companies and the extension of the wartime workers' councils (*consigli di gestione*) as instruments of economic planning.[20] These measures, which were intended to strengthen the working class and its system of alliances and weaken its enemies, came to be known as structural reforms.

The concept of structural reform led to the end of the separation between political and economic struggles. The latter, as Togliatti argued, were not to be carried so far as to destabilise the economic sytem itself, while, on the other hand, the battle for structural reforms was not to be fought solely by electoral or parliamentary means. The PCI encouraged, for instance, a series of occupations of the land and work-ins on uncultivated land as a means of pressing for land reform; it tried to promote strikes of sharecroppers and landless labourers in support of the same objective. And, later, the unions began to promote factory struggles for structural reform, demanding, for instance, to bargain with the employers over the size, type and location of new investments. These initiatives, however, diminished the role of the organs of bourgeois democracy to which the Popular Front strategy had committed the Party; they seemed to involve ignoring the democratic stage and the need for alliances. The revolutionary strategy which could be developed from the notion of structural reform was, in the long run, inconsistent with a rigid interpretation of the two-stage theory. These two variants of Eurocommunism coexisted within the PCI; in the early 1960s Pietro Ingrao was to make the more radical interpretation of the concept of structural reform a major element of his platform.

A policy of broad alliances and structural reforms also required a mass party rather than a Leninist vanguard. In 1944 Togliatti proposed that the PCI should become a 'new party' (*partito nuovo*), a mass party that would admit to its ranks even those with little knowledge of Marxism: 'The new party is a party of the working class and of the people that does not limit itself only to criticism and propaganda, but intervenes in the life of the country with a positive and constructive activity . . .'[21] By 1946 the PCI had over two million members.

The Popular Front policy of the Comintern opened the way to the elaboration of 'national roads' to socialism by the various Communist parties, roads different from that taken by Russia in 1917. However, the PCI took advantage of this possibility sooner and more completely than the others. While the history and situation of Italy and of the Party itself made it more receptive to such a policy,[22] the adoption of the Italian road to socialism by the PCI was also due to the battle which Togliatti fought throughout his career against the traditional, pre-1935 Comintern conception of revolution.

3. The Struggle for the Italian Road within the PCI

Togliatti's position within the International was coherent with his analysis of the Italian situation and his strategic perspective. In the late 1920s he supported Bukharin, who believed capitalism was then beginning a fairly long phase of consolidation; hence he opposed the adoption of the more aggressive, revolutionary line characteristic of the third period, which was based on the prediction of an imminent crisis of the world economy. While accepting Comintern discipline, he sought to resist as far as possible the full application of the third-period strategy of 'class against class' to Italy, even after the X Plenum of the Executive of the Comintern (1929) which sanctioned the defeat of Bukharin's line.[23] And, as Vice-Secretary-General of the Comintern, Togliatti had a major role, along with Dimitrov, in the formulation of the Popular Front strategy; he delivered the second report, on the risk of war, to the VII Congress.[24] As Comintern representative in Spain during the Civil War, he saw the Spanish Republic as a prototype of a progressive democracy that had accomplished the first part of the two-stage advance towards socialism indicated by the Popular Front strategy.[25]

The policy of the Popular Front was partially suspended during the life of the Hitler-Stalin pact (1939-41), when the Comintern defined the war as an inter-imperialist war, placing the Western democracies and the Axis powers on the same plane. But with Hitler's attack on the Soviet Union, the attitude of the Comintern and the PCI changed suddenly and completely, and in Italy all those who were prepared to fight against fascism and the Nazi invader — industrialists, landowners, 'patriots' and members of the middle classes — were invited to join the anti-fascist alliance. In April 1944 Togliatti, spectacularly reversing the PCI's position, agreed to enter a coalition government to prosecute the war against Germany without first securing the abolition of the monarchy. The anti-fascist coalition, he argued, should include both republicans and monarchists, and the solution of the 'institutional question' which divided them should be postponed until after the defeat of fascism. During the Resistance, he also opposed those Party leaders, including the majority of the Central Committee members in occupied Italy, who advocated the replacement of the old structure of the state, prefectoral and centralised, with the Committees of National Liberation. Togliatti's caution in this and other matters, such as land reform, reflected his concern to separate rigidly the two phases of the Popular Front strategy, the 'democratic' and the 'socialist', by doing nothing to alienate the potential allies in the middle classes and the bourgeoisie.

Similarly, in the post-war period Togliatti laid great emphasis on the drafting of the Republican Constitution, which was intended to lay the basis for a new type of democracy, more advanced than traditional liberal democracy. Most of the objectives of a Popular Front coalition could be subsumed under one article or another of the Constitution which was eventually approved, for it contained many programmatic norms which made the removal of social and economic inequalities, the protection of the right to work, the promotion of the health and education of the citizens, and other advanced objectives, goals of the state. The Communists' votes also secured the passage of Article 7 of the Constitution, which incorporated the Lateran Pacts. These were the agreements signed with the Papacy in 1929 which gave the Catholic Church a privileged position in Italy. The vote for Article 7 was another element of Togliatti's strategy of alliance with the middle classes, whose most important political representative had proved to be the Christian Democratic Party.

The years 1947-53 constituted a second, partial parenthesis in the Popular Front period. With the beginning of the Cold War, the United States, rather than fascism, became the principal enemy of the USSR, which sought to promote the formation of anti-American coalitions in the Western European capitalist states. These new coalitions, formed in the name of peace rather than of anti-fascism, were nevertheless to be inter-class alliances, embracing even members of the bourgeoisie who opposed American domination. Thus continuity with the previous period was maintained, even though some anti-fascist parties, such as the Italian Christian Democrats, were now on the other side of the barricade. But in other respects the Soviet leadership, through the newly founded Cominform, promoted positions which were typical of the pre-1935 period and scarcely compatible with the coherent pursuit of a policy of broad alliances, even one with different objectives and boundaries. For instance, the Yugoslav Communists were condemned in 1948 for making too many concessions to the independent peasants, and for suggesting that there could be different 'national roads' to socialism.

These criticisms could not but appear as an implicit rebuke to Togliatti too for the coherent form of Popular Front strategy he was pursuing. They were not lost on Pietro Secchia, Vice-Secretary-General and head of the organisation section of the Party, who from 1948 to 1954 was a possible alternative leader of the PCI. Secchia

did not stand for a break with the policy of alliances characteristic
of the Popular Front, but rather for a more 'closed' and ouvrierist
interpretation of it and a more orthodox Marxist-Leninist position
in matters of theory and party organisation. He was not a 'Stalinist',
as he was later labelled both inside and outside the PCI, nor did he
lead a non-existent 'insurrectionary' wing of the Party. His position
was in many respects similar to that of the present-day pro-Soviet
Communist parties which accept the strategy of alliances but refuse
to draw all the conclusions which it entails, though Secchia himself
was not unconditionally linked to Moscow. When Togliatti was
convalescing in the Soviet Union in 1951, Stalin offered him the
Secretary-Generalship of the Cominform, and his obvious successor
in Italy would have been Secchia. Togliatti succeeded in refusing
the invitation, but this affair made clear the lines of division between
the two men.[26]

The discussion of the PCI's activity in the south at the VII
Congress (April 1951) illuminates the difference between the two
interpretations of the Party's strategy. Giorgio Amendola, son of
the Liberal deputy Giovanni Amendola, martyred by the Fascists,
had been put in charge of the southern organisation of the PCI in
1947 (see Chapter 5, Section 2). Fully accepting the consequences
of the Popular Front strategy, he attempted to form links with the
southern bourgeoisie and petty bourgeoisie, who were called upon
to 'complete the bourgeois revolution' and to unite in the struggle
for the rights of the south, conceived of as an oppressed region similar
in some ways to a colony. After the 1948 election Amendola
promoted the 'Movement for the Rebirth of the South', which included
many people who were neither Communists nor Socialists, but
generically progressive. They came from the ranks of the traditional
petty bourgeoisie which, through the old Liberal parties, had
dominated the south before fascism. The land occupations of 1949-50
were organised by a similar inter-class movement, the 'Committees
for the Land', promoted by the PCI. In the same period the northern
federations of the Party, while paying lip-service to the programme of
class alliances, in practice had a closed, sectarian position. Many of
their cadres had been formed in the Resistance and preferred Secchia's
more orthodox line.

At the VII Congress Amendola put up a vigorous, emotional defence
of the Movement for the Rebirth of the South, stressing that the Party's
action in the *Mezzogiorno* needed to have its 'own, particular character'
with the struggle for regional development and agrarian reform at its

centre.[27] Secchia, on the other hand, was very critical of the way the
Party had developed in the south: its structure was too loose and poorly
articulated, membership fluctuated, recruitment was unselective and
no distinction was made between the Party and the mass organisations,
with the result that the latter — trade unions, co-operatives and peasant
alliances — were underdeveloped. Secchia remarked that after the
Liberation 'there were even some comrades who theorized that the
Party had necessarily to assume the form of a "movement" in the
South' because of the region's backwardness and social disorganisation.
This he labelled an 'anti-Leninist' theory, caused by faintheartedness in
the face of difficulties and by electoralism. He laid the greatest stress
on the struggle for peace, and criticised the Southerners' emphasis on
the campaign for rebirth and agrarian reform.[28]

At the Congress the Vice-Secretary-General won an apparent victory,
and it was decided to send a large number of cadres (the *costruttori*)
from the north and centre to the south to help create a 'Leninist'
organisation there. In the end, this experiment failed to produce the
desired results, not simply because of cultural differences between the
costruttori and the southern cadres, but also on account of a difference
in political line between the majority of southerners, who supported
Amendola, and their guests.[29]

In 1953, however, Secchia's influence began to decline. First,
the new group of Soviet leaders who succeeded Stalin initiated a
policy of *détente*, which made Secchia's policy position, based on
the need to avert an imminent threat of war, outdated. Furthermore,
the 1953 election demonstrated the success of Amendola's strategy:
in the south the PCI more than doubled its 1946 popular vote, while
in the north and centre, where Secchia's line was most influential,
it suffered losses or scored only marginal gains.[30] The PCI had
prevented the Christian Democrats and their allies from reaching
an absolute majority of the popular vote, and thus receiving 65 per
cent of the seats in the Chamber as the new electoral law (*legge truffa*,
or swindle law, the Communists called it) provided. But the presence
of two lines within the Party prevented it from fully exploiting its
victory. Secchia's policy of defensive struggles and husbanding the
Party's strength for a decisive future moment did not allow the PCI
to use the crisis of the centrist political formula initiated by the 1953
election to broaden its alliances and put the DC in difficulty. Indeed,
some comrades thought that, with the election victory, the time
had come to 'seize the occasion' and prepare for the final battle with
an already beaten enemy.[31]

At the December 1953 Central Committee meeting, Togliatti
launched the campaign that would lead to Secchia's fall. He called
a series of provincial congresses, in which the northern and central
federations were to be urged to imitate the example of the Party in
the south by creating a broad people's movement, open to the middle
classes and to non-Communists. He proposed that the slogan of
'Rebirth' (*Rinascita*) be adopted in the north and centre as well, and
that a series of objectives which would involve different strata of
society be included in a plan of *Rinascita*:

> As far as our concrete work is concerned . . . I don't believe we
> can say we have obtained good results in all fields. Without doubt,
> we have had our best results in the *Mezzogiorno* and in Sicily, where
> before, during, and even after the election campaign we really
> succeeded in organizing a mass movement for the rebirth of the
> South and of Sicily. This movement is healthy and strong, it is
> developing autonomously, it is energetically demanding concrete
> solutions to the age-old problems which afflict the people of the
> South and, as a consequence, the whole of Italy.
>   In the North, have we succeeded in creating something
> similar?[32]

In the provincial congresses, the whole Party was made aware that a
shift in orientation was underway. And finally, in January 1955,
Secchia was removed as Vice-Secretary-General; Giorgio Amendola was
chosen to succeed him as head of the Party's organisation section.
With this move Togliatti definitely re-established his own pre-eminence
and that of his Italian road to socialism within the PCI. This was the
major turning-point in his struggle, though the XX Congress of the
CPSU in 1956 gave him further weapons to overcome the remaining
resistance, open and covert, to his line.

Even without the dramatic denunciation of Stalin which Khrushchev
delivered in his secret speech, the XX Congress of the CPSU would
have marked an important departure in the history of the international
Communist movement. In his report to the Congress Khrushchev
denied that war between the capitalist and socialist blocs was inevitable;
peaceful coexistence and peaceful economic competition could ensure
the triumph of socialism. While Stalin's main objective in foreign policy
had always been to defend the USSR from aggression, he had operated
on the premiss that war was more or less inevitable. The campaigns
for 'peace' in the European capitalist countries in the period 1948-54

were essentially designed to keep those states neutral should the USA attack the socialist camp.[33] For Khrushchev, the socialist states were now strong enough to dissuade the United States from such an enterprise.

This altered international situation created new prospects for revolutions in the non-socialist world. The might of the USSR could protect them from foreign intervention. Hence the possibility of different roads to socialism from that followed by Russia. Khrushchev was in fact simply drawing the logical conclusion from the Popular Front strategy, which implied another, more gradual form of passage to socialism.

The cue given by Khrushchev was taken up in Italy: for Umberto Terracini, a member of the Executive of the PCI who had belonged to the original editorial group of *l'Ordine Nuovo* with Gramsci, it meant the rejection of the necessity of the dictatorship of the proletariat.[34] Since, in Lenin's definition, dictatorship is 'a power founded directly on violence and not limited to any law', and the dictatorship of the proletariat is associated with the violent suppression of the bourgeois state apparatus and the limitation of democratic rights for the class against whom the dictatorship is exercised,[35] Terracini argued that it was incompatible with progress towards socialism according to the rules of bourgeois democracy. This call for clarity did not find favour either with Togliatti's supporters or with his orthodox opponents within the PCI. The latter considered that a violent reaction by the bourgeoisie to any progress towards socialism was 'very probable', and hence wanted to keep open the perspective of an armed insurrection, though they were not prepared to state openly that it was inevitable. The former, on the other hand, practically excluded the possibility of an armed conflict, trusting to the dissuasive power of the alliance organised around the working class, but they did not wish to abandon the term 'dictatorship of the proletariat' explicitly, stressing its democratic character and the supposedly democratic form it had taken in the USSR.[36] Togliatti stated that 'The dictatorship of the proletariat, that is the political direction by the working class of the construction of a socialist society, is an historical necessity', but went on to say that it could take different forms.[37]

At its VIII Congress, held in December 1956, the PCI passed a Programmatic Declaration which resolved the question by implicitly rejecting the need for the dictatorship of the proletariat. A transition to socialism within the framework of the Constitution was possible, and the ruling class could be discouraged from reacting violently.

In practice, the possibility of violence was not contemplated, nor the denial of political rights to the bourgeoisie. Parliament would not be suppressed in the socialist stage, but simply supplemented by organs of direct democracy.[38]

The Programmatic Declaration summed up all the other main features of the *via italiana al socialismo* as well. It laid great stress on the role of the Resistance in creating the conditions for a broad alliance of the working class with other strata of the population. The Party's immediate aim, it asserted, was the establishment of a 'new power' resting on the support of the workers, the peasants and the 'working middle class', under which the state would be neither bourgeois nor socialist. It made specific promises to the potential middle-class allies: for instance, 'for decisive middle-class groups the passage to new socialist-type or socialist relations will take place only on the basis of their economic advantage and of free consent'.[39] The Declaration also further specified the content of the major structural reforms: the monopolies to be nationalised included electrical energy, public services, credit institutions, large chemical, steel and mechanical firms and 'basic industries' generally, while a universal social security system and the complete implementation of the Constitution were added to the list of reforms.

Togliatti, more than any other Communist leader, developed the Popular Front strategy into a viable line for a mass working-class party in Western Europe. He gradually eliminated those residues of the Comintern's pre-1935 perspective that were incompatible with the Popular Front, while his concept of structural reforms provided the basis for an alternative to the breakdown theory of revolution. Such an alternative strategy was formulated by the left-wing opposition within the PCI in the early 1960s in response to the difficult situation which the Italian economic miracle and its political consequences had created for the Party.

Notes

1. See G. Amyot, 'What is Eurocommunism?', *Canadian Dimension*, vol. 13, no. 4 (Nov.-Dec. 1978), for a fuller discussion of these points. Cf. also K. Kautsky, *La via al potere*, 1909 (Bari, 1969), esp. Ch. 4 on the role of trade-union action.

2. Cf. Kautsky, *La via al potere*; the polemic on the mass strike in the German SPD showed how reluctant the Marxist 'centre' was to contemplate even purely political strikes.

3. J.V. Stalin, *The Foundations of Leninism*, 1924 (Peking, 1970), p. 27.

4. Cf. N. Harding, *Lenin's Political Thought*, vol. 1 (London, 1977), for this interpretation.

5. See F. Hayek, *Storia dell'Internazionale comunista* (Rome, 1969), pp. 252-3, 290-1.

6. Quoted in F. De Felice, *Fascismo, democrazia, Fronte popolare* (Bari, 1973), p. 125.

7. See P. Togliatti, 'Sulle particolarità della rivoluzione spagnuola', *Sul movimento operaio internazionale*, ed. F. Ferri (Rome, 1972), pp. 190-2, where the bourgeoisie are explicitly included in the Popular Front.

8. The essay first appeared as a chapter of *History of the Communist Party (Bolsheviks) of the Soviet Union* (New York, 1938).

9. De Felice, *Fascismo*, p. 153.

10. *The Road to Socialism in Canada – the Program of the Communist Party of Canada* (Toronto, 1972), pp. 33, 45-6.

11. *Manifeste du parti communiste français – Pour une démocratie avancée, pour une France socialiste!* (Paris, 1969), p. 23.

12. *The Ninth Congress of the Communist Party of Greece* ('Exterior'), n.p. (1973), pp. 110-11.

13. See E. Berlinguer, *La proposta comunista* (Turin, 1975), pp. 49-50, quoted below, Ch. 13, p. 214.

14. 'Elementi per una dichiarazione programmatica del PCI!, *VIII Congresso del Partito comunista italiano – Atti e risoluzioni* (Rome, 1957), pp. 907-9.

15. In *L'Internazionale comunista e il fascismo* (Milan, 1971), originally published in *L'Internazionale comunista*, Aug. 1928. On the (significant) differences between Togliatti's approach to revolutionary strategy in Italy and Gramsci's, see, among others, L. Colletti, 'Antonio Gramsci and the Italian Revolution', *New Left Review*, 65 (Jan.-Feb. 1971).

16. P. Togliatti, *Lezioni sul fascismo* (Rome, 1970), pp. 9-10 and *passim*.

17. Ibid., p. 136.

18. A. Tasca, *The Rise of Italian Fascism* (New York, 1967), provides an excellent account of this period and a critique of the PSI's line. Togliatti's analysis owes much to that of Tasca, who was a member of the PCI until expelled in 1929 for right deviationism.

19. P. Togliatti, *La politica di Salerno* (Rome, 1969), p. 13.

20. A. Cecchi (ed.), *Storia del PCI attraverso i congressi* (Rome, 1977), pp. 57, 71.

21. Quoted in S. Tarrow, *Peasant Communism in Southern Italy* (New Haven and London, 1967), pp. 121-2.

22. See Tarrow's excellent treatment of this question in 'Communism in Italy and France: Adaptation and Change' in D.L.M. Blackmer and S. Tarrow (eds.), *Communism in Italy and France* (Princeton, NJ, 1975).

23. See esp. De Felice, *Fascismo*, pp. 209, 211, 218.

24. Togliatti, 'La preparazione di una nuova guerra mondiale da parte degli imperialisti e i compiti dell'Internazionale comunista' in *Sul movimento operaio internazionale*.

25. Togliatti, 'Sulle particolarità della rivoluzione spagnuola' in ibid.

26. See G. Bocca, *Palmiro Togliatti* (Rome-Bari, 1973), Chs. 25 and 26, and P. Secchia, *L'azione svolta dal partito comunista in Italia durante il fascismo 1926-1932* (Milan, 1970), pp. xxiii-vii. G. Amendola, *Un'isola* (Milan, 1980), pp. 180-1, confirms that in the 1930s Secchia was much more critical of Soviet policy than Amendola himself.

27. *VII Congresso del Partito comunista italiano* (Rome, 1954), pp. 65-73.

28. Ibid., pp. 165, 166-8 and *passim*.

29. Cf. Tarrow, *Peasant Communism*, pp. 229-30.

30. See table in P.A. Allum, 'The Italian Elections of 1963', *Political Studies*,

XIII, 3 (Oct. 1963); in the south and islands the PCI went from 10.3 per cent to 21.7 per cent, in the north-west from 23.4 per cent to 22.3 per cent, in the north-east from 13.3 per cent to 12.6 per cent, in the centre from 32.3 per cent to 33.7 per cent, in Italy as a whole from 18.9 per cent to 22.6 per cent.

31. G. Amendola, *Il rinnovamento del PCI*, interviewed by R. Nicolai (Rome, 1978), p. 21.

32. *L'Unità*, 8 Dec. 1953.

33. See F. Claudin, *La crisi del movimento comunista – dal Comintern al Cominform* (Milan, 1974), pp. 362-9, 445 ff.

34. 'Dittatura del proletariato e democrazia socialista', *l'Unità*, 1 Aug. 1956; see the comments on Terracini's article by A. Vaia and M. Alicata in *l'Unità*, 18 July and 8 Aug. 1956 respectively, and Terracini's reply in *l'Unità*, 22 Aug. 1956.

35. V.I. Lenin, *La rivoluzione proletaria e il rinnegato Kautsky*, 1918 (Moscow, 1949), pp. 10-14; the definition quoted appears on p. 11.

36. See articles by A. Colombi, *l'Unità*, 28 July 1956; C. Salinari, *l'Unità*, 22 Aug. 1956; L. Longo, *l'Unità*, 29 Aug. 1956; L. Romagnoli, *l'Unità*, 5 Sept. 1956.

37. Cecchi, *Storia del PCI*, p. 159.

38. 'Elementi per una dichiarazione programmatica', *VIII Congresso*, pp. 907-11.

39. 'Elementi' in Cecchi, *Storia del PCI*, p. 177.

3 LEFT-WING EUROCOMMUNISM: THE INGRAO LEFT

1. The Economic Miracle and the Crisis of the PCI's Strategy

The *via italiana al socialismo* was the Italian variant of the Popular Front strategy, which Togliatti had espoused with enthusiasm and developed into a coherent perspective as a result of his reflections on the defeat of 1922. His own personal preferences no doubt predisposed him to choose the more moderate, gradualist approach which the ambiguity of the Comintern's position after 1935 left open to him.[1] These factors, among which the international predominate, lie at the root of the *via italiana*. But this line was also supported and justified by an analysis of the Italian economy and Italian society, which was not less significant for being elaborated largely *ex post*.[2] Though Togliatti's and Gramsci's strategic perspectives were different, the PCI's analysis purported to be based on that of Gramsci (see Chapter 1, Section 2). For Togliatti, the underdevelopment of the south, the continued existence of 'semi-feudal' relations of production in agriculture, such as sharecropping and large estates, and the oppression of women were all evidence of the backward nature of Italian capitalism. (So too, paradoxically and in apparent contrast to Marx's predictions, he considered the dominance of monopoly capital a sign of backwardness.) As fascism itself had been the product of the backwardness of Italian capitalism, the structural reforms aimed at eliminating the social bases of fascism would also solve the various questions, such as the southern question, left unsolved by Italy's incomplete bourgeois revolution. And a broad alliance was necessary to 'complete the bourgeois revolution'.

This analysis led to the conclusion that Italy's economy, backward and strangled by the monopolies and large agrarian proprietors, with their tendency to restrict production, was incapable of rapid economic growth. Furthermore, while Togliatti did not have a catastrophic view of the prospects of world capitalism, he did believe it was entering a general crisis which would tend to worsen and bring in its train stagnation, immiseration and increasing unrest. As late as 1956 he affirmed that 'for the population in general we cannot deny that there remains a tendency to impoverishment'.[3] This was the perspective shared by the entire international Communist movement in the late

54

1940s and early 1950s; Stalin himself, in his *Economic Problems of Socialism in the USSR* (1952), foresaw a steadily worsening crisis of overproduction in the capitalist world, which would have difficulty finding markets for its products.[4] This was consistent with his own theory of capitalist crisis, outlined in 'Dialectical and Historical Materialism'.[5] For Togliatti, it was the task of the working class not to aggravate this crisis, but to form a broad coalition to lead the country out of it. The struggle for structural reforms, then, he saw as a struggle against the social bases of fascism that was at the same time a struggle over the quantity of economic growth (but not its quality). Hence it was largely defensive, aimed at protecting democracy and the living standards of the working class and middle strata which were threatened by the monopolies and the crisis. He did not see structural reforms as a way of furthering the direct transition to socialism.

The Italian 'economic miracle' of the decade 1953-63 seriously undermined the analysis which justified the PCI's strategy. It proved that the monopolies, far from promoting stagnation, were capable of generating rapid economic growth and rising living standards. Hence it was no longer possible for the PCI to propose a coalition with the object of economic development *tout court*; it would have to call into question the quality of that development. With development and growth, too, the legacies of the 'incomplete bourgeois revolution', such as the southern question, seemed to be losing their importance. And at the same time the weight of the middle strata, the focus of the PCI's policy of alliances, declined with industrial development. (The percentage of self-employed in the workforce fell from 44 in 1951, to 37 in 1961, to 29 in 1971.[6]) The monopolies were no longer politically isolated, as the DC regime was able to attract support in the north and centre on the basis of the new prosperity, and in the south by means of a system of subsidies, favours and corruption. In particular, the DC strengthened its political hold on the middle strata. Some of the democratic and anti-monopolistic structural reforms, it now seemed, could be carried out by the bourgeoisie itself to strength its own position.

The miracle dealt an even more serious blow to the catastrophic perspective of the economic breakdown of capitalism, which was still that of many among the older generation of PCI militants. More disturbing yet were the climate of *détente* in international relations after the death of Stalin and Khrushchev's theorisation of the possibility of peaceful coexistence; many had come to expect that the 'X hour' of the socialist revolution was likely to be precipitated by a war. For this reason the Chinese critique of the policies of the USSR and of Togliatti, which became publicly known in 1960, struck a responsive chord. The Chinese reaffirmed the traditional Leninist thesis that 'imperialism is the eve of the socialist revolution', and held that a revolutionary crisis, in the form of a war, was to be expected.

In the late 1950s, then, both the more orthodox militants of the PCI and those who had understood and accepted Togliatti's line came to doubt the bases of their positions, which they had previously considered certainties. This theoretical crisis was reflected in a major organisational decline, as party membership, recruitment (especially among the young) and activism fell off sharply.[7] The crisis was aggravated by the delay with which the Party perceived and adjusted to the new reality of economic growth, as it continued to wage defensive struggles and was still, in many areas, led by men and women whose political outlook was that of a past era. The 'X hour' mentality led many cadres to adopt a passive, waiting attitude and to close themselves within the Party organisation. An event emblematic of this loss of contact with the new situation was the defeat suffered by the CGIL in the 1955 Fiat grievance committee election.

Not only did the 'miracle' lead to a weakening of the PCI's organisation; potentially as serious was the loosening of the Party's links with the Socialist Party. After 1953 the PSI began to be attracted by the possibility of social-democratic reforms on the North European model. In 1956 it did not renew its long-standing unity of action pact with the PCI and initiated talks with the Social Democrats about the eventual reunification of the two parties. At the same time it made it clear to the DC that it would be available for a reforming governmental coalition. These developments posed a clear threat to the PCI: the end of the alliance with the PSI could lead to the loss of power in local government and splits in the trade unions and other mass organisations which it controlled with the Socialists. And there was the spectre of a large social-democratic party, born of the fusion of PSI and PSDI, that could supplant the Communists as the largest force on the left. These dangers became much more concrete with the formation of the centre-left coalition, including the DC, the PSI, the PSDI and the Republicans, in 1962-3.

The centre-left seemed to demonstrate that the monopolies, far from being unable to gain the consent of the other classes in Italian society, were attracting new forces to their camp. While some Communists argued that it could be the first step towards breaking down the anti-Communist prejudices of the DC, the new governmental formula seemed to most a threat and an attempt to isolate the PCI.

At the same time the economic growth of the period 1953-63 put Togliatti's strategy into question in another way: by the early 1960s a labour shortage had developed in the northern industrial triangle, and this along with long hours, speed-ups and the poor housing and social services for the thousands of recently arrived southern workers led to a new wave of working-class militancy, after the passivity of the 1950s. The new militancy encouraged a tendency to see the working class as the focus of the Party's strategy, and to minimise the importance of the alliance policy. Many Communists now considered the struggle for democratic objectives out of date and wanted to fight for immediate socialist goals.

A new youth movement also grew up in the early 1960s. In July 1960 demonstrators, many of them very young, provoked the fall of the Tambroni government, which had come to power thanks to neo-fascist parliamentary support. Leftist young people, reflecting the spirit of their times, displayed impatience with the PCI's two-stage strategy and called instead for a direct struggle for socialism. These ideas permeated the leadership of the Young Communist Federation (FGCI), whose journal called as early as 1961 for the reopening of debate on the thought of Trotsky. For the editors of the journal, Trotsky had had the merit of emphasising the importance of the Western proletariat as the agent of socialist revolution.[8] The following year Achille Occhetto, a left-wing critic of the Party's strategy, was elected Secretary of the FGCI.

2. Ingrao's Platform

The crisis of the *via italiana* in the late 1950s and early 1960s led some Communists to reformulate the Party's strategy. Structural reforms, they argued, must strike not at the backward elements of Italian capitalism but at its very heart: the large corporations, the most advanced manifestations of capitalist development. They must be part of a strategy of direct struggle for socialism, rather than simply for a first stage of progressive democracy. The most important leader in this group was Pietro Ingrao, a member of the Executive and former editor of *l'Unità*, the Party daily. This Communist left rejected, as Togliatti had, the breakdown theory and the any kind of *politique du pire*. But they also rejected the view that monopoly capitalism generated stagnation and thereby facilitated the formation of an anti-monopoly coalition. Rather, they saw that it had the capacity to promote growth and believed, perhaps too pessimistically, that it could provide reforms and broaden the basis of consent on which it rested. Therefore, for them the Party's aim had to be not an acceptable quantitative level of economic growth, but rather a qualitatively different type of economy. As Lucio Magri put it in 1962:

> What is today the real discriminant between the plan of development which the bourgeoisie proposes or is historically able to propose for our society, and the opposing plan which guides the working class in the determination of its allies and in the definition of its objectives of mobilization and struggle? Is it the traditional discriminant, no matter how revised, between an autocratic, immobilist, and tendentially authoritarian capitalism and a movement of democratic forces which is, on the other hand, united around a platform of completing the bourgeois revolution? Or does the question present itself in qualitatively new terms?[9]

This position, however, created a serious problem for the Communist left: if the Party's aim was not to save capitalism from stagnation and crisis, but rather to break with capitalism and construct a socialist society, how could it avoid pursuing a policy which was certain to bring about a crisis in the system? The commitment to avoiding a crisis seemed to entail accepting the priorities of the system. The answer to this question provided by Ingrao was the 'alternative model of development', a credible, positive alternative programme. Togliatti, in his Yalta promemoria (1964), had written of the need for such a plan when discussing the trend towards centralised economic planning in Western Europe:

> This requires a development and co-ordination of the workers' immediate demands and of the proposals for reforms of the economic structure (nationalisations, agrarian reforms, etc.) in a general plan of economic development to oppose to capitalist planning. This will certainly not yet be a socialist plan . . . but it is a new form and a new means of struggle to advance towards socialism.[10]

This programme provided an outlet for the workers' militancy. If workers' struggles remained purely economistic, concerned simply with wage increases, they could provoke a crisis, but they could not be linked to the political goal of socialism; whereas, if they included among their objectives qualitative changes in investments and production they could be part of the fight for the alternative model of development. Thus Ingrao's strategy finally abolished the distinction between economic and political struggles and allowed trade-union action to be more than defensive in character. The very strength of the capitalist economy which it postulated gave the working class a margin of manoeuvre to fight for changes in the economic structure.

The economic content of the 'alternative model' was only sketched out by some members of the Communist left. It meant a change in consumption patterns – i.e. a change in values. Investment had to be controlled and directed towards collective and essential goods: capital goods and subsistence goods rather than consumer durables. Priority was to be given also to investment in agriculture, the development of the south and social services. As Alfredo Reichlin, a prominent member of the left, wrote, these reforms were 'intermediate objectives that the working-class movement recognizes as its own and that are not immediately socialist'.[11] They had to involve a shift in the relations of force in society in favour of the working class. This shift would give it new positions of power from which to go on and further undermine the monopolies' strength and decision-making power.

This approach clearly involved the danger of a technocratic, authoritarian application of the concept of the 'alternative model'. But the model had a political content which was perhaps even more important than its economic side. Ingrao developed and carried further Togliatti's reflections on the causes of Stalinism, laying great stress on the absence of any structure in civil society other than the party as one of the roots of the abuses of the Stalinist period.[12] He saw these roots as reaching deeper into the fabric of Soviet society than most other PCI leaders of the centre and right were prepared to admit.[13] Therefore, he reasoned, in order to prevent the appearance of Stalinism in Italy it was necessary to decentralise power by creating a network of centres of local power and direct democracy, which he identified with the institutions of local government, with eventual forms of workers' control and with independent organisations in civil society such as trade unions.[14]

Furthermore, Ingrao believed that this network of autonomous powers could not be constructed *ex novo* after the victory of socialism, but had to be prefigured in present-day capitalist society. Hence the object of structural reforms, for him, was not only to attack the

monopolies' power over investment, the organisation of work and the
pattern of consumption,[15] but also to create such a fabric of autonomous bodies. He wanted to begin to break down the division
between state and civil society by creating counterweights to the state
in civil society; in particular he was opposed to the attempts to involve
the trade unions in an incomes policy which were being promoted by
the centre-left government at that time. He feared this would limit the
unions' autonomy while creating a corporatist decision-making
structure that would reduce the power of elected assemblies and
political parties.

The FGCI leaders took these ideas even further; they foresaw
the coexistence of two types of democratic bodies in a future socialist
society: organs of direct democracy (factory councils or soviets) and
assemblies elected on a territorial basis. This would not take the form
of 'dual power', as in Russia in 1917, but would be a permanent 'co-
presence in a form which will be determined by the class struggle'.[16]

The first and most notable revision of the PCI's Togliattian
strategy which the Communist left's position entailed involved the
policy of alliances. In the perspective of a struggle for progressive
democracy, it was crucial to form firm alliances with the middle strata
and non-monopolistic bourgeoisie. For the left, who aimed directly
at socialism, alliances were important but not central: the working
class, in particular in the large factories, was the most important agent
in the struggle. This tendency was clearly perceived by Amendola,
the foremost representative of the right, who defended the Togliattian
strategy:

> Certain conceptions lead at a certain point to a negation of the
> growing importance of the working class's alliance policy, at the
> very moment when the expansion of the monopolies and its
> consequences create on the contrary new possibilities for widening
> our system of alliances, broadening the basis of the alliances of
> the working class to all the strata that are hurt by this monopolistic
> expansion, rather than reducing this basis.[17]

The left argued that petty commodity production and other pre-
capitalist relationships were losing their importance. Occhetto, the
FGCI Secretary, called for the explicit abandonment of the Popular
Front strategy by the Western Communist parties, and for a new
system of alliances suitable to the direct struggle for socialism. He
argued that Togliatti had in the last years of his life abandoned the

line of the VII Congress of the Comintern and recognised that capitalism, not fascism, was the enemy. He had realised that economics and politics were closely linked in advanced capitalism and that the purely political anti-fascist alliances of the 1930s and 1940s were no longer sufficient. For Occhetto, the Yalta promemoria with its reference to an alternative economic plan represented an innovation with respect to the VIII Congress of the PCI and raised the *via italiana* to the level of a strategy for the European working-class movement.[18]

While the left's argument rested on the advanced nature of Italian capitalism, the right did not consider itself bound to the thesis that it was backward. In an important series of articles in 1964,[19] Amendola argued for a policy of broad, Popular Front alliances from the *advanced* character of Italian capitalism and its similarity to that of the rest of Europe, rather than from its backwardness and particularity. For Amendola and the right, the policy of alliances and the two-stage strategy were valid irrespective of the stage of development of capitalism.

For Ingrao, on the other hand, the new situation put the struggle for socialism directly on the agenda and required the formation of a 'new historic bloc' of social forces. This bloc would include many, if not all, of the traditional allies of the old Popular Front, but it was to be formed primarily in civil society rather than at the political level. Ingrao argued that his alternative model of development would not alienate members of the intermediate strata who might agree with some points but not others, but rather would help the Party win allies by dissipating the suspicion that its reform proposals were simply tactics aimed at attracting votes, rather than part of its real programme.[20]

At the same time, developments within the unions were also pointing towards a greater role for the working class in the Party's overall perspective. From the mid-1950s the CGIL had begun to respond to the new conditions in the factories by extending the scope of collective bargaining beyond wage rates and hours to the organisation of work, its speed, sanitary conditions and many other fields. In the long run, the attempt to control the organisation of work entailed bargaining over the type of machinery to be installed, and therefore over the firms' investment plans. This naturally led on to the demand for a new model of economic development, to give a sense to the unions' proposals over investment, and Ingrao's strategy was therefore a logical complement to the unions' new tactics.

But the proposal that the unions themselves should use their bargaining power to control the large firms' investment plans meant

that alliances with other classes were less necessary and that the elected
assemblies (parliament and local government) could be bypassed. The
assemblies were the place in which political alliances with the middle
classes, through their political representatives such as the DC, were
most easily made, and the PCI's commitment to bourgeois democracy
as part of its two-stage strategy meant that they should be recognised
as the central decision-making bodies in society. Similarly, schemes
involving decentralisation of power and direct democracy, such as
Ingrao's, were potentially incompatible with the PCI's commitment
to bourgeois democracy as it existed. So in yet another way the left's
position meant a revision of the PCI's traditional policy of alliances.

The left also broke with the two-stage strategy explicitly. Not only
did they wish to direct their programme of structural reforms at the
heart of Italian capitalism, the monopolies, rather than simply at its
backward elements; they denied that the gradual implementation of
these reforms during an intermediate phase was possible. They believed
that the capitalists' reactions to any left-wing victories would be sharp
and rapid, and would soon precipitate a crisis. As Bruno Trentin, a left-
wing trade-union leader, put it, 'The danger is not so much that we
shall be absorbed as that we shall be overrun.'[21] Therefore, an organic
plan was necessary, in the left's view, to deal with these capitalist
reactions; otherwise, the Party's reform programme would not appear
credible. It would be seen as simply the prelude to economic crisis.

Amendola and the right, on the other hand, were more sanguine
about the margins for reformism within Italian capitalism; this was in
part because they contemplated less radical reforms. They believed that
capitalist reaction was possible, but that state intervention and the
'mobilisation of the masses' could prevent it. Luciano Barca, one of
the Party's economic experts, foresaw an intermediate phase between
capitalism and socialism, a two-sector economy dominated by the
public sector and governed by 'democratic planning'. For the left, this
kind of reformed capitalism was impossible.[22] They quoted in support
of their position one of Togliatti's last articles, in which he implied
that the big bourgeoisie in Italy was not ready to accept 'even a group
of moderate measures of bourgeois reformism'.[23] Their own action
would precipitate a crisis for which they wanted to have ready a
positive solution.

In the third place, the left's position led it to challenge democratic
centralism as practised in the PCI. Their critique flowed both from their
concern to prefigure the future socialist society in the course of the
struggle within capitalism, and from their conception of revolution.

Healthy intra-party democracy was a bulwark against the appearance of authoritarian tendencies in a future socialist regime. Moreover, the democratic centralist model of the party was adapted to the view of revolution as the seizure of power by a small, disciplined group in a moment of crisis — the Leninist strategy. A strong party discipline was also necessary in Togliatti's Popular Front strategy, in order to brake and restrain the corporative, economic demands of various groups, in particular the working class, for the sake of the Party's overall political strategy, the formation of a broad alliance. (One of Lenin's principal reasons for advocating the formation of a vanguard party in Russia in 1902 was his conviction that the immediate task of the Russian Social Democrats was the political struggle for the overthrow of tsarism rather than the struggle for socialism itself. Hence the need, in a predominantly peasant society where the working class was a small minority, to forge an inter-class alliance, to which the economic, corporative interests of the working class had to be subordinated.[24]) The Communist left, on the other hand, sought to integrate political and economic struggles rather than superimpose political requirements and goals on the economic and social life of the working class. As the Italian working class, unlike the Russian workers in Lenin's time, was the majority or at least the crucial social group, its corporative, economic concerns were also the central political questions of the day. And it could give birth to a network of relatively autonomous institutions in civil society only if the Party did not exercise tight control over the actions of Communists in these institutions.

Ingrao himself argued, in an article of 1964, that the party needed fuller internal debate because there was no longer a 'military-type conception of the party (as a detachment which essentially had to prepare itself for the decisive armed struggle)'[25] whose strategy was already given; as the question of strategy was open, more freedom to discuss and find new roads to socialism was necessary. Democratic participation by members of the Party in its life was also necessary if the PCI was to gain intellectual and moral hegemony over society, which Gramsci had laid down as a precondition for the achievement of power. Finally, he wrote, young people and intellectuals would be attracted only by a relatively open party. Therefore he proposed organisational decentralisation and the formation of working groups around specific problems at the grassroots to supplement the territorial and workplace organisations. Furthermore, he argued that the leading bodies of the Party (i.e. Central Committee and federal committeees) should really make decisions, rather than simply be

consulted by the Secretariat and Executive (*Direzione* or *direttivo*).
To facilitate this, he proposed that the reports presented to the
committees by the secretariats should not deal with the *whole* situation
and the *whole* policy of the Party, but only with the main points at
issue or proposed changes in the Party's position, which could even
be presented 'in problematic form' (i.e. with alternative solutions
proposed). The higher bodies, Executive and Secretariat, should take
up clearer positions on one side or the other, but explain how they
arrived at their decisions so that the rank and file could really take
part in the discussion as well. At the same time Ingrao declared his
opposition to the formation of factions (*correnti*) in the party, because
they tended to crystallise differences of opinion and perpetuate divisions.
The experience of factionalism in the PSI had not been positive.

Further, the left's position led it to take a much more pessimistic
view of the possible results of the centre-left coalition than the right
did, and therefore to adopt a much more intransigent stance towards
it. The left believed that capitalism was capable of integrating the
working-class movement, and saw the centre-left as an attempt to do so
which had good chances of succeeding in isolating and weakening the
PCI. It therefore was prepared to abandon the older strategy of seeking
alliances at the political level with other parties, such as the PSI, which
it judged to be on its way towards integration, and to build instead a
new historic bloc, anti-capitalist and opposed to the centre-left,
directly in civil society, drawing on working-class and left-wing
elements from all political traditions, including the Catholic. Some of
the left saw this almost as a desperate rearguard action against the
advance of neocapitalism.[26]

For the right, on the other hand, the centre-left was bound to fail
to solve the problems of Italian capitalism: its 'secondary contradictions', such as the southern question, were too intractable, and the
system was bound to enter a new phase of crisis and stagnation.
Therefore the centre-left would, in the long run, bring new votes to the
PCI as disillusionment set in and at the same time prepare the way for
the Communists' entry into government as the only party capable of
ensuring the success of a reform programme. For these reasons the
right envisaged a solution at the political level, to be reached between
the parties, and was consequently concerned to maintain good relations
with the PSI. The left, on the other hand, believed that the PCI had no
common ground with most other political forces, because it did not
believe a first stage of bourgeois reforms could be a prelude to further
advance.

In the debate over the centre-left the differences between right and left in the PCI first became evident. Before its formation, many right-wing PCI leaders showed their sympathy for the experiment and criticised the left wing of the PSI for obstructing the achievement of the new governmental formula. They saw the 1963 general election, in which the PCI advanced 2.7 per cent while both the DC and PSI lost ground, as vindicating their argument that the centre-left would strengthen the PCI. (Ingrao and the left saw it as a rejection of the centre-left itself by the electorate and a stimulus to develop a more aggressive, radical strategy.) In January 1964 the left wing of the PSI, which had refused to vote confidence in the first centre-left cabinet the previous month, left the party to form the Italian Socialist Party of Proletarian Unity (PSIUP). While the Communist left greeted the new party with enthusiasm, the majority of the PCI would have preferred to keep a foot within the government through the PSI left wing.[27] They feared that the presence of the PSIUP would exacerbate tensions between the PCI and the PSI, and provoke the exit of the latter from local government coalitions and mass organisations.

Amendola demonstrated his desire to maintain links with the Socialists later in the year in a controversial article, 'Hypotheses on Reunification'.[28] He proposed the fusion of the Communists and Socialists into a single party of the working class. Shocking some older PCI militants, he argued that both social democracy and communism had failed to create a socialist society in Western Europe in the previous fifty years. The end of the Cold War, peaceful coexistence and the adoption of the Popular Front strategy by the Communist parties had made the reasons for the split of 1921 anachronistic. In an advanced capitalist country, such as Italy was becoming, the Popular Front was, in Amendola's view, the policy the reunified party should adopt.[29]

The article reflected not only Amendola's long-term political perspective, but also a more immediate preoccupation: after the PSIUP split the reunification of the PSI and PSDI became a feasible proposition. (It in fact occurred in 1966; the unified party split again in 1969.) The PSDI was fiercely anti-Communist, and a unified PSI-PSDI might try to break with the PCI in local government and the unions, and perhaps even form a 'socialist' trade-union confederation. (The PSI's creation of a socialist peasant organisation in competition with the older unitary *Alleanza contadini* did not go unnoticed.)

Amendola also believed that the political situation was approaching a crisis, and that if a left-wing alternative to the centre-left could not be found there was a grave danger that the monopolies would resume control and perhaps impose a right-wing, authoritarian solution.[30] (The De Lorenzo affair, which came to a head in the summer of 1964, demonstrated that some elements in the Christian Democratic Party, including the President of the Republic, Segni, were contemplating such a solution: General Giovanni De Lorenzo, commander of the Carabinieri, drew up a plan for the arrest of left-wing politicians and unionists. He consulted only President Segni before doing this.) This was, in his view, a further reason for seeking an immediate solution at the political level rather than attempting the long-term task of constructing a new historic bloc in civil society. The danger of a political crisis made a broad democratic alliance necessary, just as fascism had dictated such an alliance in the past. (Again, Amendola's commitment to the Popular Front strategy was *a priori* and did not depend on his analysis of the situation of the moment, which indeed was shaped by his strategic perspective.) He hence proposed that unification should embrace all the '48 per cent of Italians to the left of the DC' (i.e. not only PCI, PSI and PSIUP, but also PSDI and PRI). In keeping with this strategy, he proposed in December 1964 that the PCI support Giuseppe Saragat, leader of the PSDI, as candidate for President of the Republic.

The left within the PCI criticised Amendola's proposal because the 48 per cent of Italians to the left of the DC had no common programme to unite around. Their reasoning was in terms of social classes rather than traditional political 'families' and parties; their aim was to unite the 50 per cent of Italians who were working class. They preferred to seek alliances with left-wing Catholics rather than with the bourgeois parties of the lay left, in the hope of building a largely proletarian historic bloc. For this reason they were more inclined to support Fanfani, the representative of the DC left, for the Presidency in 1964. The Communist left also wanted to restrict the ambit of any eventual left-wing unification to the PCI, the PSIUP and the Lombardi wing of the PSI, who had come out against continuing the centre-left experiment.[31]

Finally, the Communist left took up a much more critical stance *vis-à-vis* the USSR than did the right. They aimed at the construction over a fairly long time of a new historic bloc, and the success of this project depended to a large extent on whether they could present a credible model of socialism different from that offered by the Soviet Union. Ingrao's reflection on Stalinism and its causes was connected to this preoccupation. Amendola and the right, on the other hand, saw the next phase as a democratic, rather than a socialist one, so that for them the development of a credible socialist perspective was less urgent. Furthermore, Amendola believed that a crisis was imminent in Italy and that in this situation the PCI would need to maintain above all its unity; hence a debate on the nature of the USSR and a break with the Soviet Union would be counter-productive because they would divide and weaken the Party.[32] After the Sino-Soviet split, Ingrao was much more sympathetic than Amendola to the Chinese position, while not by any means embracing it, and he opposed a break with the Chinese Party. Amendola, on the other hand, became increasingly pro-Soviet in his pronouncements.[33]

3. The XI Congress

The struggle between left and right came to a head after the death of Togliatti in August 1964. He was succeeded by Luigi Longo. Since 1960-1 Amendola had been losing favour with the leader — the December 1961 Central Committee meeting was the scene of a serious difference of opinion between them over the pace of de-Stalinisation. At the same time Ingrao's star was on the rise, as Togliatti appeared to move to a more left-wing position. Longo's Secretary-Generalship appeared as an interim solution, with Ingrao, Amendola and Giorgio Napolitano, a Neapolitan protégé of Amendola, the favoured candidates to succeed him. The debate on unification did not increase Amendola's popularity with the rank and file, so much so that he withdrew his direct and vigorous support after the proposal had been taken up by the party leadership, while the Ingrao group adopted it in the form of a limited unification with the PSIUP and the Lombardians.

The first shots in the battle proper between the two tendencies were fired at the Genoa conference of Communist workers at the end of May 1965. Before the conference, rumours circulated that there were 'Ingrao theses' prepared for it; in fact the theses were prepared by a committee chaired by Amendola to which Ingrao did not belong.[34] But the influence of the latter was undoubtedly strong. Many of the worker delegates stressed the need for a clear connection between the day-to-day struggle in the factory and the Party's general reform programme; the alternative plan proposed by the *ingraiani* was the most credible answer to these complaints. For example, the delegate from the Trieste shipyards criticised the Party's struggle against closures in the industry as 'sectorial', when it should have been linked to a general programme of reform for the whole maritime sector, involving port construction, the merchant fleet and, ultimately, Italy's foreign policy and trade relations. A railway worker similarly stressed the need for a general plan for the transport sector, especially in view of the centre-left's intention to reduce the public, social-service aspect of the state railway network, and a militant from the RIV ball-bearing plant in Turin noted that the Party had been too slow in responding to lay-offs with a demand for state intervention. Generally the Party was criticised for being insufficiently present and active in the factory, leaving the field to the union, or for being present only with practical work of a trade-union type and limiting political activity to a purely theoretical, ideological level. The Party's general line, based on Amendola's favourite concept, 'democratic planning', was too remote from the workers' day-to-day struggles.

These calls for a more pronounced working-class orientation in the Party's activity were taken up by one of the representatives of the left, Luciana Castellina. She insisted that the centre of the Party's work should be the most advanced, rather than the most backward, sectors of the Italian economy. The workers themselves should contract the number of hands required for each job, the rhythm of work and a reform of technical education and of the career structure. Amendola in his comments took issue explicitly with this proposal to concentrate on the 'advanced' sectors only.[35]

When, approximately a month later, the Central Committee chose a committee to prepare the 'theses' for the forthcoming congress, differences of opinion reappeared. After lively discussions in the theses committee, the actual drafting was delegated first to one sub-committee, then to another, before finally being taken in hand by the Party Executive and Secretariat. The Party rank and file, however, received no information about this long gestation process, which lasted roughly four months.[36]

The theses eventually drafted substantially reflected the line of the centre and right of the Party. When the Central Committee met at the end of October 1965, a major debate ensued.[37] On the question of the PSI and the centre-left, the spokesmen of the left expressed their pessimism, holding that the integration of the PSI into the capitalist system, if not irreversible, was well under way. As it became a party of government, the social base of the PSI and its cadres were changing; access to patronage was corrupting it. The right wing was winning the PSI provincial congresses then underway. The left therefore contested the theses' formula 'failure of the centre-left' as partial and inexact, because only its 'reformist' aspect had failed, while it had succeeded in integrating the PSI.

The left also proposed again 'more advanced' objectives and a link between mass struggles and proposals for reform, both of which implied an 'alternative model of development' rather than partial objectives, and posing the question of power at the grass roots. The theses had only in part accepted this conception. Some speakers (e.g. Chiaromonte) opposed making any distinction between 'advanced' and 'backward' sectors of the economy, while Amendola explicitly opposed more 'advanced' slogans. Few examples of 'more advanced' slogans were given during the debate: Natoli referred to the way in which the nationalisation of the electricity industry in 1962 had been carried out from above, without any participation by the mass of the workers or any demands by the PCI for a more advanced form of nationalisation.

The crucial battle at the October Central Committee, however, was joined on the question of intra-party democracy. Ingrao, who had participated in the drafting process, had finally agreed to the version of the theses proposed by Mario Alicata and Alfredo Reichlin, who was very close to Ingrao's positions. Nevertheless, he voiced a number of criticisms of them in the course of the meeting. He defined the formula 'failure of the centre-left' as inadequate and called for a model of development rather than partial objectives. The Party's programme, he said, should provide a link between mass struggles and reforms by posing the question of power at the grass roots. He then entered a plea for more debate within the Party: the Central Committee should spend more time on crucial decisions; otherwise there was a harmful discrepancy between 'the breadth of the debate and the corresponsibility for the decisions taken'.

Ingrao insisted in making public his disagreement in order to allow the whole party to take part in the discussion. But his criticisms of the theses gave rise to very strong protests within the Central Committee, because he had broken the unwritten rule of 'cabinet solidarity', the unity of the higher bodies towards the lower, even in the decision-making process (see above, Chapter 1, p. 29). Macaluso challenged him: if he was in favour of the formation of factions, he should say so openly. Pajetta stressed the role of the leadership of the Party (*gruppo dirigente*) in preserving its particular characteristics, and argued that democracy should make the party function better rather than constitute an end in itself. One of the strongest attacks came from the traditionalist leader Arturo Colombi who stated that the Party rank and file was 'perplexed' by the appearance of divisions in the leadership, and went on:

The publicising of the debate has been requested by comrade Ingrao. He has not waited for the Central Committee to decide to make this debate public: he has taken this liberty off his own bat. This act damages the party and, in the first place, comrade Ingrao himself.[38]

Amendola himself criticised Ingrao: the theses, he said, were the result of four months' hard work of mediation, and Ingrao should have accepted them as a 'unitary' result. The publicising of debate was not advisable on all occasions. Majorities and minorities should form in the Party on specific concrete questions, not general ones – otherwise they would crystallise and degenerate into factions. Amendola, who had been strongly in favour of greater intra-party democracy in 1956 and in 1961, now began to moderate his position, since Ingrao's demands were out of tune with the sentiment of much of the rank and file and threatened Party unity.

In this same Central Committee many of the traditionalist group (Roasio, Secchia and Vidali) intervened in favour of freedom of debate; whereas only Colombi took a strong stand against Ingrao. Secchia attempted to assume a mediating position between the two sides, while adding his own criticism of the theses for stressing the struggle for peace too much as opposed to the struggles for national liberation.

Alicata, who had co-ordinated the formulation of the theses, replied to the debate, rejecting the criticisms of the formula 'failure of the centre-left' and arguing that Ingrao's request for more advanced objectives and an alternative plan was satisfied by the theses. He agreed to insert a more complete analysis of the PSI, while criticising the attempt to restrict the proposed unification to the PSIUP and the Lombardi group. Longo, in drawing the final conclusions of the debate, stressed that freedom of criticism, even to criticise the general line, existed in the party, but took Ingrao to task for criticising the theses he had agreed to in committee.

At the congress itself, Longo took up the question of intra-party democracy again in his opening remarks. Repeating his strictures on factionalism, he pointed out that the debate within the party had been amply publicised, so that he could not understand what the request for 'publicising of the debate' meant. Some recent criticisms of the Party's line, he said, were 'general and abstract' or 'hermetic and allusive', and therefore difficult for the comrades to understand.

Ingrao spoke on the need for unification with the PSIUP and the *lombardiani*, as a step towards a wider unity with a clear positive alternative programme, a 'cartel of yesses' (*cartello dei si*) rather than a simple protest vote. It was a fairly complete statement of many of the characteristic elements of his position, without any explicit criticisms of the theses; indeed, he said he might have stressed too much the 'new elements' of the political situation in the October Central Committee meeting. At the end he referred to internal democracy: 'Comrade Longo has expressed his criticisms and his preoccupations on the question of the publicising of debate. I should not be sincere if I said to you that I have been persuaded'.[39] He went on to confirm his own 'reinforced support' for the Party line and his opposition to the formation of factions. Expressing respect for Longo's opinion he also conceded that the higher organs of the Party should decide whether a question should be taken to the rank and file or not.

Though Ingrao's criticism involved not the theses themselves but the procedural question of the 'publicising of debate', it caused a vehement reaction and demands for counter-measures, especially from Pajetta and Alicata.[40] The next day Pajetta launched a severe attack, telling Ingrao to state clearly what his disagreement with the Party was, since it clearly went beyond the question of the 'publicising of debate'. Ingrao had not clarified what he meant by this phrase.[41] Alicata intervened later; after making some concessions to Ingrao on the question of an alternative programme, he too asked if Ingrao was not expressing doubt about the substance of the Party line as well. He agreed that comrades had the right to have doubts, so long as the doubts were not permanent, but they should express them openly. He concluded with a strong plea for party unity. Enrico Berlinguer took up the criticism of Ingrao, but in less sharp tones, suggesting that debate should not be made public on all occasions. Several speakers, however, came to Ingrao's defence: Secchia, Luporini and Alfredo Reichlin, who made a conciliatory appeal for party unity and for a less dramatic view of the question of democratic debate. Longo's conclusions were milder than might have been expected on the question. He stated that Ingrao had still not specified concretely what he wanted done to better 'publicise debate' within the Party, and expressed his 'shock' at the request for more debate than there had already been. Taking up Reichlin's appeal for unity he repeated a firm no 'to the group spirit, to insincerity and disloyalty towards the Party and its leading bodies'.[42]

Ingrao had nevertheless suffered a serious, indeed humiliating, defeat. In the debate on substantive questions, he did not fare any better. In spite of Alicata's concession on the need for an 'organic programme', the term 'model of development' was rejected. Berlinguer,

one of the inner leadership, also rejected Ingrao's notion of reforms
when he said that the structural reforms' main objective was to broaden
the alliances of the working class, and only secondarily to change the
relations of force in society. Quick, concrete results were not necessary,
since even lost battles could lead to future successes.[43] Similarly, on
reunification, 'advanced' objectives, international policy and the centre-
left, the left wing's position was rejected.

In the organisational sense, the congress was a defeat for the left as
well. It signalled the beginning of a systematic, wide-ranging purge of
pro-Ingrao elements within the Party. Even before the congress,
Alicata had *de facto* taken Rossana Rossanda's place as head of the
cultural section of the Central Committee, and removed the director
of the cultural weekly *Il Contemporaneo* (Rago), the secretary of
the theoretical monthly *Critica marxista* (Ledda) and A. Curzi of the
propaganda section. Aniello Coppolla had also lost his post at
l'Unità.[44] After the congress, the 'purge' of *ingraiani* took on even
vaster proportions, especially in the central apparatus where they had
been particularly strong on the editorial boards of *Rinascita* and *Critica
marxista* and in the cultural section. Similar purges occurred in some,
but not all, pro-Ingrao federations (e.g. Venice).[45]

The reasons for this defeat, which, though serious, was not definitive,
will be examined in a later chapter. Here we wish to point out that the
theme of intra-party democracy came to take on such importance at
the XI Congress not only because of its major place in Ingrao's own
political thought, but also because the tide of pressures on the Party's
Popular Front line generated by factory militancy, the Sino-Soviet
dispute and the centre-left inevitably generated a desire to discuss and
revise it. It is indicative of the strength of the tradition of 'democratic
centralism' that the *casus belli* was precisely the problem of intra-
party democracy.

Notes

1. This is the thesis of G. Bocca, *Palmiro Togliatti* (Rome-Bari, 1973); see e.g.
Chs. 8 and 9.

2. Some of the earliest Communist analyses in this school are P. Grifone,
Il capitale finanziario in Italia (Rome, 1945), and E. Sereni, *La questione agraria
nella rinascita nazionale italiana* (Rome, 1946).

3. A. Cecchi (ed.), *Storia del PCI attraverso i congressi* (Rome, 1977), p. 151;
cf. G. Amendola, *Il rinnovamento del PCI*, interviewed by R. Nicolai (Rome,
1978), pp. 88-9.

4. In *The Essential Stalin*, ed. B. Franklin (Garden City, NY, 1972); see p.
469.

5. See Chapter 2, note 8.
6. See Table 4.2 below.
7. See below, Chapter 4, pp. 76-8.
8. 'Perché non siamo trotzkisti', *Nuova generazione*, 15 Dec. 1961; cf. D.L.M. Blackmer, *Unity in Diversity* (Cambridge, Mass., and London, 1968), pp. 204-5.
9. *Tendenze del capitalismo italiano* (Atti del convegno di Roma 23-25 marzo 1962), vol. I, Rome, 1962, p. 323.
10. P. Togliatti, 'Promemoria sulle questioni del movimento operaio internazionale e della sua unità', *Sul movimento operaio internazionale*, ed. F. Ferri (Rome, 1972), p. 368.
11. *Critica marxista*, III, 5-6 (Sept.-Dec. 1965), p. 110.
12. 'L'origine degli errori', *Rinascita*, XVIII, 12 (Dec. 1961).
13. Cf. G. Amendola, 'Le nostre corresponsabilità', ibid.
14. See, e.g., PCI, *V^a Conferenza nazionale – Atti e risoluzioni* (Rome, 1964), pp. 112-16.
15. 'Un nuovo programma per tutta la sinistra', *Rinascita*, 25 Dec. 1965.
16. A. Occhetto, 'Relazione al Consiglio nazionale della FGCI', *l'Unità*, 13 Mar. 1965; see also A. Occhetto. 'Il significato di una opposizione al centrosinistra'. *La città futura*, I, 1 (Feb. 1964), and 'Gestione sociale dei mezzi di produzione', ibid., I, 9 (Apr. 1965), and P. Marconi, 'Constant e Marx, liberta e socialismo', ibid., I, 8 (Mar. 1965).
17. *Tendenze del capitalismo italiano*, pp. 326-7.
18. 'Relazione al Consiglio nazionale'; 'Il proletariato al bivio fra socialdemocrazia e comunismo', *La città futura*, I, 6 (Jan. 1965); 'D'accordo chiari e unilaterali però', ibid., I, 7 (Feb. 1965).
19. 'Problemi e prospettive di unità della sinistra europea', *L'Astrolabio*, 10 Apr. 1964; 'Il socialismo in Occidente', *Rinascita*, 7 Nov. 1964; 'Ipotesi sulla riunificazione', ibid., 28 Nov. 1964.
20. 'Un nuovo programma per tutta la sinistra'; see also L. Magri, 'Unità e programma', *Rinascita*, 15 Jan. 1966; cf. H. Weber (ed.), *Parti communiste italien: aux sources de l'eurocommunisme* (Paris, 1977), pp. 159-83.
21. *Critica marxista*, III, 5-6 (Sept.-Dec. 1965), p. 141.
22. See Barca in *l'Unità*, 29 May 1965; L. Turci in *l'Unità*, 4 Dec. 1965; M. Figurelli in *l'Unità*, 21 Jan. 1966.
23. 'Capitalismo e riforme di struttura', *Rinascita*, 11 July 1964.
24. Cf. Chapter 2, note 4.
25. 'Democrazia socialista e democrazia interna di partito', *Rinascita*, 25 Apr. 1964.
26. R. Rossanda in *Il Manifesto*, 24 Mar. 1972.
27. L. Pintor, 'Mutata col PSIUP la scena politica', *Rinascita*, 25 Jan. 1964; E. Berlinguer, 'Nuova unità e svolta a sinistra', ibid., 15 Feb. 1964.
28. 'Ipotesi sulla riunificazione', *Rinascita*, 28 Nov. 1964.
29. See articles cited in note 19 above and 'Battaglia unitaria per il socialismo', *Rinascita*, 12 Dec. 1964, and *l'Unità*, 23 Apr. 1965.
30. 'Battaglia unitaria'.
31. Cf. L. Magri, 'Unificazione: su quale linea?', *Rinascita*, 6 Mar. 1965.
32. P.A. Allum, *L'Italia tra crisi e emergenza* (Naples, 1979), p. 106.
33. See the different views of the two men over the Soviet invasion of Afghanistan in *Avanti!*, 6 Jan. 1980.
34. *L'Unità*, 23 Apr. 1965.
35. Ibid., 30 and 31 May 1965.
36. L. Maitan, *Il movimento operaio in una fase critica* (Rome, 1966).
37. For this debate, see *l'Unità*, 27-31 Oct. 1965.
38. Ibid., 30 Oct. 1965.
39. *XI Congresso del Partito comunista italiano – Atti e risoluzioni*, p. 265.

40. Cf. L. Januzzi, 'La scure di Longo', *l'Espresso*, 6 Feb. 1966.
41. *XI Congresso*, pp. 335-8.
42. Ibid., p. 643.
43. Ibid., p. 593.
44. *L'Espresso*, 2 and 23 Jan. 1966.
45. R. Rossanda, 'Note sul PCI dagli anni '60 al XIII Congresso', *Il Manifesto*, 24 Mar. 1972.

4 THE SOCIAL ROOTS OF LEFTISM AND RIGHTISM IN THE PARTY

1. The Diffusion of the *Via Italiana* in the Federations

While Togliatti was attempting to secure the acceptance of his line at the national level, he was also engaged in a more difficult struggle against the traditional, orthodox mentality of the leaderships of many federations. While the 'renewal' of the Party (*rinnovamento*) is commonly held to have occurred during and after the struggle against Secchia,[1] the whole period from 1943 to the present has seen the gradual winning over of the federations, or at least of their leaders, to the *via italiana*. Even when this strategy began to be called into question by economic development and its consequences in the late 1950s and early 1960s, the process of persuasion continued, for there was still powerful 'sectarian' resistance at the federation level to the Togliattian strategy of the Party leadership.

Of the five federations studied in this book, Naples was the first to be won over to the Italian road to socialism. Amendola, on becoming Chairman of the PCI's Southern Commission in 1947, began to work as an enthusiastic proselytist for the Party's line. In Perugia a new leadership committed to Togliatti's line came to power in 1951-4. The defeat of 1955 in the Fiat grievance committee election led to a radical renewal within the Turin PCI. After repeated efforts by the national centre of the Party, the federation of Modena embraced the *via italiana* in the early 1960s. In Bari, on the other hand, only a very few leaders fully understood and supported the national policy of the Party until the beginning of the 1970s.

The timing of the acceptance of the *via italiana* was related to the openness of the different federations to Ingrao's positions. However, the different orientation of the federations in the Amendola-Ingrao dispute can also be explained by the magnitude of socio-economic change and the social composition of the Party membership in the different provinces. We shall discuss these factors after a brief overview of the effects of *rinnovamento* and the 'economic miracle' on the structure of the Party as a whole in the decade 1956-66.

75

Table 4.1: Membership of the PCI and the FGCI (Young Communist Federation), 1956-66

Year	PCI	FGCI
1956	2,035,353	358,126
1957	1,826,928	245,199
1958	1,826,098	241,747
1959	1,787,269	229,703
1960	1,792,968	211,743
1961	1,728,620	221,042
1962	1,630,550	183,563
1963	1,615,112	173,701
1964	1,641,214	173,699
1965	1,615,296	173,465
1966	1,575,935	154,485

Source: L. Magri and F. Maone, 'Problemi di organizzazione nell' esperienza del PCI' in Il Manifesto, *Classe, consigli, partito* (quaderno No. 2), Rome, 1974, p. 177, and M. Barbagli and P. Corbetta, 'Partito e movimento: Aspetti del rinnovamento nel PCI', *Inchiesta*, a. VIII, no. 31 (Jan.-Feb. 1978), p. 11.

2. The PCI Organisation, 1956-66

On the national level 1956-66 saw a major decline in the size and quality of the PCI's organisation. The number of Party members fell from 2,035,000 in 1956 to 1,576,000 in 1966 (see Table 4.1), while the Youth Federation went from 358,000 to 154,000 adherents. As we shall see below, this decline was very unequal in the different parts of the country. While the proportion of workers in the entire population was increasing (Table 4.2), the percentage of PCI members who were workers remained at roughly 40 per cent throughout the decade (Table 4.3). Only half of the workers enrolled in the Party were employed in industry; the rest were in construction, transport, services, the state sector etc. The Party's membership did not reflect immediately the fall in the peasant population or the rapid increase in the number of white-collar workers: the former continued to be overrepresented, the latter seriously underrepresented, in the PCI. Moreover, the only social category to substantially increase its share of PCI membership in the decade were the pensioners; this was not a good sign for the vitality of the organisation.

Table 4.2: Social Composition of the Italian Active Population,
1951-71 (percentages)

		1951	1961	1971
I	Bourgeoisie	1.9	2.0	2.6
II	Middle Classes	56.9	53.4	49.6
(a)	Dependent Petty Bourgeoisie (white-collar)	9.8	13.1	17.1
	1. Private Employees	5.2	6.9	8.9
	2. Public Employees	4.6	6.2	8.2
(b)	Relatively Autonomous Petty Bourgeoisie	44.4	37.2	29.1
	1. Peasant smallholders, sharecroppers, etc.	30.3	21.6	12.1
	2. Shopkeepers, etc.	6.7	7.6	8.7
	3. Artisans and others	7.4	8.0	8.3
(c)	Particular Categories (religious, military and others)	2.7	3.1	3.4
III	Working Class	41.2	44.6	47.8
	1. Agriculture (*braccianti*)	11.8	8.4	6.2
	2. Industry and construction	22.9	29.0	33.0
	3. Other fields (transport, commerce and others)	6.5	7.2	8.6
N		20,075,000	20,305,000	19,620,000

Source: P. Sylos Labini, *Saggio sulle classi sociali* (Bari, 1975), pp. 155-6.

At the same time, the Party was no longer present in as many
social milieux as before. For instance, the number of workplace cells
fell from 10,732 in 1956 to only 4,158 in 1966.[2] The number of
territorial cells also declined,[3] as there were no longer enough activists
to maintain them. Furthermore, the activity of many local
organisations came to be increasingly centred on organisational
maintenance — the routine of distributing party cards, fund-raising, or
major celebrations such as May Day — and they ceased to be centres of
political and social action.[4] This was doubtless a result, in part, of the
disenchantment of many of the militants formed in the period 1943-54
with the Party's new course: they were often uninterested in taking
initiatives along the lines now indicated by the national Party leadership. Thus not only membership, but also activism, fell off drastically.

Table 4.3: Social Composition of PCI Membership, 1954-67 (percentages)

	1954	1960	1964	1967
Workers	39.9	37.4	40.1	40.2
Braccianti (agricultural labourers)	17.8	15.4	11.0	10.4
Peasant smallholders	16.2	18.0	14.6	12.4
Artisans, shopkeepers, etc.	5.2	5.9	6.4	6.5
White-collar workers, technicians, professionals and intellectuals	2.7	2.5	3.1	3.3
Students**	0.3	0.3	0.4	0.6
Housewives and cottage workers	13.5	14.1	13.2	12.8
Pensioners and others	4.4	6.3	11.2	13.8
N	2,145,317	1,792,972	1,641,214*	1,534,704*

* Excludes a small number of members who belonged to federations abroad.
** Only students who are members of the Party are counted. Most students were enrolled in the FGCI only.

Source: Magri and Maone, 'Problemi di organizzazione', p. 181.

The organisational decline continued, furthermore, even into the 1960s, after the revival of working-class and youth militancy. Some of the new social movements were now growing up outside the Communist Party, though often in close proximity to it. Many youth and radicalised workers found the political perspectives both of the older militants and of those who had embraced the *via italiana* uncongenial, and therefore sought to express themselves politically through other channels. This deflection of new social movements away from the PCI was to become the rule after 1968; before then, it was especially noticeable in a few of the more advanced situations. For instance, the radicalised youth in Turin often ignored the Communist Party, after some initial unhappy attempts to work within it, and supported instead groups such as *Quaderni rossi*. The workers there often preferred to work through the union. Thus organisational deterioration continued because of the sedimentation of the political perspective of a previous period in the sections and cells and because the *via italiana* was not designed for these newly radicalised groups and their demands.

3. Differential Effects of Economic Growth

The economic growth of 1953-63, however, had very different effects on different areas of the country, and, as a consequence, the social bases and organisation of the PCI were affected in different ways. The 'model of development' of the Italian economy was based on the expansion of the consumer durables industries (automobiles, domestic appliances, office machinery etc.), which exported a large part of their production. Therefore it was especially important for them to be able to keep wages low so as to maintain their competitive position on world markets. In the early 1950s Italy had large reserves of under-employed manpower in agriculture which could be drawn by relatively low pay to the industrial centres. Hence the miracle was characterised by massive internal migrations as peasants fled from the land to the cities. Most industry was concentrated in the north, particularly in the industrial triangle of Milan, Turin and Genoa; peasants came there from all regions of Italy, but particularly from the south. Thus some provinces experienced rapid demographic growth, while others suffered depopulation. Even those regions which had little net gain or loss in population saw important intra-regional shifts to the cities.

The class structure underwent important changes. The rural population, in particular the sharecroppers of various types, declined drastically, while the number of urban workers increased. Even more significant was the increase in the urban white-collar group (Table 4.2). Once again, different regions were affected in a far from uniform way by these changes: in some there was a large increase in the size of the working class; in others, only the white-collar group grew substantially. There were also intermediate cases of more balanced development or slight changes.

The five provinces chosen for our study illustrate a variety of changes in social structure. Turin, for example, one of the centres of the miracle, enjoyed a large increase in population. The active population increased 29 per cent in twenty years. These people went to swell the working class and the growing white-collar category. Perugia, by contrast, suffered a 24 per cent decline in active population in the same period. Here, the rural exodus was particularly massive and sudden. Some ex-peasants found work in industry in the province, but many others emigrated. Modena experienced a similar flight from the land, but was able to absorb most of the peasants in its local industries. While Perugia, a hilly central province far from major industrial areas, was outside the zone of the miracle, Emilia was able to prosper from

Table 4.4: Social Composition of the Five Provinces, 1951 and 1971
(percentages of active population)

	Turin	Modena	Perugia	Naples	Bari
1951					
Workers	54.0	26.8	24.6	50.1	28.4
Braccianti	1.3	9.7	6.1	7.1	30.9
Peasant smallholders and sharecroppers	15.4	43.7	52.7	13.1	19.4
Artisans, shopkeepers etc.	12.4	11.3	8.2	14.4	11.5
Managers and white-collar workers	14.6	6.4	6.8	12.7	7.5
Entrepreneurs	2.3	2.1	1.6	2.6	2.3
N	691,228	231,155	255,766	642,552	401,919
1971					
Workers	57.0	45.8	44.8	52.6	39.5
Braccianti	0.3	6.2	6.2	6.1	21.3
Peasant smallholders and sharecroppers	4.5	12.6	15.4	5.0	7.8
Artisans, shopkeepers etc.	12.8	17.9	14.3	12.4	13.2
Managers and white-collar workers	23.7	15.9	17.4	21.7	16.5
Entrepreneurs	1.7	1.6	1.9	2.3	1.9
N	893,354	233,597	193,843	714,584	406,743

Source: Data elaborated from ISTAT census returns.

it, developing smaller plants and industries which provided components
for the large firms of the north. Thus the miracle allowed Modena to
experience more balanced growth. In Bari many of those who fled the
land were *braccianti*, who had been the majority of the agricultural
population. The province's active population did not decline as a
result because of the creation of an industrial 'pole of development' in
the capital city, as part of the programme of special assistance for the
south designed to offset the growing regional disparity caused by the
miracle. Finally, Naples alone had no major transformation of the social
structure of its population. The flight from the land was modest, and
the only group to grow appreciably were the white-collar workers.

Our first hypothesis is that the strength of the left in a provincial

federation will be positively correlated with the magnitude of demographic and social change in the province itself, whatever the direction
or nature of that change. Even changes that did not involve proletarianisation of the population and the decline of the traditional middle
strata favoured the left; they were likely to lead to difficulties and some
defeats for the PCI, and either a revision of previous strategy by the
local leadership or their replacement by a new group. Since the Ingrao
left was proposing a break with the hitherto accepted strategy of the
via italiana, any new problems which forced the local party leadership
to rethink some of the basic aspects of their strategy were likely to
favour it. Problems of this sort were the increase in working-class
strength and militancy in Turin, on the one hand, and on the other the
near disappearance of the Party's firmest base of support, the sharecroppers, in Perugia. Bari and Modena are intermediate cases, in which
the rural exodus was significant, but much of it was absorbed by the
industries of the province itself. Finally, Naples, though it certainly
experienced some industrial growth, had a relatively stable social
structure throughout the miracle.

4. The Role of Intellectuals

Our second hypothesis is that a necessary, but not sufficient, condition
for a federation to adopt a leftist position or have a strong leftist
minority is the presence of a critical number of intellectuals. Without
this important element the correlation between demographic and social
change and leftism will not hold. As Gramsci pointed out, any
innovation in political thought or ideology requires the contribution of
intellectuals. On the other hand, the Italian intellectuals, as a social
group, are a petty-bourgeois stratum who belong to the dominant
historic bloc and have their own class interests to pursue in politics.
Their greed for public employment and other spoils of political office
is well known and documented.[5] Therefore, if a large number of them
are present in a party organisation, it is possible that they will try to use
the party to further their own class interests. In this case they are not
'traitors to their class', as are the few intellectuals who typically join a
left-wing party; and they are most likely to support the right wing.
Therefore, the most favourable situation for the left is that in which
there is a moderate number of intellectuals.

On this dimension, too, the five provinces studied demonstrate
significant differences. As far as the Party membership as a whole was

Table 4.5: Percentages of Intellectuals, Professionals and Students in the Five PCI Federations, 1954-67

| | | Turin | | | Modena | |
	1954	1960	1967	1954	1960	1967
Intellectuals and professionals	0.4	1.2	0.6	0.2	0.3	0.2
Students	0.2	—	0.2	0.1	0.1	0.1
N	54,016	30,249	29,655	87,135	82,767	71,823

| | | Perugia | | | Naples | |
	1954	1960	1967	1954	1960	1967
Intellectuals and professionals	0.4	0.4	1.8	0.8	1.8	2.6
Students	0.4	0.4	2.8	1.1	1.2	2.1
N	31,302	28,145	25,541	76,049	53,350	33,977

| | | Bari | |
	1954	1960	1967
Intellectuals and professionals	0.6	0.4	0.6
Students	0.6	0.2	0.6
N	32,157	31,654	20,619

Sources: *Forza e attività del Partito* (1955); *La forza del PCI per la pace, la democrazia, il socialismo* (Rome, 1967); *Dati sulla organizzazione del partito* (Rome, 1968).

concerned, Naples had the largest proportion of intellectuals throughout the period; Turin, Bari and Perugia were in the intermediate range, and Modena consistently had the smallest ratio of intellectuals to members (Table 4.5). (Students have been included in the table as they were future intellectuals and capable of playing the catalysing role of intellectuals in their own right.) Perugia appears to have markedly increased its recruitment of intellectuals and students in 1960-7, however, almost reaching the combined total of Naples.

An analysis of the social composition of the federal congresses for which data are available confirms the above classification of the federations (Table 4.6). Insufficient data are available to test this

Table 4.6: Percentage of Intellectuals, Professionals and Students among the Delegates at Some Congresses of Four Federations, 1954-66

Federation	Year	Percentage of intellectuals, professionals and students	N
Turin	1954	4.5	614
	1956	7.5	577
	1960	5.0	400
	1962	8.1	432
	1966	9.7	462
Modena	1954	1.6	567
	1956	3.9	552
	1960	4.4	540
	1966	3.6	472
Perugia	1966	4.2*	283
Naples	1962	13.0	385
	1966	13.7	372

* This figure is for university graduates only; it therefore excludes students.

Sources: Congressional minutes in archives of Turin, Modena and Perugia federations; Naples Federation, X Congress, *Risoluzioni e nuovi organismi dirigenti* (Naples, n.d.), and XI Congress, *Risoluzione politica e nuovi organismi dirigenti* (Naples, 1966).

classification at the level of the federal committees as well. The percentage of intellectuals and professionals in the Perugia federal committee varied between 28 and 38 in 1954-66; approximately half of these were elementary school teachers (*maestri*).[6] In Turin their number increased from 7.9 per cent in 1956 to 20 per cent in 1966.[7] In Modena 10.3 per cent of the federal committee were intellectuals or professionals in 1960.[8] And in 1968 fully 53 per cent of the members of the Naples federal committee were intellectuals, professionals and students.[9] Thus the above analysis would appear to find confirmation at this level also.

Our analysis of several levels of Party membership, then, suggests a threefold grouping of the federations, with Naples and Modena at the extremes and the other three occupying intermediate positions. We should expect the latter three to have the critical number of

intellectuals necessary for the formation of a strong left-wing
tendency.

5. The Marxist Subculture in Central Italy

The above two hypotheses ought to be sufficient in themselves to
explain the differences in political orientation of the five federations.
However, an examination of the federations of the traditionally 'red'
regions (Emilia-Romagna, Tuscany and Umbria) suggests a further
special hypothesis to help account for differences in leftism and
rightism among them: in those provinces where the left is securely
entrenched in the most important local government bodies and where
it controls an extensive network of collateral organisations, such as
co-operatives, sports associations etc., the PCI federation is more likely
to be on the right than in those 'red' provinces where its local power is
felt to be threatened by the DC and where the co-operatives and other
secondary associations are less important. In the former type of
province, mostly found in Emilia, much of the Party's energy will be
devoted to the maintenance and management of the subcultural and
economic network; hence it will tend to be less politicised and less open
to new political orientations. The possession of such a network may
also make the Party somewhat fearful of radical change (especially
economic instability) and generally more conservative. On the other
hand, where the PCI is in danger of losing control of local government,
there is a powerful stimulus to reconsideration and revision of
traditional strategy and hence a chance for the left to obtain a hearing.

Modena was a province of the first type where the PCI was secure
in its local power and had a large number of important organisations
under its control. Only small mountainous communes were governed
by the DC. In Perugia, on the other hand, the Party saw important
formerly left-wing communes, including Todi, Spoleto, Foligno and the
provincial capital pass under the control of centre-left *giunte* (executive
committees); and left-dominated organisations played a much less
significant role in the social and economic life of the province.

Evidence of the greater attention paid in Perugia to political questions, and particularly general issues of national and international
importance, is provided by an analysis of the subjects discussed by the
federal committees of the two federations (Table 4.9). These differences should lead us to expect that, other things being equal, leftism
will be stronger in Perugia than in Modena.

Table 4.7: Composition of the *Giunte* of the 27 Communes of the
Province of Perugia with over 5,000 Inhabitants and the Communes
of the Province of Modena, February 1965

Type of *giunta*	Number of communes	
	Perugia	Modena
PCI or PCI-PSIUP	10	4
PCI-PSI-PSIUP	7	24
Centre-left	6	2
DC or DC and right	4	15
Other	0	2
Total	27	47

Sources: PCI, Federazione di Perugia, *Per l'Unità del Movimento Democratico*,
Assemblea degli eletti e dei dirigenti di Partito, Perugia, 21 Feb. 1965; Atti del
XII° Congresso provinciale, Archives of the Modena Federation.

Table 4.8: Strength of the Co-operative Movement in Perugia and
Modena, 1962-4

	Perugia	Modena
Number of co-operatives	66	332
Total number of members	24,945	82,670
Members per 1,000 population	55	177

Source: See Table 6.3.

In the following chapters we shall investigate the political
history of the five federations with a view to testing these hypotheses
about the conditions for the emergence of a strong left wing. In so
doing, we shall also evaluate the relative importance of the various
issues which were being debated within the Party, such as the centre-
left, reunification with the PSI, the Sino-Soviet split and internal party
democracy. And finally we may be able to explain not only the rise
of the Ingrao left in certain areas of the country, but also its failure to
become a majority within the PCI as a whole.

Table 4.9: Subjects on Agenda at Federal Committee Meetings in Modena (1956-60 and 1962-6) and Perugia (1962-6)

| Subjects | Modena | | | | Perugia | |
| | 1956-60 | | 1962-6 | | 1962-6 | |
	No.	%	No.	%	No.	%
General political topics	7	15	11	19	13	27
National	7		7		10	
International	0		4		3	
Sectoral political topics	14	29	21	36	20	42
Elections	4		12		9	
Other (women, youth, peasants etc.)	10		9		11	
Organisational maintenance	27	56	26	45	15	31
Distribution of memberships, press	8		6		)	
Party organisation and budget	11		12		) 13	
Cadres policy, resignations etc.	4		7		1	
Other	4		1		1	
Total	48	100	58	100	48	100

Source: Elaborated from archives of the federations.

Notes

1. See G. Amendola, *Il rinnovamento del PCI*, interviewed by R. Nicolai (Rome, 1978).

2. L. Magri and F. Maone, 'Problemi di organizzazione nell'esperienza del PCI' in Il Manifesto, *Classe, consigli, partito* (quaderno No. 2), Rome, 1974, p. 190.

3. G. Sivini, 'Struttura organizzativa e partecipazione di base nel Partito Comunista Italiano' in G. Sivini (ed.), *Partiti e partecipazione politica in Italia* (Milan, 1969), pp. 151-2.

4. See e.g. below, Chapter 7, p. 123.

5. See e.g. P. Sylos Labini, *Saggio sulle classi sociali* (Bari, 1975), pp. 47-62. On intellectuals as a pressure group within the PCI, see G. Bonazzi, 'Problemi politici e condizione umana dei funzionari del PCI', *Tempi moderni*, 22 (July-Sept. 1965).

6. Archive of the Perugia federation.

7. Archive of the Turin federation.

8. See Table 8.5.

9. P.A. Allum, *Politics and Society in Post-War Naples* (Cambridge, 1973), p. 234.

5 THE DOMINANCE OF THE RIGHT IN NAPLES

1. The Neapolitan Political Background and the Early Years of the PCI

The Neapolitan federation was won to the *via italiana* very early thanks
to the efforts of Giorgio Amendola and his group. The class structure
and political make-up of southern society, in which middle-class
intellectuals played a key role as mediators between the masses and the
state, made the alliance policy particularly suitable there. In Naples,
with its large sub-proletariat and particular political culture, the
southern political system, based on clientelism, took on a pathological
form. The Neapolitan federation hence was typical, in many respects,
of the south, where most of the Party supported Amendola and the
right. It was exceptional because it was the southern federation with
the largest concentration of intellectuals and, above all, of workers.
An opposition to Amendola's group was therefore able to form, particularly after the early 1950s, when his project of an alliance with the
southern middle class became less and less practicable as this group
was incorporated in the dominant historic bloc. Nevertheless, his
position in Naples, which he had built up since 1947, was strong
enough to withstand this challenge.

Naples has long been known for its distinctive political culture,
typical of large pre-industrial Mediterranean cities.[1] For centuries
the capital of a kingdom and seat of an opulent court, it swelled
in size with the vast army of retainers, artisans and hangers-on who
lived off the incomes which the king and his nobles extracted from the
peasantry. The Neapolitan crowd (*popolino, lazzaroni*) was more often
than not royalist and Catholic in sentiment, as the leaders of the
Parthenopean Republic of 1799 learned to their undoing. So long as
the king provided sufficient bread to ward off dire need, the *popolino*
were his faithful subjects. If he did not, it was their prerogative to
riot. They never advanced beyond this stage of political consciousness
because industry did not come on any large scale to Naples; they
remained a collection of impoverished small artisans and urban poor,
many with no fixed occupation, living by their wits from day to day.
This large sub-proletariat has remained an important part of the
Neapolitan population even in recent years: its size has been estimated
at 300,000.

Modern industry grew up late in the city, and was not sufficient to absorb the entire population. In the last years of Bourbon rule the state attempted to foster a commercial and industrial bourgeoisie, but unification spelt the death of these beginnings of capitalist development. The elimination of tariff barriers between the Kingdom of Two Sicilies and the north, which was hardly more advanced industrially in 1860, did not in itself expose southern industry to fatal competition. Rather, the northern bourgeoisie controlled the new Italian state and used it systematically to favour its own development. Public works were concentrated in the north; control of credit was transferred there with the subordination of the Bank of Naples to the northern *Banca Nazionale*; the new common tariff was not high enough for Naples's industries.[2] The northern bourgeoisie, after a short period of conflict between the largerly southern 'left' and the Cavourian 'right', secured the political support of the southern landowners, to the detriment of the capitalist class of the *Mezzogiorno*.

The landowners, through their agents the petty-bourgeois intelligentsia, founded their political power on a clientelistic relationship with the voters, providing favours, generally to individuals rather than groups, in return for votes. This system made good relations with the government important; hence the 'transformism' which characterised southern deputies in the late nineteenth century — their willingness to 'transform themselves' into government supporters. When transformism failed, more direct forms of governmental pressure could be used to influence southern elections. The prefects were used as election agents, government employees were reminded to be grateful, and funds were liberally spent.[3] These practices earned Giovanni Giolitti, several times Prime Minister from 1892 to 1921, the appellation *il ministro della malavita* ('the minister of crime'). In Naples the clientele system found a particularly fertile terrain for its growth among the subproletariat, who could not be organised in stable occupational groups or mass class-based parties, and who were used to looking to benefactors and protectors for favours. This southern political system, the result of the introduction of a parliamentary system in a preindustrial society, has been brilliantly described in Gramsci's 'Southern Question'.[4] Parties were weak and unstable coalitions of local notables, who were linked to their voters by a pyramidal structure of *grandi elettori* and *capielettori* and in their turn were often grouped around a few great notables of national stature.

Naples, however, was different from the rest of the *Mezzogiorno* because it had the largest concentrations of intellectuals and of workers. In the late nineteenth century it was the most important centre of large-scale industry (steel) in Italy, and had a combative working class, divided between a transformistic reformism and a revolutionary consciousness which sometimes took an extremist form. Amadeo Bordiga, the first (1921-4) Secretary-General of the PCd'I, had been a dominant figure in Neapolitan socialism.[5] He advocated an intransigent, revolutionary version of the Marxist orthodoxy of the II International; he held that Lenin was not an innovator, but had simply restored true Marxism.

In many southern centres the end of fascism saw the emergence of groups of Communist leaders who had been out of touch with the Party leadership for years, and who had not accepted the new course of 1935. It took the national leadership three to four years to remove all the 'sectarian' and 'extremist' elements from the federations of the *Mezzogiorno*. In Naples there were two groups, only one of which had accepted the new Party line. The struggle between them took a particularly acute form when the leftists founded a rival organisation, the 'Montesanto federation', led by Mario Palermo, a progressive lawyer and Enrico Russo, an engineering worker.[6] The Montesanto group were not all Bordighists or Trotskyists; their main criticism of the PCI was that it lacked internal democracy. The split in the Naples federation lasted only two months (October–December 1943) before, as elsewhere, a new leadership which was loyal to the national Party line was put in place. Under Amendola's leadership, the remnants of the extreme leftist tradition in the south were eradicated.

2. Amendola Introduces the *Via Italiana* to Naples

The next phase of the PCI's development in Naples is intimately connected with the career of Giorgio Amendola. Amendola's father, a professor of philosophy and journalist as well as a politician, had represented the most advanced wing of the southern petty-bourgeois intelligentsia. He had been a minister under Nitti, and was the most outstanding spokesman of the Liberal opposition to Mussolini in 1924-5. His parliamentary constituency was Nocera Inferiore, an agricultural centre between Naples and Salerno, where political life was dominated by the clienteles typical of the south.[7] Young Amendola received his grounding in politics by participating in his father's campaigns. In this period Giorgio developed the traits of wilfulness and self-confidence that were to assist him in his later political career.

During his studies in Naples he came into contact with Croce, but he was eventually to forsake his earlier political friends of liberal-democratic leanings to join the Communist Party.

Returning from abroad during the war, Amendola was a key member of the PCI's Roman leadership during the Resistance. In 1947 he was chosen to head the Party's southern commission, whose office, significantly enough, he transferred to Naples. From this position he began to fashion a southern organisation in keeping with his own conceptions; as a sincere supporter of the Popular Front strategy, he laid stress on alliances with the middle classes and on building the *partito nuovo*, i.e. a mass party rather than a traditional Leninist party. He was responsible for placing the southern question, seen practically as a national question or as the completion of the bourgeois revolution, at the centre of all the Party's activities in the south. Because of the importance of the middle classes, particularly the intellectuals, in southern politics, the south was the most favourable terrain in the country for the introduction of the Popular Front line.[8]

The PCI in the south may have been loose and discontinuous in its organisational structure, and its electoral support may have been personalistic in some areas, but Amendola, building a party on the basis of his own experience, knew what was necessary in the southern milieu. He himself became regional secretary of Campania and of Basilicata; Mario Alicata, at this time his close associate, was appointed to run the Calabrian organisation. At a later stage he gained influence in Abruzzo and Molise as well. Among the young Communists at the University of Naples cell, he recruited other associates, including Giorgio Napolitano and Gerardo Chiaromonte.

While the PCI in the south accepted the policy of alliances from the beginning, internal Party democracy was not highly developed in this early phase. Most of the federations were in practice controlled by a small group, and the cultural distance between the federal officials and the ordinary membership was much greater than in the north. This was a result in part of the way in which the Party had been founded in the south, as a vast movement impelled from above, and in part of the great differences in education, class background and exposure to the media and current events between the federal leaders and the militants in the sections. The Party, like all southern parties, was staffed at the federal level by many intellectuals of bourgeois origin. The ordinary members were Stalinist, and were not very highly politicised. This situation was only somewhat attenuated in Naples itself, with its large numbers of intellectuals and more politically sophisticated workers. As Amendola

himself once said about the period, 'We were enlightened despots.'[9]
Nor did he take any initiative to alter this situation.

It is not surprising, then, that orthodox, not to say Stalinist,
attitudes were prevalent in the Party even in Amendola's Neapolitan
headquarters. The most important episode of resistance to the Popular
Front strategy before 1956 had its centre in the Communist youth
movement.[10] In 1949-50 an historical study group, the 'Gramsci
Circle', was founded within the university cell. After the VII Congress
they began to polemicise with Amendola for his alleged failure to
apply the decisions of the congress; they accused him of continuing to
put the southern question ahead of the struggle for socialism and peace.
This, they held, was an 'economistic' and 'democratic' deviation. They
took the question to the mass membership in late 1953, under the
leadership of Piegari, Secretary of the FGCI. Apparently the potential
support for the group was fairly extensive: not only the youth, but
some of the pre-1943 members of the Party agreed with Secchia's line,
which the Gramsci circle was in fact promoting; there was also support
from outside the province. The secretary of the Naples federation
itself, an experienced worker, Salvatore Cacciapuoti, was ambiguous or
hesitant on the main questions at issue. He embodied *doppiezza* in
himself: when in Naples he was with Amendola, but at the same time
'he was waiting for orders from Secchia'.[11]

After Piegari sent a 36-page letter to *Rinascita* outlining his position,
Togliatti, having ascertained that there was no direct connection with
Secchia, decided to have him elected to the provincial congress of 1954
and to reply to him in person. The opposition group was surprised
when Togliatti concluded the congress with a complete endorsement of
Amendola's positions. Most of the Party rank and file did not even
know the real terms of the dispute, and after the congress those who
had been in contact with the Gramsci circle were removed from Party
posts or expelled, and most of Piegari's supporters did not renew their
Party memberships.

In spite of this defeat in the Piegari episode, orthodox, 'Secchian'
positions continued to be expressed at the Naples federation. At the
VIII Congress of the federation (1956), for instance, one comrade
disagreed with the XX Congress's conclusion that war was now not
inevitable, fearing that this would weaken the Party's initiative for
peace, while other delegates voiced their reservations over the XX
Congress's position on Yugoslavia, and over the 'excessive criticisms of
comrade Stalin'. At the same time these speeches also called for more
democracy in the Party, as had Secchia himself in an article in *l'Unità*

the previous July.[12] With clear reference to the defenestration of Secchia, one speaker said, 'Often we have not stimulated debate about the diverse positions which have developed within the national leadership of the Party.'[13]

This left opposition group's firm support at the VIII Congress, measured by the pattern of cancellations of the names of some leaders in balloting for the federal committee, amounted to about 8 to 9 per cent of the delegates.[14] While many members of this group left the Party or became inactive in the next two or three years, even in 1962 the federal committee noted in its report that the lessons of the XX Congress had not been fully absorbed, and that 'positions of nostalgic attachment to the political and organisational schemes of the past' were still present even among leaders of the federation. Nor had the XXII Congress led to any clarification:

> In practice, caution and preoccupation prevailed in the face of the emotional character of certain discussions. Thus the document of the Secretariat of the Party on the XXII did not become the basis for further discussion and elaboration of the themes of our political line, but instead marked the closure of the debate.[15]

3. The Rise of an 'Ingraian' Opposition

While the orthodox opponents of Amendola's line remained a signifi-cant group in the federation, an 'Ingraian' tendency began to appear as well in the early 1960s. The increasing difficulties of the PCI's traditional southern policy and the stagnation of the Party's vote in the south provided this new tendency with its arguments; however, that such a group formed in the Neapolitan federation but not in other southern federations subject to Amendola's influence, was largely due to the great number of intellectuals in its ranks. It was they who 'politicised' some of the federation's members and introduced the ideas of Ingrao and his followers to them; where there were no intellectuals to do this, the rank and file members remained largely unaware of the discussions between the Party leaders and several years behind the times in their political consciousness.

But the presence of so many intellectuals was also a major cause of the ultimate victory of the right, for, in spite of its positive effect on the level of political discussion, it also increased the personalism typical of all southern parties. As Gramsci has shown, intellectuals are a necessary element in the southern clientele structure. The Party had been constructed in the south by Amendola to take account of the peculiar characteristics of the region, and intellectuals had therefore been given an important place in it. While the left could profit from this situation to win some short-term advantages, in the long term personalism within the Party was bound to give the advantage to those who held power at the highest levels, the right, because of the pyramidal structure of personalistic political relationships within the federation. The fragility of the position of the few left-wing intellectuals can be graphically illustrated by the career of Massimo Caprara: he owed his promotion to regional secretary of Campania in 1962 to the influence of Togliatti, whose secretary he had been. After Togliatti's death, his power and prestige began to wane and, in spite of his popularity, real power in Naples remained in the hands of Amendola and his group. When Caprara was expelled from the PCI as a member of the *Manifesto* group in 1969, he took very few followers with him.

Changes in the organisation and practices of the federation after 1956 also helped the left. Decentralisation and democratisation were promoted in order to overcome 'every deformation of a hierarchical, paternalistic and bureaucratic type' in relations between federation and sections, as well as 'the persistent zones of confusion, primitivism and political and ideological backwardness' in the Party.[16] Amendola, in the early post-war period, had not been prepared to undertake demo-cratisation of the Party in order to shake the rank and file out of its Stalinism. This task was carried out by Abdon Alinovi, who became federal secretary in 1954, and the group around him, who were 'centrist' rather than linked to Amendola. Amendola and Alicata, while promoting *rinnovamento* at the national level, were opposed to changing the old methods of work in their own southern regions. Now democratisation offered space to left-wing critics of the official line. For instance, certain sections were unified after the X Congress to create larger units (the new Ponticelli, Curiel and 'G. Quadro' sections) in the hope that the new sections would see livelier political debate. This result was achieved, but some of the new sections became centres of leftism. The election of the federal committee at the X Congress in 1962 was also indicative of a new style in Party life. There were 73 candidates for 61 positions, and although 295 delegates voted, the highest vote obtained by any candidate was 244, while the lowest among those elected was 112.[17]

Amendola's southern policy had entered a crisis, its critics pointed out, because its bases were being undermined by the formation of the new historic bloc whose main component in the south was the 'state bourgeoisie'.[18] The agrarian reform laws and the *Cassa per il Mezzogiorno*, while they did nothing to solve the southern question, allowed the government to weaken the 'Movement for the Rebirth of the South' by means of corruption. The movement was divided on the position to take *vis-à-vis* the *Cassa*, for the PSI and other groups did not fully agree with the PCI's decision to vote against it in Parliament. After the election of 1953 the DC intensified its efforts to win over the southern intelligentsia, who had played the decisive role in denying it an absolute majority. The 1953 election was in fact the last success of the PCI's old southern policy: most of the middle-class elements who had been attracted to the *Movimento* had already left it or were soon to do so.

In Naples the formation of the new historic bloc meant the demise of the Monarchists, led by Achille Lauro, and the rise to power of the Christian Democrats, represented by the Gava family. Lauro, Mayor of Naples from 1952 to 1958, built his political position on an old-style network of clienteles, distributing small favours to the subproletariat. He and his closest associates were involved in commercial and speculative activities, like construction and shipping, which they furthered through their control of the city government. While given to regionalist rhetoric in election campaigns, Lauro had in practice served as a willing instrument of the Christian Democrats on several occasions. The Gavas, on the other hand, represented the newer state bourgeoisie: while not disdaining to use the older methods of corruption (on the contrary), they brought a new efficiency to the process of converting public funds into votes, using the various state agencies and state corporations, ISVEIMER, the *Cassa*, the development *Consorzio* and the peasants' association, to name only a few, to distribute jobs and other benefits on a larger scale than Lauro could ever do. Their system was more akin to a 'clientelism of the bureaucracy' than to Lauro's classic 'clientelism of the notable'. They also brought some industry to the area, always with the aid of the central government; these new plants were used as another source of rewards for the clients of the Gava clan. The Gavas themselves developed extensive interests in various enterprises. But the PCI was rather slow to recognise that its traditional southern policy, which had proven so successful in 1947-53, had been made obsolete by the creation of this new structure of power in the *Mezzogiorno*.

In the early 1960s, however, left-wing critics began to question the Party's support of industrialisation *tout court*, based on the premiss that the south was suffering simply from the absence of capitalist development. In reality, the left argued, the south's plight was the product of the capitalist development of Italy as a whole, rather than of its absence, and functional to the development of northern industry. Therefore the struggle in the south had to be explicitly anti-capitalist, not a 'two-stage' struggle, first for capitalist industrialisation, then for socialism.

For the left, economic development had to be seen qualitatively, not simply quantitatively. It was necessary to distinguish different types of development which could come to the south, and to favour only that type which was not purely subordinate to the needs of northern capital (as, for instance, oil refineries were). Both in the north and in the south the enemy was the same: the monopolies. Industrial development had to be redirected towards the production of capital goods for agriculture. As Alfredo Reichlin, Apulian regional secretary and a supporter of Ingrao, noted, the struggle for democratic planning had made no progress at the governmental level; whereas, at the mass level, some conquests had been achieved. The aim of day-to-day struggles, he concluded, should be power: they should 'mobilize the masses, cement a new unity on more advanced lines, favour a shift in the relations of force and the formation of a new power bloc, and modify the organization of the State'.[19] The left-wing position found a vehicle in *Cronache meridionali*, a journal founded in 1954 as an organ for Amendola's southern policy, until it was closed as a result of intervention from above.[20]

While the establishment of the new historic bloc in the south meant the PCI's traditional alliance policy could not function, the Party in Naples suffered no permanent electoral loss as a result of the loosening of its links with some of the middle classes and the intellectuals. While it fell from 21 per cent to 19 per cent of the vote in the 1956 municipal election, the PCI was able to profit, in a small measure, from the decline of Lauro's Monarchist Party, another result of the growth of the new bloc in the south.[21] The Party did, however, suffer some defections of prominent personalities to the right in 1956; and Party membership fell by half from 1956 to 1966, a more serious decline than in most other parts of the country. These difficulties the left could attribute in part to the Party's outdated southern policy.

The centre-left was another sign of the crisis of the PCI's traditional alliances and strategy in the south. The first centre-left commune in the country was Torre Annunziata, a major coastal industrial city in the province of Naples, where a DC–PSI coalition came to power in 1957.

Table 5.1: General and Municipal Election Results for City of Naples, 1946-68 (percentages)

Year		PCI	Socialist	DC	Right
1946	(G)	8	7	24	52
1946	(M)		32	13	53
1948	(G)		20	48	25
1952	(M)	22	5	24	45
1953	(G)	21	7	30	39
1956	(M)	19	5	16	58
1958	(G)	25	8	32	33
1960	(M)	23	8	26	42
1962	(M)	21	12	28	39
1963	(G)	25	16	30	27
1964	(M)	25	14	35	27
1968	(G)	29	14	29	26

Source: P.A. Allum, *Politics and Society in Post-War Naples* (Cambridge, 1973), p. 145.

Table 5.2: Membership of Five PCI Federations, 1956-66

	1954	1956	1960	1966	Loss 1956-66 %
Perugia		29,346	28,145	27,201	7.3
Modena		87,286	79,767	73,035	16.3
Turin		44,235	30,249	29,653	33.0
Bari	32,157		31,654	20,619	35.9
Naples		72,491	53,350	34,690	52.1

Source: See Table 4.5.

These developments, while not as important an issue in Naples as in areas where the PCI had major positions in local government to defend, nevertheless provoked unease and confusion. As the 1962 report of the federal committee put it:

The objective difficulties of our relations with the PSI have not been dealt with correctly: positions going from accusations of

betrayal directed at the PSI to attitudes of compliance *vis-à-vis*
the positions of surrender adopted by that Party have had currency
in our Party.[22]

However, in spite of the possibilist attitudes of some of the Party's
cadres, influenced no doubt by Amendola's line and by the hope of
using the PSI to gain a share of influence in the decisions, great and
small, of local government, the hostility of the base to the experiment
was almost unanimous. This attitude was in part a product of the way
that the centre-left was introduced in Naples, under the complete
hegemony of the Christian Democrats. This explained, in the PCI's
view,

> the conditions of particular backwardness and of undisguised trans-
> formism which characterised the advent and development of the
> centre-left in the province of Naples [and] the humiliating condition
> of inferiority and grave risks of degradation for the PSI as a result of
> its acceptance of these political operations and combinations.[23]

The rank and file of the Party were convinced that the process of social
democratisation of the PSI was completed, that it had been integrated
into the capitalist system, and that its fusion with the PSDI was a
certainty. There was considerable opposition to Amendola's reunification proposal, especially from older members of the Party, who saw it
as a betrayal of revolutionary principles. The issue undoubtedly
contributed in some degree to Ingrao's following.

The revival of working-class militancy was felt very strongly by the
Neapolitan federation of the PCI,[24] and suggested to the left an
alternative to Amendola's southern strategy. While the first ten years
after the war saw the closing of many factories in the area, an absolute
reduction in the number of industrial workers in the province, and a
series of bitter defensive struggles by the CGIL and the PCI, the
situation began to change in the late 1950s. The unions began to
organise workers in small and medium industries and in building. The
earlier struggles had combined defensive objectives, such as the
maintenance of employment levels and the elimination of wage
differentials between south and north, with generic, maximalist
campaigns, like that for peace. By 1960, however, the workers felt
sufficiently strong, even in the south, to begin factory-level bargaining,
occasionally winning benefits even in excess of those provided by
the national collective agreement. The CGIL decided that wage

demands could not be subordinated to the need to overcome the
historic backwardness of the region.

By the X Congress the federation recognised also that new working-
class nuclei had grown up, many of them beyond its reach. These were
products of the subsidised industrial development encouraged by the
DC in the south, where workers were recruited from the countryside
on the basis of the recommendations of the priests. In 1962 the federation had formed a series of workplace or occupational sections with the
aim of increasing the participation of workers in Party life and of
encouraging the emergence of working-class cadres. Six sections,
grouping over 10 per cent of the total membership in the city, were
formed. Even more important, the federation decided that its recruitment in 1963 had to be centred on the factories.[25]

This revival of interest in the working class provided a fertile
terrain for the spread of Ingrao's ideas about the linking of factory
struggles to the movement for reform. The real leaders of the pro-
Ingrao group, those who brought his ideas to Naples and propagated
them, were a small group of intellectuals in the Party, like Caprara.
However, they were able to influence a small but significant group of
intermediate cadres, including some of the new working-class militants
who emerged in the early 1960s.[26] The most original and accomplished
defence of Ingrao's positions at the XI Congress was delivered by a
delegate of the Italsider factory section, Giovanni Scherillo. (Italsider
is a state steel plant, the largest factory in the Naples area.) He argued
that the Party must elaborate an alternative plan for the steel industry,
and make it an objective of workers' struggle in the factory, 'in order
that these programmes for which we fight be achieved, become
concrete as a result of our decisive contribution, and not be delegated
instead, in a very general and uncertain way, to a not better defined
public intervention'.[27] Steel production, though controlled by the
state, was oriented towards the needs of the monopolies, producing
the type of product they wanted and offering them favourable prices.
It should, instead, Scherillo maintained, be producing steel components
for the capital goods sector and for prefabricated housing for workers.
The Party had to conduct 'more advanced political battles, with a
different scope, in which one aim, however, should be clearly present:
a different society, a socialist society'. Caprara himself spoke of the
need to conquer new positions of power for the working class, stating
that 'today the capitalist system is being contested' in a 'direct conflict
between capitalism and the socialist forces'![28] So strong was the
current in favour of this new line in the factories that Napolitano

himself, now federal secretary, did not oppose it. He mentioned in his report the need for the workers to gain new powers in the factories, in spite of the defensive character of the battles they had been forced to engage in during the previous two years, and spoke of 'the model, the line, the programme of development that we propose for the Italian economy'.[29]

International questions provided another potential terrain for convergence between the *ingraiani* and the orthodox opponents of the federal leadership. They were also perhaps the most hotly debated issue within the federation in the period 1956-66. At the X Federal Congress (1962) the policy of peaceful coexistence came under very strong attack, especially in view of what was perceived as Khrushchev's retreat in the Cuban missile crisis.[30] The congress's final resolution shows how widespread these views were:

> 1. Peaceful coexistence: The Congress, while it approves the formulation contained in the theses on the subject, emphasizes the need to give an even clearer answer to the perplexities and reserva- tions which came to the surface in the debate concerning the Cuban crisis and recent international events. This [is necessary] in order to overcome, without any possibility of equivocation, the positions of those who demonstrate that they are not convinced of the non- inevitability of war and interpret coexistence as the crystallization of the present relations of force between capitalism and socialism on the world scale . . .[31]

The resurgence of anti-imperialist activity in the early 1960s, especially among youth, at first had to seek an outlet outside the Communist Party. A 'Neapolitan Anti-Colonialist Committee' was formed, and in 1964 enjoyed wide support. Imperialism seemed to be gaining ground everywhere — in Cuba, the Dominican Republic, Vietnam and Latin America — while the socialist camp, divided, reacted only weakly. This put the PCI on the defensive. Longo, at the 1965 congress of the Resina section, near Naples, was led to characterise this as simply a 'counter- attack' by imperialism after the advance of the national liberation movements and of socialism (e.g. in China, North Vietnam, Cuba, Algeria). Replying to numerous criticisms, he was forced to defend Soviet foreign policy, pointing out that the USSR had sent arms to Algeria, though this was not given publicity for diplomatic reasons, and had sent everything the North Vietnamese had asked for.[32] Longo lamely attempted to present the Cuban missile crisis as a victory, because it had forced the USA to recognise the independence of Cuba. The USSR had also offered to undertake the air defence of Hanoi, and to send men for the purpose, but the North Vietnamese had declined the offer. Other comrades of the Resina section had asked why the USSR had not sent troops to Vietnam, or used the atomic bomb to stop imperialist aggression; Longo replied that China would probably not have allowed Soviet troops to pass through its territory, and that in any case the Vietnam war was a guerrilla war for which regular Soviet forces would be unsuited.

Just as worrisome to the ordinary members as the apparent resurgence of imperialism and the failure of the policy of peaceful coexistence was the disunity in the world socialist camp. Only a minority took sides with either the USSR or China: the almost unanimous view was that a greater effort had to be made to restore international unity. This view implied a criticism of the leaders of the PCI, some of whom, like Alicata, had taken strongly anti-Chinese positions. The leadership as a whole was often criticised for not doing enough to bring about a reconciliation. Both orthodox and pro-Ingrao sections voiced the same type of criticism of the Party's official international positions.

In spite of the undoubted support which the positions of the left enjoyed at the XI Congress on many issues, it was the right which emerged victorious nevertheless. The paragraph in the final resolution on economic policy and the southern question referred to 'democratic planning' as the Party's solution to the problems generated by mono-polistic accumulation, while the new ideas promoted by the Ingrao group were scarcely referred to, and only some vague references to the new terms of the southern question were included.[33] The new federal committee was elected by the system of the closed list with open voting, in contrast to the liberal procedure adopted in 1962, and the left, while represented, was in a clear minority in the new leadership of the federation. When Napolitano passed to Rome on a full-time basis in February 1966, he was replaced by Antonio Mola, a former worker who was not identified with either the Amendola or the Ingrao groups and who was expected to mediate between them and resolve the tensions that had developed in the federation.

The Neapolitan federation, then, remained basically under the control of Amendola and his friends in 1966, in spite of a significant amount of left-wing dissidence. The crisis of the PCI's pre-1953 southern strategy did not lead to major electoral losses; nor did Naples experience the same rapid social and economic change as other provinces during the decade 1956-66, though some new industry was created towards the end of the period. The sections in the working-class and intellectual quarters of the city were the most politicised, and most likely to provide opposition to the leadership, while the sub-proletarian and peasant sections were often social clubs which transformed themselves when necessary into electoral committees.[34] The presence of a substantial body of intellectuals permitted the left to put forward its own point of view and strike a responsive chord among the rank-and-file membership. They were unable to win, because of the structure of power which the right had established, but they did make a significant impact on some sectors of the Party, as future manifestations of dissent, culminating in the *Il Manifesto* episode, were to prove.

Notes

1. Neapolitan political culture is very well described in P.A. Allum, *Politics and Society in Post-War Naples* (Cambridge, 1973). See also M.A. Macciocchi, *Lettere dall'interno del P.C.I. a Louis Althusser* (Milan, 1969) and E. Hobsbawm, *Primitive Rebels* (Manchester, 1959).

2. E.M. Capecelatro and A. Carlo, *Contro la questione meridionale* (Rome, 1972), Ch. III.

3. See C. Seton-Watson, *L'Italia dal liberalismo al fascismo 1870-1925* (2 vols., Bari, 1973), vol. 1, pp. 61-3, 108-10; and Allum, *Post-War Naples*, pp. 68-9.

4. A. Gramsci, 'Alcuni temi della questione meridionale' in *La costruzione del Partito comunista 1923-1926* (Opere, vol. 12, Turin, 1971); on Naples, see G. Procacci, *Le elezioni del 1874 e l'opposizione meridionale* (Milan, 1956), pp. 81-2.

5. See A. de Clementi, *Amadeo Bordiga*, Turin, 1971.

6. C. de Marco, 'La costituzione della confederazione generale del lavoro e la scissione di "Montesanto" (1943-44)', *Giovane critica*, no. 27 (Summer, 1971); cf. S. Cacciapuoti, *Storia di un operaio napoletano* (Rome, 1972).

7. On Giovanni Amendola, cf. Allum, *Post-War Naples*, p. 71; cf. above, Chapter 2, p. 47 ff., see also Giorgio Amendola's autobiographical *Una scelta di vita* (Milan, 1976).

8. Cf. S. Tarrow's *Peasant Communism in Southern Italy* (New Haven and London, 1967), which argues on the contrary that the *via italiana* was designed for the north and unsuited to the south.

9. G. Amendola, *Gli anni della Repubblica* (Rome, 1976), pp. 345-7, himself described how he built up his network of power; cf. Tarrow, *Peasant Communism*, pp. 230-3.

10. Sources for the following are Amendola, *Gli anni*, p. 349, and *Il rinnovamento del PCI*, interviewed by R. Nicolai (Rome, 1978), pp. 48-51, and interview, 12 Jan. 1972.

11. Interview, 17 Dec. 1971.

12. *L'Unità*, 14 July 1956; cf. ibid. (Naples ed.), 24 and 25 Nov. 1956.

13. Ibid. (Naples ed.), 25 Nov. 1956.

14. Interview, 8 Dec. 1971.

15. *Rapporto di attività del Comitato federale*, X Congresso della Federazione Napoletana del P.C.I., Napoli, 16-17-18 novembre 1962 (Naples, 1962), p. 15.

16. *Risoluzioni e nuovi organismi dirigenti*, X Congresso della Federazione napoletana del P.C.I., Napoli, 16-17-18 novembre 1962 (Naples, n.d.).

17. Ibid., pp. 4, 21-2.

18. See Chapter 3, Section 1, above. Cf. Amendola, *Gli anni*, pp. 327-30, and S. Tarrow, *Peasant Communism*, Chs. 12 and 13, and S. Tarrow, 'The Political Economy of Stagnation: Communism in Southern Italy, 1960-70', *Journal of Politics*, 34, 1 (Feb. 1972).

19. 'Appunti sul centro-sinistra nel Mezzogiorno', *Cronache meridionali*, IX, 12 (Dec. 1962), p. 40; cf. A. Reichlin, 'Verso le elezioni', ibid., X, 2 (Feb. 1963), and his reply to V. Fiore, ibid., X, 3 (March 1963).

20. Interview, 6 Dec. 1971.

21. See P.A. Allum, 'Comportamento elettorale e ceti sociali a Napoli', *Nord e Sud*, n.s., X, no. 45 (106), Sept. 1963.

22. *Rapporto di attività*, p. 13; cf. *l'Unità* (Naples ed.), 23 Jan. 1960.

23. *Rapporto di attività del comitato federale*, XI Congresso della Federazione napoletana del P.C.I., Napoli, gennaio 1966 (Naples, 1966), p. 2.

24. Interview, 7 Dec. 1971; A. Mola, 'La classe operaia nell'organizzazione comunista napoletana', *Cronache meridionali*, XI, 1 (Jan. 1964). Also P. Valenza, 'Il rinnovamento del P.C.I. nel Mezzogiorno: a che punto siamo?', ibid.; A. Alinovi, 'Lotte operaie e rinascita del Mezzogiorno', *Rinascita*, XVII, 4 (Apr. 1960).

25. *Rapporto di attività*, X Congresso, pp. 5-7; *Risoluzioni e nuovi organismi dirigenti*, X Congresso, pp. 18-20; data on sections kindly supplied by P.A. Allum.

26. Interview, 12 Jan. 1972. Cf. Macciocchi, *Lettere*, pp. 232-6, on the role of intellectuals in the PCI in Naples.

27. XI Congress, speech by G. Scherillo, Archives of the Neapolitan Federation (AFN).

28. *L'Unità* (Naples ed.), 10 Jan. 1966.

29. 'Rapporto del compagno Giorgio Napolitano all' XI Congresso della Federazione comunista napoletana', AFN, p. 24.

30. See e.g. speech by G. Hermann, 16 Nov. 1962.

31. *Risoluzioni e nuovi organismi dirigenti*, p. 5.

32. Congress of Resina section (Dec. 1965), tape recording (courtesy of Ciro Olivieri).

33. *Risoluzione politica e nuovi organismi dirigenti*, XI Congresso della Federazione napoletana del P.C.I., Napoli, 6-9 gennaio, 1966 (Naples, 1966).

34. Interview, 8 Dec. 1971; cf. Macciocchi, *Lettere*, pp. 31, 251.

6 THE PARTY IN PERUGIA

1. The Socio-economic Setting

The Perugian federation of the PCI was one of the most clearly left-wing federations in 1966. Its leaders, who had been orthodox Togliattians when they first took office in the early 1950s, reached this point after unsuccessfully using Togliattian formulas to deal with the rapid social change that was eroding their mass base. Many of them came from the minor professions and were therefore open to new ideas; furthermore, the federation had a considerable number of student and intellectual members. All these factors, as well as the federation's poor relations with the PSI, helped make Ingrao's ideas popular in Perugia.

The province of Perugia, incorporating the larger part of Umbria, is in a traditionally 'red' region. Its social structure at the unification of Italy was similar to that of neighbouring Tuscany: a small number of large proprietors, the *agrari*, owned most of the land. Their estates, of several hundred hectares each, consisted of a number of family farms which were let to peasants on a sharecropping basis; a typical estate would be composed of thirty or forty farms (*poderi*). The peasants' contracts were of short duration (often only one year), though in practice the same peasant sharecropper (*mezzadro*) usually remained on the farm for life, in a nearly feudal relationship with the landlord. The peasant often brought the landlord produce, or carried out other services such as acting as gatekeeper in his villa or castle. The landlords dominated not only the peasants, but also the whole of the rest of society. The minor professionals typically found in a rural society, such as surveyors, schoolteachers — and, in many cases, the local priest — were either in their direct employ or linked to them through clientelistic relationships. The widespread dependence of the priests on the landlords was in part a result of the confiscation of the Church lands by the state after unification, which left the clergy with scant means. The towns of Umbria were largely administrative and market centres; the landlords' pre-eminence was therefore unchallenged.

At the same time, the sharecropping system generated intense antagonism between landlord and *mezzadro*. The renewal of the contract and the division of the crop (the landlord usually taking more

103

than 50 per cent) were only the most important occasions for conflict.
The landlord usually supervised the work in the fields as well, and the
choice of crop, investments and methods of cultivation were ultimately
his. The *mezzadro* was in this process constantly reminded of his
inferiority, which was also emphasised in non-economic relationships —
e.g. in seating at church or at public entertainments.[1] In this context, it
is not surprising that many *mezzadri* supported the Socialist, and later
the Communist, parties. They were won over all the more easily to
socialism because the clergy, perceived as clients of the landlords, had
lost their political influence, though not always their religious authority.
Memories of papal rule also generated anti-clerical sentiment, which
early found expression in support for left-wing candidates.

After the fall of fascism the region returned a left-wing majority
(see Table 6.1). But Umbria was the third 'red' region; the PCI's vote
was not as large as in Tuscany or Emilia-Romagna. The landlords and
the Church retained a substantial following, particularly among the
white-collar, professional and petty-bourgeois element in the towns
and in the hills and mountains, where there were concentrations of
small peasant proprietors. The DC, with 33.1 per cent of the vote in
1958, was the largest single party. While the PCI and PSI controlled
the provincial councils and the major municipalities, there was no
extensive network of co-operatives, as in Emilia or, to a lesser extent,
in Tuscany (see Table 6.2). The institutions of civil society were still
largely dominated by the traditional ruling class. The Party appeared
to be an embattled force, rejected by this ruling class which, as in many
regions of the south, still retained much of its economic and social
power. The absence of major industrial development in the province of
Perugia allowed this social structure to survive into the 1960s.

2. The Adoption of the *Via Italiana*

The Perugia federation was headed in the early post-war period by
Armando Fedeli, a Party member since 1921. Fedeli was a near-
legendary figure who had been imprisoned by the Fascists for five
years and had then continued Party work abroad clandestinely. He had
led the Resistance in the province. Like many comrades formed in that
school, he had a traditional conception of communism. In 1951,
however, Fedeli was sent as part of the movement of *costruttori* to
direct a Party school in Sicily, and under the leadership of the new
federal secretary, Raffaello Rossi, a younger group began to take up

Table 6.1: Share of Popular Vote Won by Left-wing Parties in 'Red'
Regions, 1895-1958

		Umbria	Perugia province	Emilia	Tuscany	Italy
1895	Socialist	1.9		20.7	9.3	6.8
	Radical	29.5		24.6	10.5	11.7
1900	Socialist	7.2		26.5	16.2	13.2
	Radical and Republican	27.8		25.8	15.5	13.3
1904	Socialist	22.9		37.8	24.5	21.3
	Radical and Republican	24.2		19.5	19.3	13.3
1909	Socialist	22.8		39.5	21.6	19.0
	Radical and Republican	18.2		16.9	19.8	14.4
1913	Socialist	17.0		44.9	29.6	22.9
	Radical and Republican	25.0		16.3	14.7	15.1
1919	Socialist	46.8		60.2	43.9	32.3
	Radical and Republican	11.2		4.7	8.0	4.0
1921	Socialist and Communist	24.8		41.9	41.6	24.7
	Radical and Republican	5.0		6.2	5.0	1.9
1946	PCI	27.9	27.6	37.6	33.7	19.0
	PSI	22.8	24.3	28.0	21.9	20.7
1948	FDP*	47.2	46.6	51.3	48.0	31.0
1953	PCI	28.2	27.8	36.7	35.1	22.6
	PSI	23.7	23.9	14.3	13.4	12.8
1958	PCI	30.7	30.6	36.7	34.4	22.7
	PSI	21.4	21.4	16.4	16.8	14.2

* PCI–PSI joint list.

Source: Ministry of the Interior, *Compendio dei risultati delle elezioni politiche
dal 1848 al 1958* (Rome, 1963).

Table 6.2: Strength of the Co-operative Movement in the 'Red' Regions, 1963

	Emilia	Tuscany*	Umbria	Perugia province	Italy
No. of co-operatives	2,339	944	93	66	8,860
Total no. of members	548,255	195,695	42,580	24,935	1,844,391
Members per 1,000 pop. (1961) census	151	72	55	45	38

*   Excluding Lucca and Massa-Carrara.

Sources: Elaborated from *Annuario generale della cooperazione italiana*, 2nd edn (Rome, 1965), p. 99; *Annuario parlamentare 1963-64*, vol. I (Rome, 1963), pp. 1246-9.

positions of responsibility. Rossi himself identified the years 1953-4 as a turning-point in the history of the federation, when the Party shifted its emphasis from general propaganda on national issues to concrete struggles over local problems.[2] This was a federation where the national 'turn' of 1953-4 was immediately applied: the PCI organised 'reverse strikes' in which peasants and others undertook needed improvements on neglected estates; it calculated the value of the landlords' incomes and showed how they could be used for investment and improvement. In local government as well, the 1952 elections brought in a new group of administrators who went beyond simple honest correct administration by setting up neighbourhood councils to reduce tax evasion, undertaking road and school building in the outlying hamlets and enforcing sanitary regulations strictly. A major aim of these initiatives along the lines indicated by Togliatti at the December 1953 Central Committee[3] was to win over the intermediate strata with a plan for the 'rebirth' of the region.

The mass of the Party's membership now came from the peasantry (see Table 6.3). The period 1945-50 had seen the breaking-up of the largest concentrations of the working class in the province, the miners of Bastardo and Spoleto. The federal committee, on the other hand, was chiefly made up of workers, professionals, and teachers (see Table 6.3 (b)). Relatively few intellectuals with university degrees, however, were part of the inner leadership, and even fewer were functionaries (one in 1954, two in 1956, none in 1966). The Party was directed, therefore, to a large extent by members of the minor professions which did not require a university degree — in particular elementary-school

Table 6.3

(a) Social Composition of PCI Membership, Perugia (percentages)

	1954	1960	1967
Workers	20.6	20.9	29.5
Braccianti	5.7	5.9	8.0
Sharecroppers	49.4	49.7	30.1
Smallholders	2.9	2.9	5.9
Artisans, shopkeepers etc.	3.5	3.4	7.0
White-collar workers and technicians	0.7	0.8	0.7
Professionals, teachers and students	0.8	0.7	4.6
Housewives	15.0	13.7	5.7
Pensioners and others	1.3	2.0	8.5
Total	99.9	100.0	100.0
N	31,302	28,145	25,541

(b) Social Composition of the Federal Committee of the Perugia
Federation of the PCI, 1954-66 (percentages)

	1954	1960	1967
Workers	26	32	30
Braccianti	0	2	2
Sharecroppers	7	18	22
Smallholders	0	0	0
Artisans, shopkeepers etc.	5	0	0
White-collar workers and technicians	12	14	15
Professionals, teachers and students	31	30	28
Housewives	2	0	0
Pensioners and others	17	6	2
Total	100	102	99
N	42	37	46

(c) Social Composition of the Active Population of Perugia Province
and of the Active Portion of PCI Membership in the Province

	Province 1951	PCI 1954	PCI 1960	Prov. 1961	PCI 1967	Prov. 1971
Workers	24.6	24.7	24.9	36.8	35.6	44.8
Braccianti	6.1	6.9	7.0	4.3	9.6	6.2
Sharecroppers	25.0	59.3	59.2	17.6	36.3	4.0
Smallholders	27.7	3.5	3.4	21.1	7.1	11.4
Artisans, shopkeepers etc.	8.2	4.3	4.0	10.3	8.4	14.3
White-collar workers and technicians	6.8	0.9	0.9	8.9	0.8	17.4
Professionals and entrepreneurs	1.6	0.4	0.5	1.0	2.1	1.9
Total	100.0	100.0	99.9	100.0	99.9	100.0
N	255,766	26,066	23,632	226,814	21,181	193,843

Sources: See Tables 4.4 and 4.5; data on federal committees from archive of
Perugia federation.

teachers (*maestri*). One group of schoolteachers, in particular, from one zone of the province, the upper Tiber valley around Umbertide and Città di Castello, were co-opted by Rossi as bearers of the line of *rinnovamento* and came to play a leading role in the federation from 1954 on. In 1954 fully 25 per cent of the functionaries elected to the federal committee were former *maestri*, and in 1956, 29 per cent.

Perugia, then, experienced an early and fairly painless 'de-Stalinisation'. However, a small group within the federation wanted to move even further and faster than Togliatti in the direction of *rinnovamento* and a policy of offensive demands and structural reforms.[4] They were not prepared to maintain a rigid distinction between the democratic and the socialist phases; nor would they accept Togliatti's compromises with the orthodox group within the Party. At the 1956 federal congress these dissidents called for a bolder pursuit of structural reforms, in particular the struggle for agrarian reform and the revival of the post-war workers' councils (*consigli di gestione*). They criticised the traditional, trade-unionistic type of sharecroppers' actions, which concentrated on winning improved contracts from the landlord rather than changing basic property relations. Their second major theme was the need for greater intra-party democracy and the complete elimination of all Stalinist survivals. The PCI leadership itself had been too slow in recognising the need for *rinnovamento*, had shared the theoretical errors of Stalin, and had encouraged a cult of Togliatti's personality; after the XX Congress, at the time of the Hungarian invasion, Togliatti had retreated from *rinnovamento*.

These positions foreshadowed in many respects the themes of the Ingrao left. While in Naples the opponents of the official line in 1956 were traditionalists or Stalinists, the Perugian dissidents were more typical of the opposition expressed by small but significant groups throughout the country. About one-eighth of the delegates to the Perugia congress supported them with write-in votes for the federal committee (19 to 21 out of 159 valid votes). While the *rinnovatori* who led the federation received the votes of all three groups present (traditionalists, *rinnovatori* and dissidents), the traditionalist candidates were supported only by the first two.[5] Though defeated, the dissidents, in part because of the prestige of some intellectuals among them, had established a tradition of legitimate debate and discussion in the federation; more important, they had publicised a more advanced interpretation of the *via italiana* in Perugia, which the leadership was later to adopt itself after a series of setbacks and experiments.

Table 6.4: Active Population by Branches of Activity — Perugia
Province

	1951 No.	%	1961 No.	%	1971 No.	%	Net change 1951-71
Agriculture	153,317	59.9	98,688	43.5	42,787	22.1	−110,530
Industry }	102,449	40.1	73,380	32.4	80,993	41.8	+ 48,607
Other }			54,746	24.1	70,123	36.2	
Total active pop.	255,766	100.0	226,814	100.0	193,843	100.1	− 61,923

Source: ISTAT census data.

3. Crisis and Left Turn

No sooner, in fact, had the *rinnovatori* come to power in Perugia than
they were faced with the disappearance of the Party's social base. The
mainstay of the region's economy was agriculture. In the 1950s Italian
agriculture as a whole entered a serious crisis, which precipitated a
massive flight from the land. In Umbria this exodus was even more
serious because the traditional estate run on the *mezzadria* system was
an obstacle to investment and the creation of large, rationalised
operations.[6] The *agrari* lacked capital and seldom showed entre-
preneurial spirit, while the *mezzadri* were unwilling to make improvements which might revert to the landlord, without any compensation,
the following year. In the province of Perugia the number of peasants
(*mezzadri*, proprietors and family members working on the farm) and
braccianti fell from 153,000 in 1951 to 43,000 in 1971 (see Table 6.4).

The *mezzadri* were especially hard hit in this period, though the
major exodus was delayed until the early 1960s. The number of farms
let in *mezzadria* fell from 20,106 in 1962 to only 7,590 in 1970.[7]
While industry and (even more) the tertiary sector grew, they did not
absorb the loss of manpower in agriculture. The population of the
province fell from 578,000 (1951) to 557,000 (1961).[8] In the 1960s,
therefore, the Party was threatened with the loss of its firmest base of
support.

For this reason the PCI was particularly interested in promoting an
experiment undertaken in Umbria in the late 1950s and early 1960s:
the formulation of a regional economic plan by the local political

forces. Umbria was the only region to do so, and this is not surprising in view of the risks of depopulation and decay to which the 'economic miracle' subjected it. A committee was set up by the two provincial administrations (Perugia and Terni), the two provincial Chambers of Commerce and the *Centro per lo sviluppo dell'Umbria*, a research body created by the DC. This structure, formed in 1959, was the result of an agreement between the PCI, PSI and the left wing of the DC, the *fanfaniani* who had just taken over power in the local party from the traditional right. The initiative offered the PCI a chance to apply the directive issued by the Party in December 1953 to formulate local plans for the 'rebirth' of each particular area and thereby form alliances with other classes and parties: indeed, it was a perfect example of a local application of the Popular Front strategy and was frequently mentioned with favour by Togliatti. It also owed something to the ideas of Ingrao, who had become a deputy for the constituency of Perugia–Terni–Rieti in 1958, because it was a manifestation of local autonomy.[9] But the PCI wanted above all to stop the flight from the land and thereby halt the erosion of its *mezzadro* base.

The planning committee set up a research centre and a scientific committee, chaired by Prof. Siro Lombardini, a noted Christian Democratic economist. By 1961 it had produced a series of studies on various aspects of the region's economy – demography, agriculture, industry, tourism, credit, commerce and handicrafts. The principal suggestion for the industrial sector was to make credit more easily available; as most enterprises in the region were small, and even the largest in Perugia were family firms (Perugina and Spagnoli), little capital came from the outside; furthermore, the banking system did not direct such saving as there was in the countryside into local industries. To replace *mezzadria*, the experts proposed either co-operatives or fairly large capitalist farms, with a marginal role for small peasant properties.[10]

The plan, however, was never implemented. First, it required assistance and collaboration from the national government which were not forthcoming. Secondly, the economic boom came to an end in 1963; whereas the planners had assumed that it would continue and eventually spread to Umbria.

From a political point of view the plan was also a failure for the Party because it did not mobilise the hoped-for mass movement behind it. In the first place it was a 'unitary' plan, formulated with DC and PSI participation, and therefore could not propose solutions that went beyond the framework of capitalism. Thus it was more concerned with productivity and efficiency than with full employment and the solution of the peasant question; it did not support the distribution of the land to the peasants (*mezzadri* and others), as the PCI's programme demanded. At the same time it contained no analysis of accumulation — i.e. profits and wages — in the region. These weaknesses of the plan illustrate the potential contradiction between the policy of alliances and that of structural reforms; the fact that it was drawn up with other political forces meant that it could not contain incisive structural reforms. In the second place, it had been formulated by the leaders of the parties and experts without any mass participation. There was a good deal of resistance to the plan within the PCI itself from traditionalist members who labelled it 'social-democratic'.[11] It was not well explained to the masses, nor were enough struggles for its implementation organised, though a general strike was called in the region on 22 June 1965 to support the demand that the government supply the necessary financing for a credit agency for small and medium industry and for an agricultural development agency. The strike won no concessions from the government and was not a complete success in mobilising workers either.

As a result of the plan's failure the PCI in Umbria was forced to look elsewhere, to the growing working class, for a new social base. It realised the need, too, for an alternative national plan. But it also became sceptical of planning in itself as an economic panacea when it realised the Umbrian plan could become 'a great bureaucratic-corporative operation, mediating between the interests of all the politico-economic forces of the region'.[12] And it had experienced the limits of the policy of alliances. Since alliances and 'democratic planning' were Amendola's major themes, the Umbrian experience made the Party there less likely to support him and his ideas.

By the early 1960s, in any case, the flight from the land was of such proportions that the regional plan would have arrived too late to preserve a substantial peasant population. Therefore the PCI saw the working class as its chief future source of support. In its expansion among the *mezzadri*, the PCI had devoted insufficient attention to the workers. In 1961, 37 per cent of the active population of the province were workers, but only 25 per cent of the economically active members (1960 membership figures) of the PCI; and people employed in agriculture constituted 43 per cent of the province's active population, but 70 per cent of the active members of the Party (see Table 6.3). The latter's social composition, which had scarcely changed since 1954, had not kept pace with changes in the province.

By 1962 the lack of a strong working-class base was recognised as 'the most serious insufficiency' of the Party.[13] Proselytising work was undertaken in this direction; and this allowed the left-wing forces within the federation, especially the young Communists, to extend their influence. A document of the federation's Worker Commission of December 1963 pointed out the need for 'new instruments of direct democracy' in the factory.[14] These organisational efforts undoubtedly had some success, if the percentage of workers in the federation rose from 20.9 in 1960 to 29.5 in 1967 (35.6 per cent of active members — see Table 6.2). The prevalence of 'Ingraian' themes in the factory work of the Party is evident from the following report of the first conference of Communist workers at the Perugina plant, in preparation for the May 1965 national conference:

> We cannot be content simply to solve the crisis in which the country has fallen; we must, on the contrary, indicate a solution that questions the capitalist system which objectively and by its very nature causes crises; this means calling the working masses to struggle for objectives which are in themselves socialist.[15]

At the conference, chaired by Luigi Pintor, a well-known supporter of Ingrao, attempts to classify the Perugina Company, a chocolate factory with 1,500 full-time workers, a 'small or medium industry', were defeated. The newspaper put out for the occasion by the Worker Commission stressed other left-wing themes:

> The working class . . . must transfer its action onto the political and revolutionary terrain, contest bourgeois control of the state, struggle uniting around itself a vast grouping of alliances . . .

> A class-based union must realize and make known that its demands undermine, disturb, and compromise the capitalist social equilibrium; they act, that is, in a tendentially anti-capitalist direction.[16]

The experience of organising a new working-class base had a radicalising effect upon the Party as a whole, for it meant a break with established routines and an effort to come to grips with working-class problems without relying on preconceptions or past practices.[17]

Another factor which shifted the Perugian federation of the Party to the left, in spite of the Togliattian orthodoxy displayed by its leaders in the period 1954-60, was the impact of the centre-left within the province. While Perugia was a 'red' province, the PCI was weak enough to feel threatened in its power positions by the centre-left. Its fears were not groundless: in 1965 the PCI-PSI administration of the commune of Perugia was replaced by a centre-left coalition. As the Perugia PSI moved to the right, its gradual *rapprochement* with the DC broke up the unity with other parties which the PCI had so carefully constructed during the formulation of the regional plan. As early as the X Congress (1962), the Perugian PCI federation expressed its discontent with the caution and lack of clarity in the national leadership's public positions on the centre-left, which had not prepared the Party in time for this new threat.[18]

The question came to a head in the 1964 local election campaign, in which the PSI threatened to form centre-left *giunte* (local administrations) wherever possible after the vote. The PCI replied sharply, and a very bitter battle between the two parties ensued.[19] The PCI did very well in the province as a whole, gaining 39.6 per cent of the popular vote, but the sequel to the election was most disturbing to the Party. The PSI federation decided to seek a centre-left coalition in every commune where this was numerically possible, and to go into opposition wherever there was a PCI or PCI–PSIUP majority. Where the only majority possible was a left-wing coalition including the PSI, the Socialists agreed to accept only if they obtained the post of mayor for themselves and the PSIUP were excluded from the *giunta*. These decisions were, as a PCI document said, 'on the extreme right of the PSI's pre-electoral positions', and the way in which they were applied was even more clearly anti-Communist. By February 1965, after most of the *giunte* had been formed to take account of the elections of the previous November, the situation in the communes with over 5,000 inhabitants in the province was as follows:

(i)   in eleven communes where the PCI had a majority alone or with the PSIUP, the PSI was present in the *giunta* in only one;
(ii)   in seven where both a centre-left and a left majority were possible, four (including Perugia, Foligno and Città di Castello, three major centres) had centre-left administrations, and three had left-wing ones;
(iii)   in four where only a centre-left majority was possible, the DC had formed the *giunte* alone, with support from other parties;
(iv)   finally, in five communes where the only majority possible was a left-wing one including the PSI, three had left-wing *giunte*, but in two other major centres (Todi and Spoleto) the PSI had actually

combined with the DC to elect a minority administration with a DC mayor.[20]

The cases of Todi and Spoleto, in particular, demonstrated the PSI's desire to break the alliance with the Communists: the only other important case of a minority centre-left *giunta* was at Crotone, in Calabria. The rapid social change the province had experienced, if it had undermined the social base of the PCI, had completely altered the leadership of the Socialists. Relations further deteriorated when the PSI attempted to set up its own peasant organisation, withdrawing from the PCI–PSI *Alleanza contadini*. In these circumstances, it is no wonder that the PCI in Perugia was strongly opposed to the centre-left, and resented the ambiguous or possibilist statements on the subject by the national leadership.[21] Amendola's reunification proposals, needless to say, were received with undisguised hostility.

While the setbacks of the regional plan and the centre-left had a direct impact on the thinking of the PCI leaders, other forces had in the meantime also been at work within the Party. The events of July 1960 marked a turning-point, because they brought a new group of young people into the Party. (A circle of Young Communists had been formed at Perugia University in 1959.) At the national FGCI congress in 1962, they allied themselves with the 'Roman' tendency strongly influenced by the IV International. This Perugian youth group was to provide support for various anti-imperialist organisations and initiatives on the margin of the Party in the next few years. It was also very active in the federation's Worker Commission, where it was responsible for many of the more left-wing statements and positions. The number of students in the Party increased from 104 in 1960 to 720 by 1967 (see Table 6.3), fully 2.8 per cent of total membership. The Sino-Soviet dispute caused considerable disarray in Perugia as well. At the 1962 provincial congress the delegates criticised above all the way in which the USSR and China had carried on the debate between themselves – the USSR by attacking Albania and China by castigating Yugoslavia. This method of discussion by indirection aroused 'the most serious preoccupation'.[22] Meanwhile, the *Associazione Italia-Cina* was founded in Perugia in October 1962 by Dr Lanfranco Mencaroni, a PCI member. It gained little support among the rank and file; but the national Party leadership was seriously worried, and the Federal Control Commission, reportedly acting on direct instructions from Togliatti, expelled M. Pizzoni of the University FGCI circle and Mencaroni in February and March 1963.[23] Most of the support for the *Associazione* appears to have come from students, many of Trotskyist sympathies. But, as in Naples, most delegates to the XII provincial congress (1966) insisted that the PCI should try to promote a reconciliation between the USSR and China; no one agreed with the national Party's substantially anti-Chinese position, expressed in the theses and in the statements of Pajetta and Alicata.[24] In this period, other signs of unrest appeared: a Party member of long standing, Prof. Mario Mineo, presented a document to the XI Federal Congress (November 1962) which outlined a complete critique of the *via italiana*, proposing a struggle for an immediate transition to socialism, by means of 'dualism of power'. These positions do not seem to have attracted much support, either, though Gino Galli, the federal secretary, felt it necessary to reply to them at length in his report.[25]

At the XII provincial congress almost all the leadership supported Ingrao's platform. Particular opposition was expressed to the formula 'failure of the centre-left'. The political resolution on the theses, therefore, did *not* approve them, but suggested an alternative plan ought to be more clearly outlined:

> We must better define a programme which, starting from a more thoroughgoing analysis of the economic and political forces and the current situation, indicates the basic lines of the struggle against monopoly power and offers our reply to the major problems of contemporary man . . .[26]

Besides an alternative programme, which should explain what a socialist society is, the congress came out strongly for more internal party democracy and for caution in unification with the PSI, especially in the light of the dialogue with Catholics. This almost unprecedented act of defiance brought a very strong reaction from Rinaldo Scheda, the representative of the Party leadership sent to hold the congress. Instead of drawing the conclusions, he attacked the line adopted by the delegates in no uncertain terms. The members of the Political Commission were so incensed that they demanded a special meeting after the close of the congress, in which they severely criticised Scheda's behaviour.[27]

The leadership as well as the rank and file of the Party in Perugia were prepared to support Ingrao's theses in 1966. The attempt to stop the old base from melting away through the regional plan had failed, and incidentally had shown the limits of 'democratic planning' and pointed to the necessity of a more radical, comprehensive and national alternative. And the leadership, without a secure network of co-operatives or local governments under their control, felt vulnerable and were open to suggestions from other, culturally better prepared groups, such as Ingrao (the local deputy) and the young leftists of the FGCI. Ingrao's personal prestige with the Party membership was very great. And there was a history of dissidence, support for internal Party democracy and prodding from the left in the federation. All the above factors are consequences of the presence in Perugia of the two necessary conditions for a break, implicit or explicit, with the Popular Front strategy as it had been codified in the PCI. The province was subjected to a wrenching social and economic upheaval during the economic miracle, and, at the same time, the local federation was led by a group which was sufficiently open to new ideas that it could adopt the main lines of Ingrao's platform. As a result, Perugia distinguished itself as one of the most left-wing federations in 1966.

Notes

1. Alan Stern's description of the consequences of the sharecropping system in Tuscany in D.L.M. Blackmer and S. Tarrow (eds.), *Communism in Italy and France* (Princeton, 1975), pp. 228-31, applies equally well to Umbria (see p. 231 n. 29). See also S. Silverman, *Three Bells of Civilization* (New York and London, 1975), Ch. 3. Arts. 2141-63 of the Civil Code illustrate the semi-feudal features of the *mezzadria* relationship.

2. Interview, 3 Nov. 1971.

3. See Chapter 2, p. 49.

4. Sources for the following discussion are interviews 4 Nov. 1971 (2) and 6 Nov. 1971, and 'Intervento del compagno Riccardo Schicchi al IX° Congresso provinciale di Perugia del P.C.I. (Perugia, 1° dicembre 1956)', in Archive of the Federation of Perugia (AFP).

5. Election results in AFP. Conclusion corroborated by interview, 6 Nov. 1971.

6. Cf. *Quaderni rossi*, 3, pp. 197, 206.

7. ISTAT, *1° censimento generale dell'agricoltura*, vol. II (Rome, 1962), and *2° censimento*, vol. II (Rome, 1970).

8. Actually resident population (*popolazione presente*) as opposed to officially resident population.

9. Interviews, 4 Nov. 1971 (1) and 6 Nov. 1971.

10. 'Documenti della programmazione regionale in Umbria', *Quaderni rossi*, 3.

11. Interview, 4 Nov. 1971 (1), and *Il piano regionale umbro di sviluppo economico* (Note informative a osservazioni), a cura del Comitato regionale umbro del P.C.I., Perugia, n.d. [1963]; *l'Unità* (Rome), 9 Jan. 1966; XII Congress, introductory report, AFP, p. 22.

12. *Il piano regionale umbro*, p. 39.

13. Report signed 'CF – ottobre 1962', AFP, p. 6.

14. 'Documento indicativo sul lavoro verso gli operai, questioni organizzative, iniziative specifiche, 5.12.63', signed 'La Commissione operaia', AFP.

15. *Battaglia operaia*, no. unico (May 1965).

16. Ibid.

17. Interview, 4 Nov. 1971 (3).

18. 'Documento dell'XI° Congresso della Federazione Perugina', 16-18 Nov. 1962 (risoluzione politica), AFP, p. 3.

19. Interview, 6 Nov. 1971.

20. PCI, Federazione di Perugia, *Per l'Unità del Movimento Democratico*, Assemblea degli eletti e dei dirigenti di Partito, Perugia, 21 Feb. 1965, pp. 4, 11-12.

21. Ibid., pp. 6-7; cf. XII Congress, introductory report.

22. 'Documento dell'XI° Congresso'.

23. Interview, 7 Nov. 1971; 'Rapporto della commissione Federale di Controllo, Perugia, 7.1.66', AFP.

24. See speeches of S. Bovini, M. Morlupi, Romeo and Fabbroni, AFP; cf. interview, 6 Nov. 1971.

25. 'Relazione all'XI° Congresso', AFP, pp. 17-22.

26. *L'Unità*, 20 Jan. 1966; see 'Risoluzione politica del XII° Congresso provinciale del PCI (Perugia, 14-16 gennaio 1966)', AFP.

27. Interview, 4 Nov. 1971 (2).

7 LEFT-WING ASCENDANCY IN INDUSTRIAL TURIN

1. The Defeat of 1955 and the Development of an Alternative Strategy

The Turin federation of the PCI was the source of many of the most important elements of the programme of the Communist left. At the centre of the economic miracle, the Turinese Communists elaborated a strategic line for the most advanced sectors of the capitalist economy which attempted to link day-to-day struggles to the long-term goal of socialism. This strategy, involving action from below to control this economy and oppose its main tendencies, became an important part of Ingrao's platform as well, a major component of the 'alternative model of development'.

The crucial role of Turin in the development of Italian communism is too well known to repeat here.[1] It was, and is, an overwhelmingly working-class metropolis. At the centre of the attention of the Turinese Communists was, and is, the massive Fiat complex, the most important industrial enterprise in Italy. Much of the history of the Party in Turin is the history of the Communists at the Fiat plant.

In the war and immediate post-war period the Communists gained a very strong position at Fiat. The complex was originally taken over by the workers themselves, on the liberation of the city, and was only later returned to the previous management.[2] In obedience to the PCI's directives, the Communists assisted in the return to normal production as part of the post-war reconstruction, allowing the owners, the Agnelli family, to regain in the process most of their prerogatives. After the break-up of the tripartite coalition, the management began to eliminate systematically Communist influence in the factory. Discriminatory hiring practices and repression were combined with paternalism and a policy of high wages in an attempt to domesticate the Fiat workforce. These policies, combined with the climate of the Cold War, soon began to take effect. The number of workers enrolled in the CGIL at the Fiat works declined from 40,000 in 1950 to 1,000 in 1960.[3] The last strikes of any significance for nine years took place in 1953.

The initial reaction of the Communists in the factory to this situation was essentially defensive. The expectation that war would soon break out, or that, at any rate, the capitalist world was headed

118

towards an economic crisis, was widespread. In this perspective
factory struggles could only attempt to defend existing living standards
and employment levels against the consequences of the crisis.

The first signs of the 'economic miracle' were therefore seriously
misinterpreted by the Communists. Proposals to condition this
capitalist development and influence its course were not pursued by
the Party. For instance, in 1950-1 Fiat reduced the hours of work.
Some Communists, even then, argued that this was the sign of a crisis
of restructuring, but the majority opinion was that it was a manifestation of capitalism's inevitable tendency towards stagnation.[4] Then, in
1952, some Turinese Communists launched the proposal that Fiat
construct a small car of about 400 cc at a reasonably low price (*c.*
400,000 lire) in order to appeal to a wider market and expand
production. (This idea was, in fact, the same one that Fiat's designers
were already working on: it was to be realised as the famous '600' and,
shortly thereafter, the '500'.) This proposal for a 'mini-car' (*vetturetta*)
was to be connected with a series of measures for increasing production
at Fiat, including a reduction of all prices by 10 per cent. A model of
the *vetturetta* was built and exhibited at the *festa dell'Unità*.[5] It was in
many ways an excellent idea, founded on a Keynesian policy of
increasing internal demand, in the spirit of the CGIL's 'labour plan'
of 1949. But, because of the prevalence of stagnationist theories in the
PCI, it was not inserted in a more general programme of structural
reforms, and remained simply a project for stimulating production at
the Fiat plant, still stricken at that time with short-time working. For
this reason it was criticised as too 'technical' and 'factory-centred' by
some PCI workers.

In keeping with the spirit of *rinnovamento*, the VIII Congress of
the Turin federation (1954) launched the slogan 'democratic control
of the monopolies' to replace earlier demands for nationalisation.[6]
Concretely, this new slogan meant a form of check on the activities of
monopolistic corporations, such as Fiat, by the elected assemblies. The
immediate object was to put an end to political discrimination and
repression and to the worst forms of 'super-exploitation'. Such a slogan
marked an apparent victory for the *via italiana* in its Togliattian version
over Secchia's supporters; it replaced a propagandistic slogan with a
seemingly more realisable demand, around which alliances could be
formed. In fact it did not satisfy those Communists who believed
revolution was an immediate possibility, nor did it convince the
entire Turinese leadership. The struggles waged under this slogan were
largely against the repression exercised against Communist workers, the

firing of militants, i.e. what was called 'Fiat fascism', with the aim of 'bringing the Constitution into the factory' (another slogan of the period). These campaigns were important, but did not create much interest among workers who were not themselves Communists, particularly the younger generation.

It was not until the momentous defeat suffered by the CGIL in the 1955 election of the grievance committee (*commissione interna*) at the Fiat works that the traditional, defensive line was effectively discredited. As Sergio Garavini, later secretary of the Turin *Camera del Lavoro* (Provincial Trades Council), wrote, 'For the working-class movement, defeat is always the most convincing objective criticism, the reality which forces it to reflect and to change course.'[7] At this time the CGIL was, in many respects, a 'transmission belt' for the PCI, so that the defeat was felt as a defeat for the Party as well. The FIOM's (CGIL metalworkers' union) share of the vote for the grievance committee fell from 63 per cent in 1954 to 37 per cent in 1955. Such a tremendous failure demonstrated how much the working-class organisations had lost touch with the mass of workers, but it also provided the impetus for the elaboration of a new line of action in the factory.

The defeat was attributed, in the first place, to repression and paternalism on the part of the Fiat management, and, secondly, to errors committed by the working-class organisations.[8] The leaders of the CGIL and the Party began to realise that their action had not been closely enough linked to the real concerns of the workers in the factory; it had been too often centred on political campaigns which meant little to many of them, or on struggles for national minimum rates which Fiat workers had long since obtained. Therefore they began to pay more attention to factory questions: not only wages, but also hours of work, the speed of the assembly lines, the level of employ-ment, bonuses and incentives etc.[9] This line, while at first introduced under the slogan of *rinnovamento*, in the end led to attempts to bargain over investment, in order to promote an alternative model of development. This went beyond Togliatti's strategy, which rested on a stagnationist analysis as much as Secchia's approach did.

The CGIL reacted first to the defeat and, at its IV Congress, turned towards plant-level bargaining and the day-to-day problems of the workers on the shop floor. The Party, however, was somewhat slower to adjust its line; in fact from 1955 on the union became progressively more independent of the Party.[10] Traditionalist resistance was very strong in the PCI. At the 1956 conference on 'Workers and Technical

Progress', Garavini noted that some comrades 'took great care to strictly delimit the extent of the technical development and the progress of the productive forces in our country'.[11] Opposing this point of view, he stated that the modern factories were the model for the future of the whole Italian economy, rather than simply 'islands'. He and Bruno Trentin, of the economic research office of the CGIL, argued that the Party should accept the fact of economic growth and technical progress, and even promote it, while attempting to condition it to limit its negative effect on the working class. One instrument of this policy was the negotiation of the system of productivity bonuses, hitherto granted at the discretion of management. In fact such a negotiated 'super-bonus' had existed at Fiat until 1950, when the union itself revoked the agreement instituting it. As Vito Damico, one of the Communist leaders in the factory, wrote: 'We fell into the most rotten economism and saw the struggle over wages as an end in itself and not as a stage from which to move on to new, more advanced objectives,'[12] for the contracting of the bonus system was the first step towards bargaining over the speed of work and its organisation. Garavini and Trentin also argued that the old defensive struggle for democratic rights within the factory could not mobilise workers unless they saw they were useful in the struggle for concrete improvements in their conditions.

The defeat of 1955 also led to widespread questioning of the institution of the grievance committee itself. Elected on a plant-wide basis from lists prepared by the three competing confederations, it was criticised as too far from the concerns of shop-floor workers: furthermore, it lacked the power to negotiate agreements with management and the knowledge necessary to implement the new policy of contracting all aspects of the work relationship in every shop. Young Communists, such as Adalberto Minucci, proposed the creation of factory councils, composed of one delegate of each shop,[13] and in 1958 two Turinese Socialists, Lucio Libertini and Raniero Panzieri, published 'Seven Theses on Workers' Control'.[14] In fact the workers themselves had already noted the inadequacy of the grievance committees: in 1951 some CGIL members of the Fiat committee resigned to create a 'trade-union factory committee' (*comitato sindacale di fabbrica*) based on a network of workshop commissars.[15] And Minucci's ideas were taken up enthusiastically by some Communists at the RIV ball-bearing plant. However, these proposals were opposed by both traditionalist Communists and orthodox Togliattians as economistic, potentially corporative and likely to lead to a neglect of the policy of alliances.[16]

They were not taken up again until the hot autumn of 1969 when factory councils were formed throughout Italy.

Another effect of the 1955 defeat was a rapid renewal of the leading cadres of the Turin federation, which spared it a long, painful de-Stalinisation. The disappointing election results prompted the Party Secretariat to send a critical letter to the Turin federation, and to replace Celeste Negarville, the federal secretary, with Antonio Roasio. Roasio, an older militant with great prestige, remained for three years as secretary and promoted a new generation of cadres, like Damico, Garavini and Minucci, who were prepared to break with the traditional outlook; in fact, they soon went beyond the bounds set by Togliatti's *via italiana* too. The federation was able to draw upon a small but important group of intellectuals, such as Garavini, who were capable of elaborating a new strategy on the basis of the experience of the working class. Furthermore, they were able to work with a group of 'organic intellectuals', such as Emilio Pugno, drawn from the Turinese working class itself. As we shall see, this early de-Stalinisation of the leadership gave rise to a growing gap between its political attitudes and those of the rank and file.

At the IX Congress of the federation in 1956, there was already some evidence of this hiatus. The situation was more complex than in Naples or Perugia.[17] On the one hand, a traditionalist group of delegates, like the Neapolitan opposition, criticised recent doctrinal innovations, called for more intra-party democracy and in particular asked for an open explanation of the defenestration of Secchia. On the other, a position critical of the limits and compromises of the *rinnovamento* process, more extreme than the Perugia dissidents', was expressed in a document on the invasion of Hungary signed by two Turinese Communists and a number of other intellectuals. It stated: 'All those who have invoked, directed, and supported the massacre of the Hungarian proletariat are not socialists and can never be considered such any more.'[18] Faced with these two opposite criticisms, the group of *rinnovatori* itself divided: Luciano Gruppi, an orthodox Togliattian functionary, made a very harsh 'anti-revisionist' speech directed at the supporters of the document on Hungary. In reply, Pugno, Minucci, Garavini and a group of other leaders presented a resolution which, while criticising purely negative attacks on the Party, deplored the tendency to create divisions between intellectuals (suspected of 'revisionism') and workers within the PCI. Thus the future Communist left appeared as a distinct group in Turin earlier than elsewhere.

2. The Revival of Militancy

The new line in the factories continued to encounter resistance after
1956 from both traditionalists and orthodox Togliattians. The political
distance between the leadership and the rank and file seemed to widen
further in the context of the general organisational decline of the Party.
Membership fell from 54,000 in 1954 to 30,000 in 1959; it remained
at this level until 1966. The number and proportion of workers fell
even more, from 44,000 (82 per cent) in 1954 to 18,000 (59 per cent)
in 1960. At the root of this organisational decline, besides the
repression in the factories, was the persistence of sectarian attitudes
among the rank and file: many of the older Communist cadres were not
prepared to see that a new situation was developing. Having lost the
perspective of an 'X-hour', they had become discouraged and ceased to
devote their energies to day-to-day struggles.[19] Some even theorised
that it was impossible to struggle within the factory, and that it was
necessary to 'encircle the monopoly' from outside, in the neighbourhoods or even in the Third World. There were workers who were in
favour of an eventual armed seizure of power, but refused to take part
in strikes. Consequently, the activity of the sections and cells became
largely routine: as one trade-union leader noted, the party cadres in the
factory still had an 'orientation . . . which sees party work in terms of
campaigns and is based on defensive themes . . . We have an organization which works exclusively at the level of the distribution of
membership cards and of the press month.'[20] This description of the
problems of one city section in 1962 graphically illustrates how this
situation made it difficult for the Party to attract young people who
had been recently radicalised:

> The lack of political initiative in the section and, at the same time,
> the decrease in activism, have their root not only in objective
> reasons but also in the conflict existing in the section between two
> different positions; there are comrades who have recently joined the
> Party who want more political activism and initiative, and tend to
> reject, because of the bureaucratic characteristics which it has
> assumed, the activity of distributing party cards and collecting dues,
> selling the party press, etc., and other comrades who, although they
> correctly fight to maintain these activities which are essential for the
> Party, are not sufficiently sensitive to the need for political initia-
> tive.[21]

At the same time the slogan 'democratic control of the monopolies' was not abandoned at once, and many PCI leaders continued to insist on the need to use the institutions of the state to influence Fiat policies.[22] This orthodox Togliattian policy may have seemed more realistic than one that stressed action by the workers themselves, in a period when the Fiat workers had been substantially reduced to passivity: after the débâcle of 1955 the FIOM and the Party continued to lose ground. In 1957 the FIOM fell to 21 per cent of the votes for the grievance committee. Furthermore, it was subject to continual harassment and intimidation: it had a great deal of difficulty finding the 300 workers needed to act as candidates and scrutineers for the committee elections, since accepting one of these responsibilities meant exposing oneself to reprisals, and very often to loss of one's job.[23]

Nevertheless, the elaboration of a new factory strategy by some workers and federation leaders continued, in spite of setbacks and resistance from all quarters. At the same time the conditions for the renewal of working-class militancy were developing. Most important, the labour market was becoming tighter as the 'economic miracle' absorbed manpower. Fiat workers, therefore, were no longer a privileged minority with wages 50 or 80 per cent above the average, for other factories had to increase pay levels to attract hands. Workers fired by Fiat could now find work elsewhere with little difficulty. The strike, therefore, once again became a potent weapon. Moreover, the lack of manpower led to attempts to increase the rate of exploitation of the workers in the factory. The Fiat management introduced the 'cumulation of tasks': one worker was supposed to do one job plus part of another (e.g. maintenance).[24] Constant technical changes in the factory increased the physical and psychic strain on the workers. Fiat also lengthened the working week; for instance, the management tried to introduce the summer week of 52 hours in February 1962.

All these modifications in working conditions made the Fiat workers ready to revolt. At the same time, their conditions outside the factory were also very difficult. Turin had grown at an exceptional rate, almost doubling in population from 1950 to 1960, and there was therefore a serious lack of housing and social services. Immigrants from the south, in particular, had to suffer discrimination and hardship outside the factory. They often had no choice but to live in a *bidonville*, and they were, as a result, among the most combative in trade-union struggles.

The revival of militancy began in some of the small and medium factories and finally spread to the Fiat plant itself. The first sign of a new season of struggles was a one-hour strike at the Fiat Spa-Stura plant on 2 February 1962, called to protest against the lengthening of the working week. The FIOM thought that the long-awaited moment had finally arrived, and called a strike in all Fiat plants for 6 February. This strike was a complete failure – only a few hundred workers responded to the call. The FIOM leaders were criticised by Togliatti himself for this premature action. Even Garavini called the strike 'hasty and untimely',[25] but it was in fact an important stage in the development of the consciousness of the Fiat workers, a stimulus to discussion and a condition for the successful strikes that were to come.

On 19 June, the second one-day national strike called by the metalworkers' unions, 7,000 Fiat workers stayed at home. This was the most successful strike in nine years.[26] From then on the barriers were broken: on 23 June 60,000 workers went on strike. By 7 July, in spite of the separate agreement already reached by the UIL and the SIDA (a company union) with the Fiat management, some 92 per cent of Fiat workers struck, and there were protest demonstrations outside the offices of the UIL (the *fatti di Piazza Statuto*). Finally, in October, after the Fiat management for the first time in seven years had agreed to negotiate with the FIOM, a collective agreement was signed. This agreement was a turning-point in that it provided for plant-level bargaining over the major bonuses (previously at the discretion of management) and over the speed and manning of the assembly line. (Once again, there was a precedent for this latter point in the history of the class struggle at Fiat: an agreement of 1951 had given the *commissione interna* the power to supervise the speed and manning of the assembly lines. However, the union had allowed management to revoke this provision without putting up strenuous resistance.[27]) On the other hand, this agreement did not win a reduction in hours of work, which was probably the demand which the workers were most anxious to see satisfied.

This major victory had been won thanks to a new generation of young militants. As the Turin FIOM secretary said, speaking of the period 1958-61:

Our factory cadre was not the determining factor in this struggle. We have had this revival of the working-class movement because of the link between a small group of comrades and the working class itself.[28]

3. Beyond the *Via Italiana*: Leftism in the Factories

After the breakthrough of 1962 the leaders of the PCI in Turin began to discuss the future direction and aims of the movement. In the context of the boom of 1959-62 there was clearly a danger that the workers would be integrated into the system by the concession of high wages by the employers, without any gains in power. As Garavini said, speaking of the union struggles of 1961:

> Do we as a union want to obtain a new stabilization of the workers' contractual relations at a higher level than the present one as far as wages, hours of work, job classification, and so forth are concerned? I'd like to be very clear about this and say very frankly that we do not want to obtain this, that this is not our objective, because, to put it brutally and schematically, this is if anything the objective of the class enemy.[29]

In return for industrial peace, the employers were ready to make considerable economic concessions. The union should engage in action, argued Garavini,

> which is not revolutionary gymnastics, therefore is not striking for the sake of striking; [but] which is striking as a form of struggle which chooses its objectives, attempts to attain them, and concretises them in union compromises, which, however, are only stages in the working class's action in the framework of a perspective, which we hold out because it is real, of a progressive sharpening of the class struggle, first of all in the major Turinese automobile and engineering factories.[30]

The natural consequence of the new line in the factories was the demand for 'control over investments, meaning not only parliamentary control, but the direct participation of the workers in the productive decisions of the great enterprises which are the mainspring of any policy of development'.[31] But many within the Party, even in Turin, continued to oppose this orientation, as they had in 1955-8, in the name of the policy of alliances. There were complaints about the 'tendency to enclose all the terms of the class struggle within the work relationship in the factory, in an over-estimation of the elements of spontaneity in the struggle, and in an over-estimation of the indubitable political value of the trade-union struggle in the factory'. These qualms led to the compromise proposal of 'a scale of controls and democratic institutions going from the factory to the highest organs of the State', and for a generalisation of the struggle to non-factory questions such as housing, education etc.[32] This generalisation would allow the Party to involve the middle strata in action for these goals. Many Party cadres, in fact, were very preoccupied: under their left-wing leadership the unions were extremely active and seemed to be taking over some of the functions of the Party itself. The left was in the end to predominate in the Turin federation.

The left was able to maintain its position in Turin in spite of the economic crisis of 1963, which threw the working class back on the defensive and reduced its combativity.[33] In two years employment in the province of Turin fell by 40,000-50,000. This crisis was correctly diagnosed as a crisis of restructuring rather than a sign of the tendency of capitalism to stagnate. Under pressure from the left, the PCI responded to threats of foreign takeover (RIV, Olivetti) and closure (CVS textile plant) with proposals for nationalisation in the context of alternative plans for the sectors concerned. These factory issues, brought on by the economic crisis, demonstrated how the new line was capable of informing the action of the Party on concrete questions, giving a 'substantive response' to the workers' problems, with a 'real programme, not a programme of propaganda only, but a programme of mobilisation and struggle'.[34]

In conclusion, the left wing in Turin owed its predominance to the particular situation of the city, at the heart of economic development; the alliance policy had a less important role for the Turinese because the working class was a clear majority in the city. Furthermore, the policy of alliances had few credible solutions to the concrete problems posed by the factory struggles, while the strength of the industrial working class, on the other hand, appeared to offer a more certain path of advance. The militancy of the workers at times almost required the Party to adopt a left-wing position. Moreover, the Turin federation had a significant number of intellectuals; a group of these, especially those involved in the union, where they worked with experienced working-class cadres, were able to elaborate and propagate a new line of action in the factories. The Turinese left, although they had their own particular themes and policies, thus formed part of the broad left wing that supported Ingrao's positions at the XI Congress.

Notes

1. One of the best of several accounts now available in English of the beginnings of the PCI in Turin is John M. Cammett, *Antonio Gramsci and the Origins of Italian Communism* (Stanford, 1967).

2. For an account of this period, see L. Lanzardo, *Classe operaia e partito comunista alla Fiat. La strategia della collaborazione: 1945-1949* (Turin, 1971).

3. S. Garavini, 'Gli anni '50 alla FIAT: una esperienza storica', *Politica ed economia*, I, 2 (Sept.-Oct. 1970).

4. Interview, 6 Oct. 1972.

5. R. Gianotti, *Lotte e organizzazione di classe alla Fiat 1948-1970* (Bari, 1970), pp. 78-84; and L. Barca, 'Per una storia della Fiat dalla liberazione alla situazione di oggi', *Rinascita*, XIV, 7-8 (July-Aug. 1957).

6. See Federazione Torinese del PCI, *L'VIII Congresso (27-30 maggio 1954) – Resoconto*, pp. 296-9, and minutes of X Provincial Congress, 21-24 Jan. 1960, Archives of the Federation of Turin (AFT), pp. 38 ff.

7. Garavini, 'Gli anni '50 alla FIAT'.

8. Gianotti, *Lotte*, pp. 110-12; see Di Vittorio's speech to the Central Committee of the PCI, *l'Unità*, 27 June 1956.

9. Cf. above, Chapter 3, pp. 61-2; see V. Foa and B. Trentin, 'Le politiche rivendicative della CGIL per gli anni '60' in *Quaderni di Rassegna sindacale*, 31-32 (July-Oct. 1971); and F. Sabbatucci, 'Il livello aziendale', ibid., 35 (Mar.-Apr. 1972).

10. See P. Weitz, 'The CGIL and the PCI: From Subordination to Independent Political Force' in D.L.M. Blackmer and S. Tarrow (eds.), *Communism in Italy and France* (Princeton, 1975), pp. 349-58.

11. See *I lavoratori e il progresso tecnico, Atti del convegno tenuto all'Istituto Gramsci*, 29-30 giugno e 1 luglio, 1956 (Rome, 1956), pp. 349-58; cf. *l'Unità*, 24 June 1956.

12. V. D'Amico (sic), 'La nuova situazione impone più iniziativa politica', Roma, Istituto studi comunisti, Frattocchie, 1955 (mimeo), p. 36; cf. Gianotti, *Lotte*, pp. 62-4; and E. Sullotto, introduction to a collection of documents on repression in the factory (mss), pp. 6-7.

13. *L'Unità* (Turin), 23 May 1956.

14. 'Sette tesi sul controllo operaio', *Mondo operaio*, Feb. 1958.

15. Gianotti, *Lotte*, p. 87.

16. P. Spriano, 'La società civile', *Il Contemporaneo*, 1 June 1956; minutes of IX Provincial Congress, 28 Nov.-2 Dec. 1956, AFT, pp. 419-24, 449; articles by P. Spriano in *l'Unità*, 8 July, 12 Aug., 21 Sept. and 10 Oct. 1958; L. Barca, 'Il controllo operaio e la lotto contro il regime', *Mondo operaio*, Oct. 1958.

17. The following account is based on minutes of IX Congress, pp. 62-76, 152-61, 297-8.

18. 'I fatti di Ungheria', supp. to *Ragionamenti*, II, 7 (Nov. 1956).

19. Minutes of FC and FCC meetings, 3 Mar. 1962, AFT, p. 52; Garavini, 'Gli anni '50 alla Fiat', pp. 47-8; minutes of XI Provincial Congress (15-18 Nov. 1962), AFT, pp. 64, 205-10; minutes of X Congress, pp. 310-19.

20. Minutes of FC and FCC (10 Nov. 1962), AFT, p. 52.

21. Minutes of Congress, 45th section, 26 Nov. 1962, AFT.

22. *Per il progresso di Torino e della Provincia, per una nuova politica nazionale di sviluppo economico*, Atti del Convegno economico della Federazione torinese del PCI, 7-9 giugno 1957 (Turin, 1957), pp. 28-9.

23. See S. Garavini and E. Pugno, *Gli anni duri alla Fiat* (Turin, 1974), for an excellent discussion by two protagonists.

24. *Cronache dei Quaderni rossi*, Sept. 1962, p. 27.

25. *Rinascita*, 5 May 1962, p. 23; cf. Gianotti, *Lotte*, p. 217.

26. On the 1962 strikes, see Gianotti, *Lotte*, p. 224; G. Amyot, 'La ripresa e la battaglia contro il neo-capitalismo (1955-66)' in F. De Felice *et al., I comunisti a Torino 1919-1972* (Rome, 1974), p. 231; *l'Unità*, 12 June 1962.

27. D'Amico, 'La nuova situazione', pp. 38-9; Sullotto, mss, p. 6; Gianotti, *Lotte*, pp. 76-8.

28. Minutes of FC and FCC (10 Nov. 1962), p. 51.

29. Federazione torinese del PCI, *Atti dell'assemblea dei comunisti della Fiat*, Torino, 15-16 aprile, 1961 (Turin, n.d.), p. 66.

30. Ibid., p. 70.

31. V. Damico, 'Unità per un' alternativa', *Piemonte cronache*, III, 1 (Jan. 1965).

32. 'Questioni di orientamento e impegni di lavoro dei comunisti torinesi in relazione alla situazione alla Fiat', Documento approvato dal CD della federazione e dal comitato di coordinamento della organizzazione comunista alla Fiat (maggio 1962), AFT, pp. 8-9; cf. minutes FC and FCC (10-11 Jan. 1962), AFT, p. 18.

33. On this period, see minutes of XII Provincial Congress (Jan. 1966), AFT, pp. 27 ff., 34-6 and 240-3; cf. also speeches by A. Surdo, E. Pugno, G. Carcassi and S. Garavini, ibid.; and U. Pecchioli, 'I compiti dei comunisti nella lotta per la programmazione democratica, per la difesa dell' occupazione e dei diritti dei lavoratori' (Relazione al CF, Torino, 18.9.65), *Piemonte cronache*, III, 3 (Sept. 1965).

34. Minutes of XII Congress, p. 183.

8 COMMUNISM IN 'RED' MODENA

1. Socio-economic and Political Background: a Sectarian Federation

The Modenese PCI was moulded by the experience of the armed
Resistance, from which it emerged as a strongly sectarian federation.
A very long and painful process of de-Stalinisation, conducted largely
by Togliatti, Amendola and the right from 1954 on, was necessary. At
the end of it, the federation was firmly aligned with the right wing in
the Party.

Emilia is the oldest and most solid stronghold of the left in Italy, the
heartland of radicalism and Marxist subculture. A century ago it was
characterised by large estates in the Po valley, while small peasant
proprietors predominated in the foothills of the Apennines to the west.
The fertility of the valley, however, led some of the landlords to
attempt to modernise, introducing full-fledged capitalist agriculture
using hired labourers (*braccianti*). It was the radicalism of the countryside which made Emilia red; as early as the 1880s the *braccianti*,
organised by the provincial trades councils, launched mass strikes. In
addition, much of Emilia had been part of the Papal States, and an anti-
clerical tradition put the region on the left of national politics even
before the rise of the Socialist Party. In 1895 the Socialists already had
21 per cent of the vote in Emilia; by 1919 they had reached the
remarkable total of 60 per cent.

Emilian socialism was of a plebeian, populist stamp; its leaders were
men of the people writ large, great eaters, drinkers and lovers, like
Prampolini and Agnini, who were held in religious veneration by their
followers. The movement soon built up a strong network of
co-operatives, unions and Socialist-controlled local governments, a
Marxist subculture which was able to rival that of the Church as a social
milieu for its members. Though its exponents were given to maximalist
rhetoric, Emilian socialism was largely reformist, even corporative. Its
co-operatives and other institutions were able to improve the economic
condition of its followers; but they refused Prime Minister Giolitti's
offer of an anti-southern alliance and were swept up in the revolutionary fervour of the *biennio rosso* (1919-20).[1]

This wave of radicalism profoundly affected Emilia, where the
Socialist movement was better organised to take advantage of it: rural

130

agitation culminated in the April 1920 victory of the *braccianti*, who imposed a collective agreement very favourable to themselves, providing in particular for a minimum number of man-days of employment per hectare (the *imponibile di mano d'opera*). This agreement, and the fact that the Socialists controlled a good part of local government in the area, prompted the landlords to finance the Fascist movement, hitherto a small, urban-based group. Togliatti, as we have seen,[2] laid the blame for the rise of fascism at the door of the Socialists, whose intransigent maximalism, along with the sometimes violent methods of the *braccianti*, alienated the middle strata in the countryside (*mezzadri*, renters etc.).

During the Fascist period, the Communist Party and the Marxist subculture remained alive in the province, though driven partly underground. The co-operatives were not all dissolved; and in many villages, where the peasants were unanimously anti-Fascist, police surveillance was very difficult. The Party organisation, though harassed, was able to keep alive: at one point the PCI had from 1,000 to 1,500 members in the entire province. In the Carpi area, a left-wing stronghold, there were 80 to 100 cells with four to five members each.[3] A clandestine provincial congress was held in an isolated farmhouse to elect delegates to the IV national congress (Cologne, 1931). Party strength was greatest in the countryside, and particularly in the plain.

Given this extraordinary continuing Communist strength under fascism, it is not surprising that the armed Resistance in Modena was extremely strong, and left a lasting mark on the political life of the area.[4] The physical characteristics of the province – much of it is flat plain – were not especially propitious to guerrilla warfare, but the total solidarity of the people allowed the partisans to move 'like fish in water'. The Resistance in Modena, under Communist leadership, developed an extensive organisation, reaching to the grass roots, with a full panoply of auxiliary bodies – women's (GDD), youth (FdG), trade-union and peasant committees, plus a capillary structure of communal and village Committees of National Liberation and four newspapers. Peasant committees prevented threshing of grain so that it could not be requisitioned by the Fascists or the Germans. The purely military record of the Resistance in Modena was also impressive. It established the first liberated zone within occupied Italy, the 'Republic of Montefiorino', which lasted through May and June 1944. The movement survived the hard winter of 1944-5, and in the new year fielded two full divisions, the 'Modena M' (Mountain), with 4,000 to 5,000 men, and the 'Modena P' (Plain), with over 6,000 partisans. The

Table 8.1: Percentages of the Popular Vote for the PCI and PSI in Elections to the Chamber of Deputies in the Province of Modena, 1946-63

	1946	1948	1953	1958	1963
PCI	44.2		42.3	41.1	45.2
PSI	26.0		12.6	15.9	13.4
FDP (PCI + PSI)		56.0			

Source: Ministry of the Interior, *Compendio dei risultati delle elezioni politiche dal 1848 al 1958* (Rome, 1963), and *Elezione della Camera dei Deputati del 28 aprile 1963* (Rome, 1964).

'Modena P' division was the only partisan formation in Italy to engage the Germans in a pitched battle in open terrain. Modena also boasted the only regular female partisan fighting brigade, the *Brigata 'G. Degli Esposti'*.

The Resistance generated revolutionary expectations, which led to experiments such as peasant collectives after the Liberation.[5] During the reconstruction period, these hopes were not forgotten, but simply deferred: the PCI limited itself, in the main, to administering and defending its impressive position in the province (see Tables 4.7, 4.8 and 8.1) in anticipation of a future 'decisive moment'. As a later federal secretary said: 'We had a perspective — let us admit it — which was at odds with Togliatti's and Gramsci's elaboration of the political line of our party.'[6]

Nor did the ethos of the Modenese Party stimulate debate and criticism of this pre-1935 cominternist perspective. On the contrary: the partisan movement left a deep imprint on the Party, creating a military style of work and outlook, mixed with a quasi-religious attachment by the militants. As one local Party secretary put it in 1956, 'We came to the Party with rifles in our hands.' The PCI rank and file continued to resort at times to military methods against opponents after the war, and the repression of the Cold War only increased the tension; so much so that Togliatti, when he visited the federation in 1949, took its leaders to task for their *doppiezza* and the continuing 'terrorism' of the partisan movement.[7] But as late as 1955 the partisans marched through the city on the anniversary of the Liberation drawn up in their old formations.

In this climate, the internal life of the Party was anything but

Table 8.2: Social Composition of the Modena Federation, 1954-67 (percentages)

	1954	1960	1967
Workers	24.3	28.2	34.3
Braccianti	21.5	14.9	7.9
Mezzadri and *coloni*	24.5	18.1	7.2
Smallholders	5.0	4.6	3.3
Artisans	5.8	6.8	5.6
Shopkeepers			3.7
White-collar workers	0.8	1.0	1.5
Professionals, intellectuals and teachers	0.2	0.3	0.2
Students	0.1	0.1	0.1
Housewives and cottage workers	13.8	18.6	22.1
Pensioners	4.0	7.5	12.1
Others			2.0
Total	100.0	100.0	100.0
N	87,135	82,727	71,823

Source: See Table 4.5.

democratic — as the federal secretary said in 1954, 'Our Federation suffers greatly . . . from its insufficient democratic life which is responsible in the first place for the small number of politically active comrades.'[8] Political education was undertaken, but the majority of members had read only the *History of the Communist Party (Bolsheviks) of the Soviet Union* (Short Course), prepared under Stalin's direction in 1938, which was the chief text in the first level of party courses.[9] The content of the *History* was hardly likely to encourage free, open debate of party policy. It laid the emphasis on 'vigilance' for enemies of the Party and of communism, inside and outside Party ranks: the history of the Soviet Party was presented as a victorious struggle against spies, traitors and deviationists of various sorts. This provided a sound basis for the passivity of the masses and the 'satrapism' of the leaders.

The mass membership was in fact scarcely 'politicised'; their attachment to the Party was of an affective type, as, for instance, the quasi-religious ceremonies and rituals that punctuated the 1954 provincial congress demonstrate. The first order of business was to appoint an honorary chairmanship: 'Marx, Engels, Stalin, Malenkov, Lenin, Gramsci, Togliatti, and all the Fallen in the cause of labour and liberty.'[10] At a break in the speeches, 'A delegation of women from the village of Secchia makes an offering (a basket of eggs)' presumably to the real chairman and platform party.[11] At the end of the congress, a number of gifts were presented to the platform party (flowers, a radio, wallets etc.), while 'Pajetta's little daughter offers a bouquet of flowers to comrade Corassori' and 'The child Rubens Veratti recites a poem *L'Italia del Ma* . . . in honour of Giancarlo Pajetta.'[12] The ordinary members' Party activity consisted largely of routine, festivals and organisational maintenance, rather than political initiative. The organisation was extremely well developed, with 87,000 members in 1954, one-sixth of the province's population, and a complete network of groups of ten (instituted by Secchia in 1948 to provide a more capillary level of organisation than the cell[13]). But the level of political debate was low — most speakers at Party congresses could deal only with the single sector in which they had been working (women, *braccianti*, co-operatives etc.) or with the problems of their own section, cell, commune or factory. Table 8.4 indicates that even after the XX Congress and the invasion of Hungary the majority of speeches at the provincial congress were sectoral.

Both a cause and an effect of this low level of debate in the federation was the 'plebeian' character of the leadership, composed essentially of the Resistance generation until the 1960s (see Table 8.5; cf. Table 8.2). Most of the few intellectuals in the federal committee were functionaries.

The Party's most popular leader in this period was Alfio Corassori, dubbed 'the Grand Duke of Modena', who had been the chief Communist organiser in the province in the 1920s, and who served as Mayor of Modena from the Liberation until the fall of 1962. The federal secretary until 1950 was Leonida Roncagli, an experienced organiser formed in the old school, who ruled the Party with an iron hand. He was succeeded by E. Silvestri (known also by his partisan nickname 'Maino'), who proved to be politically and morally unworthy of the position. Among his other faults he used physical threats and violence against suspected opponents within the Party: when, the following year, Giuseppe d'Alema was sent by Party headquarters to take over the federation and restore a healthy climate, one of his first acts was to expel Silvestri from the PCI. The 'Maino episode' demonstrates the serious limits of a military style of party organisation which concentrated power in the hands of one man or a small group whose

Table 8.3: Number of Groups of Ten and Number of Members per Group in the Five Federations, 1954

	Turin	Modena	Perugia	Naples	Bari
Number of groups	2,392	7,013	2,318	4,750	1,200
Members/group	22.6	12.4	13.5	16.0	26.8

Source: *Forza e attività del partito* (Rome, 1955).

Table 8.4: Delegates' Speeches at Modena Provincial Congresses, by Topic, 1954 and 1956

		1954		1956	
		N	%	N	%
(1) General political topics		2	(4.3)	13	(34.2)
(2) Partly general political, partly sectoral		1	(2.1)	4	(10.5)
(3) Sectoral topics		44	(93.6)	21	(55.3)
(a)	Speaker's own section, cell, geographical zone or factory	12	(25.5)	4	(10.5)
(b)	Trade-union and factory questions	3	(6.4)	3	(7.9)
(c)	Agriculture, peasants, *braccianti*	3	(6.4)	5	(13.2)
(d)	Women	8	(17.0)	3	(7.9)
(e)	Youth, FGCI	5	(10.6)	1	(2.6)
(f)	Co-operatives	4	(8.5)	1	(2.6)
(g)	Other	9	(19.1)	4	(10.5)
Total		47	(100.0)	38	(100.0)

Source: Elaborated from minutes of VIII and IX Congresses of Modena federation. The report of the secretary and the conclusions of outside Party officials are excluded.

main assets were unquestioning loyalty and long service to the Party, but whose education and general political culture were limited. Secondly, it is striking that such a serious case of political misconduct had practically no effect on the mass membership of the Party: just as they did not object to Silvestri's appointment, they did not react to his

Table 8.5: Social Composition of Modena Federal Committee, 1956-60
(percentages)

	1956	1960
Workers	32.8	39.7
Braccianti	16.4	13.8
Mezzadri and *coloni*	13.1	19.0
Smallholders	1.6	1.7
Artisans and shopkeepers	11.5	3.4
White-collar workers	8.2	10.3
Professionals and intellectuals	13.1	10.3
Students	1.6	—
Housewives	1.6	1.7
Total	99.9	99.9
N	61	58

Source: Elaborated from data in Archive of Modena Federation.

expulsion. The real facts of the case, especially the episodes of violence, were kept a secret as much as possible:[14] in 1956 even some members of the federal secretariat were not aware of everything.

2. The Struggle for *Rinnovamento*

By nominating d'Alema federal secretary, Togliatti attempted to take advantage of the 'Maino episode' to win the federation to the *via italiana* (cf. his use of Fedeli's transfer to Sicily in the Perugia federation). A vigorous, dynamic leader, d'Alema attacked head-on the routine, unpolitical nature of party activity, and the combination of reformism and maximalism, similar to that of the old PSI, which characterised its action. The old type of sectoral, trade-unionistic struggles, however militant, were in fact reformist and often corporative and municipalistic. He argued that they had to be linked to a more general plan for the *Rinascita* of Modena in order to attract support from the middle classes as well; quoting verbatim Togliatti's unfavourable comparison between the northern federations' activity and the south's *Rinascita* movement, he asked at the 1954 provincial congress: 'In the North, have we succeeded in creating something similar?'[15] He suggested concrete objectives to connect trade-union struggles to the general goals of structural reform: agrarian reform, lower taxes and low-interest loans for the commercial middle classes, demands for new public investment and a host of specific improvements in social insurance and local public works. He laid great stress on cultural activity as a way of attracting the middle classes to the Party, criticising its fairly low intellectual and ideological level: 'Doesn't [the federation] still have . . . a — let us say — plebeian character which limits its interests and activity?'[16] He also attacked its military-style internal life. He again quoted Togliatti, who in the December 1953 Central Committee had identified the two major defects of the Party as its insufficient democratic life and insufficient criticism and self-criticism, and went on:

> The error of not criticizing the leading comrades at times leads us to tolerate even situations which I should dare to call cases of satrapism, so that you find at the head of an organization, even a mass organization, men to whom you cannot speak a word of criticism without making them explode, so that you have to accept every mistake they make to the evident detriment of the whole movement.[17]

However, opposition to d'Alema within the federation was tenacious. He was a *costruttore* in reverse, taking Togliatti's line to a northern, 'closed' federation, and met the same type of passive resistance as the *costruttori* encountered in the south. A later federal secretary explained the political weakness of the federation in 1951-3 by the presence of different 'theses', especially over the campaign for the development of the region, rather than a single line.[18] This was evident in the conclusions of Celso Ghini, representative of Secchia's organisation section, to the 1954 provincial congress. Ghini was careful to set conditions and limits to the pursuit of a policy of *Rinascita*: first, it had to involve actual struggle, not simply propaganda; second, the traditional positions of the popular movement must be 'tenaciously' defended and consolidated. This meant trade-union-type struggles and objectives should not be ignored in the pursuit of the more general goals of reform: he referred to the traditional battles for a non-discriminatory hiring hall for *braccianti*, and for the annual 'closing of accounts' between *mezzadri* and landowners.[19] These reservations expressed a substantial doubt about the new line, a doubt probably shared by most of Ghini's audience.

D'Alema in fact failed to bring *rinnovamento* to Modena; he was replaced by Silvio Miana, a Modenese. Nor did the XX Congress and the invasion of Hungary have an appreciable effect. Debate was restricted to a very few comrades, 'almost to the circle of functionaries, or little more than that', and they seemed to 'have not even been shaken by the things that came out of the XX Congress'.[20] In July Prof. A. Mattioli, a functionary who was a high-school teacher by profession and a *rinnovatore* since 1954, spoke of the Silvestri case in the federal committee, causing a minor scandal and drawing criticism, in particular from Corassori.[21] It was a Modenese 'secret speech', denouncing the ill effects of Stalinism in the province, but was not to be made known to the membership at large.

When the rank and file did discuss the themes of the XX Congress, they rejected the criticisms of Stalin, but agreed, like the traditionalists in Naples and Turin, with the call for greater internal democracy in the PCI.[22] At the IX Congress of the federation, in 1956, Prof. Massimo Aloisi, president of the Formiggini Cultural Club, founded by d'Alema, criticised the limits of *rinnovamento* in terms harsher than, for instance, the dissidents in Perugia had used.[23] His speech provoked a storm of protest; only his advocacy of intra-party democracy gained widespread support, which was no doubt fuelled by resentment of the authoritarianism of the local leadership as well as concern over the Secchia affair.[24] The electoral commission's proposal of a 'closed' list for the federal committee election (containing a number of names equal to the number of places to be filled) was approved only after a vote (the result was 346 to 151), and in the balloting one candidate's name was cancelled by 23 per cent of the delegates.[25]

In spite of these signs of unrest, the themes of the XX Congress were quickly dropped in Modena, as in most of the rest of Emilia. Therefore Amendola, as head of the national organisation section, called a regional conference in 1959. The preparatory document for the conference laid emphasis on the policy of alliances, the key point of *rinnovamento*, and identified the three major errors of the PCI in Emilia: (1) its instrumental attitude to alliances; (2) a policy which was objectively corporative and reformist; (3) a conception of the Party as an 'activity in itself'.[26]

Amendola, in his speech to the conference, was brutal.[27] He mentioned the 'diffident perplexity' of many comrades at the critical thrust of the conference, and their preoccupation that the strength and compact discipline of the Party would be weakened. He attacked the tendency of the Emilian party to rest upon its laurels, to ask how it could do more than it had already done, and to excuse itself by arguing, for instance, that an agrarian reform could be carried out only

under socialism. Amendola stressed the need to intensify the struggle
for structural reforms: agrarian reform, nationalisation and democratic
control of monopolies, industrialisation and local government autonomy. But his main theme was internal Party democracy and the need
for wide discussion of general political themes: the rank and file, he
said, should be treated not as minors, but as 'revolutionary fighters'.
He stressed the need to 'accelerate the rhythm' of *rinnovamento*,
concluding with a very explicit warning to those Stalinists who
obstructed the process.

Even after the 1959 conference, many leaders of the Modenese
federation continued to have hidden reservations about the Party's
line and put up passive resistance to its implementation. As one
federal commitee member said:

> These official silences which are very common even in our Federal
> Committee . . . can hide, indeed I believe that in the past they
> definitely have hidden, substantial reservations and have given rise
> to formal acceptance of the Party's orientations and positions. It is
> a fact that very often we do not know precisely what even some
> leading cadres think of the most vital part of our policy.[28]

Khrushchev's renewed attack on Stalin at the XXII Congress of the
CPSU in 1961 provoked even more discussion than the XX Congress
had, and many members of the federal committee expressed their
reservations about the Soviet leader's positions.[29] But even in 1961 the
debate was only perfunctorily taken to the rank and file; in some
communes the leaders 'considered the XXII Congress a disruption of
their work of normal administration of the Party and the organizations
of the working-class movement'.[30] It was only during the 1960s that
the federation, or at least most of its leadership, accepted the *via
italiana*.

3. The Early 1960s: a Rightist Stronghold

During this same period the province was undergoing fairly significant
socio-economic changes. The PCI's defensive struggles of 1948-51
failed to prevent the closure of many large factories. This led to a
dispersal and fragmentation of the working class, but not to general
economic decline as in Perugia. Many of the workers laid off established small enterprises, or shops, and some of these grew into fairly

substantial undertakings. Most of these 'little bosses' (*padroncini*) of the early 1950s were Communists who retained their Party loyalty. At the same time two important forms of small industry developed in the province: Carpi, the traditional Communist stronghold, became a centre of the clothing industry, part of it based on cottage industry, and Sassuolo grew to be a major producer of tiles and ceramics. Furthermore, Modena was able to participate directly in the boom through the Fiat tractor factory located in the city, which also controlled or subcontracted to several small plants in the area.[31] Emilia, with its complex of small industries, grew as an adjunct of, rather than in opposition to, the large northern monopolies. The co-operatives also helped Emilian agriculture to survive in a relatively prosperous condition, and at least moderated the flight from the land. While other provinces were pushed to the margin of the national economy by the boom, Modena enjoyed a steady and moderate rate of growth. Its transformation was, on the other hand, less abrupt than that of the industrial triangle, and did less damage to the traditional social structure of the province than either rapid growth or marginalisation. Hence the PCI was not faced with jarring changes in its social base.

The *rinnovamento* of the federation, when it did come, was due in large part to Amendola's efforts; this fact too helps explain the fact that it was aligned with the right in 1966. Given the low level of political debate in the federation, it was sufficient for him to win over the leaders, starting from the top.[32] Silvio Miana, who succeeded d'Alema as secretary, was made a member of the four-man committee which prepared the document for the 1959 regional conference, along with Amendola and d'Alema. In 1962 he was promoted regional secretary, a sure sign that he had assimilated the Party's line. The new federal secretary, Emilio Debbi, was appointed over the heads of older leaders who were more traditionalist. And in 1962 Rubes Triva, a *rinnovatore*, succeeded Corassori as Mayor of Modena.

At the same time Amendola's positions were congenial to the older Stalinists — at least more so than Ingrao's — on many issues, such as the USSR.[33] His views on the centre-left contrasted with the sectarian attitude to the rank and file, but, on the other hand, the leadership realised the importance of the alliance with the PSI. And because no centre-left alternative was possible in most communes of the province, relations with the PSI never reached the breaking-point, as they did in Perugia. In 1964 the Modenese federations of the PCI, PSI and PSIUP reached a formal agreement on the composition of the *giunte* after the local elections; by January 1966 only two of the province's 47 communes had centre-left administrations; only one of these, Sassuolo, was a major centre. Of the 28 communes controlled by the left, the PSI belonged to the *giunta* in 24 (see Table 4.7).[34] Amendola's stress on the alliance policy was also appreciated in a region where many (though by no means a majority) small industrialists, artisans and shopkeepers were sympathetic to the PCI (cf. Table 8.2).[35] His line appealed to their material interests, while Ingrao's frightened them. The Party itself, because of its network of economic interests, was fearful of the disruptive potential of the Ingraian programme. The traditional Emilian combination of reformism and maximalism survived, if much transformed, under Amendola's aegis. The political passivity of the rank and file, and the absence of intellectuals to present an alternative position, facilitated Amendola's winning over the Modenese federation.

Only a few leaders of the local youth federation — Ronchetti, Guerzoni and Turci — had absorbed some of the left-wing ideas then circulating at the national level. The latter two were almost the sole supporters of Ingrao in the federation: Lanfranco Turci, who joined the Party in 1960, was head of Press and Propaganda in Modena in 1966. Both were cautious because they knew they were a very small minority. The themes of a new historic bloc, an alternative model of development, or the leading role of the working class did not find much support in the relative complacency of Modena. It is doubtful if they were understood by any but the leaders. They were discussed only in negative terms by the functionaries in their frequent speeches to section assemblies. Moreover, Ingrao's advocacy of more internal Party democracy and more vigorous pursuit of structural reforms, as well as his severer criticism of the USSR, ran counter to their most deeply ingrained Stalinist instincts.

The XI national congress, therefore, aroused relatively little interest in the federation. Only some 27 per cent of the members took part in cell assemblies or section congresses[36] (compared to 49 per cent in Perugia[37]). Some two-thirds of the speeches at the congress itself were sectoral; in the opinion of the local PSI secretary it was 'an old-style congress . . . We saw a fairly conformistic acceptance of the national theses, which were approved and extolled more than discussed . . .'[38] Though there were no open expressions of support for Ingrao (Turci's speech was quite careful), one of the old leadership delivered a very forceful warning against factionalism: 'The problem of the unity of the Party is always on the agenda, but today it is a necessity of the *moment*.'[39] He proceeded to attack Pintor's suggestion of unification with the PSIUP and the *lombardiani* only, and advocated involving the whole PSI and the 'social-democratic masses' (sic) in the process.[40] The congress confirmed the near-unanimous support Amendola enjoyed in the federation.

Modena, like most of the rest of Emilia, provided firm support for Amendola at and before the XI congress. The strongly ingrained habits of the Party were not disturbed by overly rapid social change – when the exodus of the *mezzadri* began, the PCI already had other firm bases of support; nor was it as rapid in Modena as in some other areas. The centre-left did not threaten the Party's local power. The coincidence of Amendola's line with the material interests of the PCI in Modena and in Emilia as a whole was also a crucial factor: the co-operative movement and the other economic interests connected with the Party wished to see steady economic growth and were attracted by the prospect of reforms held out by the centre-left. They were by no means interested in creating a revolutionary situation. These forces naturally gravitated towards Amendola and were extremely suspicious of Ingrao. An intensive campaign of more than ten years was necessary to convert the federation to the *via italiana* and the Popular Front strategy; this conversion proved permanent.

Notes

1. See Gramsci's 'Alcuni temi della questione meridionale' in *La costruzione del Partito comunista 1923-1926* (Turin, 1971), p. 149; see above, Chapter 1, p.21.

2. Above, Chapter 2, pp. 41-2; cf. A. Lyttelton, *The Seizure of Power* (London, 1973), p. 284, and I. Vaccari, 'Il sorgere del fascismo nel Modenese' in L. Casali *et al., Movimento operaio e fascismo nell'Emilia-Romagna 1919-1923* (Rome, 1973).

3. L. Casali and M. Pacor, *Lotte sociali e guerriglia in pianura* (Rome, 1972), p. 50.

4. M. Cesarini [Sforza] , *Modena M Modena P* (Rome, 1955); Casali and Pacor are the main sources for the account of the Resistance in Modena.

5. Interviews 1 Mar., 2 Mar., 8 Jan. and 4 Mar. 1972.

6. *Atti del IX° Congresso provinciale della Federazione Comunista Modenese*, Modena, 30 Nov., 1-2 Dec., 1956, Archive of the Federation of Modena (AFM), conclusions, p. 5.

7. Minutes of Federal Committee meeting, 12-17 July 1956, AFM (speech by A. Corassori); cf. speech by A. Gibertoni, ibid., and P. Togliatti, 'Le lotte del lavoro', *Rinascita*, VI, 2 (Feb. 1949).

8. G. D'Alema, *I comunisti modenesi per un nuovo indirizzo della politica italiana*, rapporto tenuto all'8° Congresso Provinciale della Federazione Modenese del P.C.I., 25-28 marzo 1954 (Modena, 1954), p. 80.

9. From 1945 to 1954, 300,000 copies of the *History* were printed in Italy,

far more than of any other Marxist classic; see A. Donini, 'Traduzione e diffusione dei classici del marxismo', *Rinascita*, XI, 11-12 (Nov.-Dec. 1954); cf. minutes of FC, 12-17 July 1956: a survey showed it was the only text read by the majority of members in Modena.

10. Minutes, VIII Congress of Modena federation, AFM, 1^a seduta, p. 1.

11. Ibid., 3^a sed., p. 16.

12. Ibid., 6^a sed., p. 11.

13. See G. Sivini, 'Struttura organizzativa e partecipazione di base nel Partito Comunista Italiano' in G. Sivini (ed.), *Partiti e partecipazione politica in Italia*; cf. P. Lange, 'The PCI at the Local Level' in D.L.M. Blackmer and S. Tarrow (eds.), *Communism in Italy and France* (Princeton, 1975), for a description of 'enclave' type sections in the peripheral towns of Milan province.

14. This account is reconstructed from the minutes of the FC of 12-17 July 1956 where, apparently, the 'Maino episode' was first discussed in a formal Party meeting; cf. also interview, 8 Jan. 1972.

15. See above, Chapter 2, p. 49 for full quotation.

16. *I comunisti modenesi*, p. 12.

17. Ibid., pp. 81-2.

18. Minutes of FC, 12-17 July 1956. Cf. S. Tarrow, *Peasant Communism in Southern Italy* (New Haven and London, 1967), pp. 229-30, on the *costruttori*.

19. Minutes, VIII Congress, 6^a sed., pp. 12-22.

20. Minutes of FC, 12-17 July 1956; ibid., conclusions, p. 1.

21. Ibid.

22. Ibid. (speech by Sainati); *Atti del IX° Cong.*, 6^a sed., p. 25; 1^a sed. (speech by Vezzani); verbale Congresso Sez. Cortile, 16 Nov. 1956, AFM, p. 4.

23. *Atti del IX° Cong.*, 1^a sed. Cf. *l'Unità* (Modena), 2 Dec. 1956.

24. *Atti del IX° Cong.*, 1^a sed. (speech by Casari); ibid., 6^a sed. (speech by Bergonzoni); see comments in minutes of FC, 12-17 July 1956.

25. *L'Unità* (Modena), 6 Dec. 1956.

26. 'Documento preparatorio della Conferenza regionale dei comunisti dell' Emilia e Romagna (Bologna 27-29 giugno 1959)' in *Conferenze regionali del P.C.I. 1959* (Rome, 1959).

27. *Per il rinnovamento democratico e socialista dell'Emilia-Romagna e dell' Italia: Conferenze regionali del P.C.I.*, Bologna, 27-29 giugno 1959 (Bologna, 1959), pp. 105-20.

28. Minutes of FC, n.d. [Dec. 1959], AFM (speech by U. Bisi).

29. Minutes of FC, 17 Dec. 1961, and minutes of FC, 15 Nov. 1961, AFM; letter, S. Miana to Direzione, 20 Nov. 1961, AFM; cf. D.L.M. Blackmer, *Unity in Diversity* (Cambridge, Mass., and London, 1968), p. 191.

30. Minutes of FC, 17 Dec. 1961.

31. 'Struttura economica e strategia politica nell'Emilia del dopo-guerra', and G.P. Caselli, 'Modena, città del ciclo FIAT', *Note e rassegne*, 33-34 (Jan.-Dec. 1971).

32. G. Fanti, 'Il partito in Emilia', *Critica marxista* I, 5-6 (Sept.-Dec. 1963). Cf. G. Fanti and R. Zangheri, 'Il dibattito sul XXII° Congresso in Emilia', *Rinascita*, XIX, 1 (Jan. 1962).

33. See above, Chapter 3, pp. 66-7, and below, Chapter 10, pp. 163-6 *passim*.

34. Atti del XII° Congresso provinciale, AFM (speech by S. Rossi).

35. See S. Hellman, 'The PCI's Alliance Strategy and the Case of the Middle Classes' in Tarrow and Blackmer, *Communism in Italy and France*, esp. pp. 392, 409.

36. *L'Unità* (Modena), 13 Jan. 1966.

37. Document entitled 'Federazione di Perugia', 18 Jan. 1966, signed 'Giometti Paolo'; and Comitato Federale, 'Rapporto sullo stato del partito nella provincia', 6 Dec. 1965, AFP.

38. T. Gandolfi in *Avanti!*, 20 Jan. 1966.
39. Atti del XII° Congresso (speech by Famigli).
40. *L'Unità* (Modena), 18 Jan. 1966.

BARI: LEFTISM IN A SOUTHERN CONTEXT

1. The Socio-economic and Political Background: a *Bracciante* Federation

The federation of Bari was 'renewed' even later than Modena. The socio-economic changes which threatened the Party in the late 1950s and early 1960s did not coincide with the process of *rinnovamento*. But they did make the cadres open to strategic innovations, and these were offered by Alfredo Reichlin, a supporter of Ingrao who was nominated Apulian regional secretary in 1962.

Of all the regions of southern Italy, Apulia offered the most favourable terrain for the Communist Party. Unlike the rest of the south, it contains broad plains which are suitable for large-scale farming on a capitalist basis. Grain crops are the chief products of the Apulian estates, which employ landless labourers (*braccianti*) for the necessary work. Only a small proportion of these labourers are hired on annual contracts; the rest must hire themselves out for shorter periods, often by the day. Apulia thus was not simply a 'vast social disintegration', as Gramsci said of the *Mezzogiorno*. It was inhabited by many people in mixed economic situations, who were, for instance, smallholders, sharecroppers and labourers at the same time, but the population could nevertheless be divided clearly into a homogeneous agricultural proletariat and semi-proletariat on the one hand and a small group of large landowners on the other, with relatively small groups of intermediate figures between them.[1] In its polarised class relations Apulia resembled some parts of Emilia. Nearly all the *braccianti* were in a similar social and economic situation, which was wretched. There was never sufficient work for all, so that they counted themselves lucky to have 200 days' work in a year. The oversupply of labour allowed the employers to keep wages low and exercise many forms of pressure on the *braccianti*.

In this situation the peasant leagues early took root among the labourers. The Socialist Party, in the pre-1914 period, appeared too moderate to the Apulian *braccianti*; it was associated with northern industry and protectionism, which was seen as a policy directed against the agriculture of the south. Many of them therefore turned to revolutionary syndicalism. After the First World War the Fascist movement, organised by the big landowners, was particularly active and violent in Apulia, in reaction to the strength and militancy of the peasant leagues.

After the fall of fascism the PCI, inheriting much of the strength of the Socialists and the syndicalists in the region, built a strong base for itself, particularly among the *braccianti* of the large 'agro-towns'[2] of the plain. This strength, which allowed it to control many local administrations, also made the Party somewhat complacent. Most cadres were ill-educated and had a very schematic political outlook: they saw the major actors in society as 'we', 'the enemy' and 'the masses'. The need for alliances with other groups in the countryside was not appreciated, nor were general political objectives pursued: as in Modena, a vision of the revolution as a mythical, thaumaturgic future event was combined with a substantially trade-unionistic struggle for the improvement of the conditions of the *braccianti*, as well as 'municipalism' and 'particularism' in the 'red' communes.[3] Party organisation was well maintained, and a Stalinist style of work was introduced by *costruttori* from the north.

Even in the epic agrarian struggles of 1947 and 1949-50, the major concrete objective in Apulia was not a general agrarian reform, as in many other zones of the south, but the furthering of the interests of the *braccianti* by the establishment of an *imponibile di mano d'opera* to guarantee more employment, by an amelioration of social security provisions, and by a programme of public works that would provide further sources of income. The main themes of the Apulian Party's agitation in this period were the general national campaigns for peace, the defence of democratic rights etc. Agrarian reform, alliances, the promotion of co-operatives and the development of a plan for the *Rinascita* of the region were not seen as important. The Apulian PCI was severely criticised in 1951 by Ruggero Grieco, Alicata and Amendola for this 'narrowness' of vision.[4] At the VII Congress of the PCI, Apulia alone of the southern regions, through its secretary the Tuscan Remo Scappini, aligned itself with Secchia rather than Amendola.[5]

Nor did the XX Congress bring about major changes in the Apulian Party. Several former deputies and functionaries, in the climate of discouragement and disarray, deserted to the PSI or PSDI, which were more likely to offer the rewards of office.[6] But the vast majority of PCI cadres remained untouched by the ideas of *rinnovamento* until after 1966. Mainly veterans of the *bracciante* struggles, they continued to engage in a traditional, trade-unionist practice. There was little debate within the Party which would have led them to update their political

ideas. A Party document of 1962 stated that the history of the
Party in Apulia had hindered the assimilation of the Party's line, and
the debate on the VIII Congress 'did not produce profound modifications'.[7] It criticised the Apulian PCI for its underestimation of the role
of alliances and of mass struggle, for its 'messianism' and the 'mythical
vision' of revolution of many Apulian Communists.

2. The Late 1950s: Social Change and Party Immobilism

While the Party's cadres remained anchored to the perspectives of the
early 1950s, the region was undergoing major socio-economic changes.
These were particularly important in the province of Bari. The
traditional small and medium-scale industries that had grown up in the
city of Bari (oil, pasta, tobacco etc.) had been largely dismantled by
1956, as a result of competition from larger firms. The PCI was thus
faced with the disappearance of its urban base. The Party in Bari, in
contrast to the situation in Naples, had also been able to gain support
among the sub-proletariat and construction workers of the old city
centre, but these were being expelled to the outlying areas with the
progress of urban renewal. At the same time the city was chosen as a
'pole of development' in the government's strategy for the south, and
new factories (e.g. Fucine meridionali, Pignone Sud) were built in Bari.
They employed a new working class, recruited directly from the
countryside. About half of them still lived there and commuted to
the city. These workers had no Communist tradition, and at first the
Party had difficulty in gaining a foothold among them. The same
period saw the rapid expansion of tertiary activities and of the middle
class employed in them in the city, and the Party was not able to gain
influence immediately with these new groups either. (See Table 9.1 for
the changes in the occupational structure of the province and Table 9.2
for the Party's lag in adjusting to them.) The 'penetration of the monopolies' into the south had created a new social situation which the
bracciante cadres of the PCI found especially difficult to grasp and deal
with.[8]

The changes in the city of Bari led to a serious crisis for the PCI.
After reaching a record total of 19.1 per cent of the vote in the 1959
communal election, the Party suffered a defeat in 1962, falling to 16
per cent. The PCI recovered in the 1963 general election, returning to
the level of 19.1 per cent in the city,[9] but its membership there
continued to fall, from 5,215 in 1960 to 2,774 by 1966. In the latter

Table 9.1: Occupational Structure of Bari Province, 1951-71 (percentages)

		1951	1961	1971
(a)	By sector			
	Agriculture	50.8	43.4	30.2
	Industry	49.2	28.7	32.2
	Tertiary activities		28.0	37.6
(b)	By occupation			
	Workers	28.4	35.4	39.5
	Braccianti	30.9	30.2	21.3
	Peasant smallholders and sharecroppers*	19.4	13.1	7.8
	Artisans, shopkeepers etc.*	11.5	10.7	13.2
	Managers and white-collar workers	7.5	9.5	16.5
	Entrepreneurs	2.3	1.4	1.9
Total		100.0	100.3	100.2
N		401,919	428,440	406,743

* Including unpaid family members (*coadiuvanti*).
Source: ISTAT census data.

Table 9.2: Social Composition of the Bari Federation of the PCI, 1954-67 (percentages)

	1954	1960	1967
Workers	12.4	17.5	25.7
Braccianti	43.5	42.9	30.3
Mezzadri and *coloni*	11.5	10.3	8.7
Peasant smallholders	2.2	1.3	4.0
Artisans and entrepreneurs	2.3	4.6	2.7
Shopkeepers			0.5
White-collar workers and technicians	0.9	0.7	0.6
Professionals and teachers	0.6	0.4	0.6
Students	0.6	0.2	0.6
Housewives and cottage workers	21.1	18.7	11.5
Pensioners and others	4.8	3.5	14.8
Total	99.9	100.1	100.0
N	32,157	31,654	20,619

Sources: PCI, *Forza e attività del Partito* (Rome, 1955); *Organizzazione del Partito Comunista Italiano* (Rome, 1961); *Dati sulla organizzazione del Partito* (Rome, 1968).

year some of the 'red' centres of the province, like Andria (4,829 members) and Barletta (3,670 members), had more Communists than the provincial capital itself.[10]

In the countryside, too, important changes were taking place. The rural exodus proceeded at a very rapid rate. It was directed to the north and abroad, as well as to the cities of the region. (From 1951 to 1961 emigrants from Bari province totalled 10.8 per cent of the population.[11]) At the same time the composition of the rural workforce was changing. After the agitation of the *braccianti* in 1949-51 many landlords began to introduce a sharecropping system, known as *colonia*, in the hope that they might eventually replace the militant *braccianti* with more co-operative *coloni*. The *coloni* received the use of the land for the duration of the contract, but, unlike *mezzadri*, without a farm-house situated on it.[12] They continued to live for the most part in the 'agro-towns'. (The growth of these towns was no doubt in part due to the landlords' desire to prevent the peasant from developing a sense of proprietorship over a specific plot of land.) Their contractual relations with the landlords were of many different types: many agreements required the *coloni* to make specified improvements to the land; their length varied considerably; the division of the product took place according to different systems. This diversity made it difficult to organise the *coloni* as a group. The data of Table 9.1 no doubt underestimate the number of *coloni* because many of them preferred to register as *braccianti* in order to benefit from the social security provisions for agricultural labourers. It was commonly reckoned that by the early 1960s there were some 200,000 *coloni* in Apulia, or one-third to one-half of the agricultural workforce.[13]

Closely connected with these economic and social developments was the change in the historic bloc associated with the formation of the centre-left. Almost from the beginning, the centre-left in Apulia appeared to the PCI an openly transformistic operation by which the PSI was admitted to the spoils of office.[14] It also seriously threatened the PCI's position: its 1962 electoral defeat in Bari was attributed to the attraction of the new centre-left *giunta*. Even more disturbing, in the same year the PSI formed a centre-left *giunta* in the left-wing bastion of Andria, and its leaders' pronouncements became increasingly anti-communist.

As well as these problems caused by external social and political change, an internal issue shook the deep-rooted certainties of some PCI cadres in Bari. While the XX Congress, and even the XXII, did little to erode their simple attachment to the USSR and the international movement, the Sino-Soviet dispute caused much preoccupation. In particular, the FGCI, which was very strong (over 6,000 members in Bari in the early 1960s), was highly involved in international affairs, and often looked on the Chinese positions with favour. They organised a demonstration in 1962 for the recognition of the People's Republic of China. When the fighting in Vietnam intensified, they argued that the USSR could do more to help the Vietnamese people. In 1963 a group of FGCI members sent a letter to the regional Party journal in which they asked in all seriousness whether the Sino-Soviet dispute was real, or was simply a ruse to fool the international bourgeoisie! They supported the Chinese in their opposition to the policy of coexistence, on the grounds that Kennedy, Nehru and Pope John XXIII were reactionary and anti-Communist in internal politics and therefore could not be expected to coexist peacefully with Communist states in the international sphere either.[15] Older Party members also shared these doubts and worries.

3. Reichlin's Programme: Leftism in a Southern Context

As we mentioned in Chapter 5, these changes led some Communists to propose a revision of the Party's traditional southern policy. One of the leading innovators, Alfredo Reichlin, a close ally of Ingrao, was appointed regional secretary of Apulia in 1962. The main lines of Reichlin's position have been presented in Chapter 5.[16] Because the industrial development of the south should be closely related to the modernisation of southern agriculture, he argued, planning and state industry had to be controlled by local organs of popular power, unions, parties, local governments and above all the regional governments, which had not yet been created and whose establishment the PCI was demanding: 'a nationalisation or a municipalisation can have different meanings, so different that they can be the opposite of one another'.[17] Similarly, the peasants and the local governments should control the agrarian reform agencies (*enti di riforma*) already in existence. These were typical Ingraian themes. The Communists and the CGIL, in this context, called for the formulation of a regional plan.

This new approach to the southern question allowed Reichlin to reformulate the traditional demand for an agrarian reform. The Communists' policy of 'the land to the tiller' was no longer an attempt to overcome pre-capitalist, semi-feudal relations of production in agriculture, such as the *mezzadria* and *colonia*, but the first step in a

policy aimed at restructuring the agrarian economy in the interests of
the peasants, rather than of the monopolies. He devoted particular
attention to the question of the *coloni*; though the Party had not
ignored them in the past, Reichlin was responsible for putting them to
the fore in its work. The system of *colonia*, he argued, was one of the
chief causes of the backwardness of Apulian agriculture, because the
colono, who could be quite easily evicted, had little incentive to undertake improvements, and the landlords were not interested in doing so;
they maintained the often inefficient *colonia* because it seemed the best
way of exercising political control over the peasants. Ownership of the
land thus was the precondition for a new strategy of economic
development; only if they became proprietors would the *coloni* and
other peasants have the right to be heard in decisions concerning the
future of agriculture, through the reform agencies and consortia, and
the possibility of organising themselves to exercise some control over
credit, marketing and other policy questions. 'The land to the tiller'
was, therefore, an advanced objective:

> We chose [to emphasise] the question of the *colonia* because we felt
> and feel the need to make the struggle for the land a struggle which
> is no longer limited to the agricultural sector, but is the essential
> lever, in the South, for disrupting the [current] investment strategy
> and dismantling the mechanism of spoliation and monopoly
> accumulation, for blocking the exodus [of population] , for
> defeating the policy of 'poles of development' and initiating a new
> economic process, a new process of industrialisation whose essential
> foundation will be a new relationship between city and country-
> side.
>   And this seemed to us actually possible, in Apulia, if we succeeded
> in liberating 200,000 *coloni* (here is our weak point, which can
> become an element of strength) by making them owners of the land
> they till.[18]

Otherwise Apulia would remain in a state of 'semi-colonial dependence'
on the north, producing only raw materials and semi-finished goods for
processing industries located elsewhere. No 'technical' change in
agricultural products or methods could be considered apart from the
problem of changing the relations of production. For instance, in the
case of Apulian viticulture, an important part of the agricultural sector,
the peasants could sell their product only to large industrial wine-
makers because they produced wines for mixing with other, superior,

vintages (*vini da taglio*) rather than varieties that could be sold directly on the market. Only if they became owners of the land could they plant new types of vines and thus end their dependence on the large firms, which naturally kept the prices of the product as low as possible.[19]

Reichlin's ideas had the advantage of providing a general strategy to which all the specific, local struggles could be linked. But many cadres still saw the agrarian question mainly as a trade-unionistic struggle to improve the condition of the *braccianti*. And many of the peasants themselves demonstrated little interest in owning the land. The few who had received farms from the land reform of the early 1950s had fared badly, precisely because they could not control the markets for their products, credit etc., and because they lacked sufficient capital and received little state assistance. (This was one of the reasons why the PCI leaders began to speak of the need for reforms in these fields as well as simply transferring ownership of the land.) Furthermore, the contractual victories of the *braccianti*, especially those won in the great strike of June–July 1962, contrasted with the failure of the Party and unions to win a collective agreement for the *coloni*.[20] They had demanded not only a guaranteed minimum wage and a more favourable division of the product and costs for the *coloni*, but also the right to participate in decisions concerning investment and new crops, and the right to dispose freely of their share of the crops. The PCI also demanded a reform of agricultural credit, assistance for peasant co-operatives and the establishment of democratic agrarian development agencies with powers of expropriation. But no contract for the *coloni* was signed in 1962 or in 1965. As a result, the *coloni* earned more as *braccianti* than they did when working on their own plots: 1,600–1,800 lire per day as against 500–700 lire per day.[21]

While Reichlin's line did not bear any immediate fruit, he was nevertheless able to win the federation over to the left. The changes of the 1950s and early 1960s threatened the PCI's position in Bari and undermined the old certainties of the 'Secchian' cadres. In this situation the Party was ready to receive new ideas, a new line, and Reichlin was able to provide it. Nevertheless, without the presence of Reichlin and a few intellectuals which he gathered around himself, it is unlikely that any fresh ideas, whether those of Ingrao or any others, would have taken root there. The presence of intellectuals was decisive; as in other areas of the south, a few prestigious personalities can have a very significant impact. On the other hand, the number of intellectuals in the PCI in Bari was very small; many had deserted in the early 1950s.

In this respect, the Party in Bari was different from the Neapolitan federation. Reichlin, on account of his intellectual force and personal prestige, was able to win over the cadres in Bari to his position. The Party had already taken action on problems such as the *colonia*, local development plans and irrigation, but Reichlin was the first to synthesise these sectoral struggles and connect them to the Party's general objectives. The mass membership was not active in the determination of the Party's line, and therefore it was necessary to convince only the cadres. The parallel with Amendola's role in Emilia is striking. So great was his success in convincing the cadres that one Party member said they were 'infatuated' with Reichlin. Furthermore, Amendola's positions on the centre-left, reunification and China were very unpopular. The Apulian delegates were, as a result, fully in support of Ingrao at the XI Congress, so much so that they were described as forming his 'claque'.[22] Reichlin's control seemed almost total, though a few influential members in Bari remained sympathetic to the right or centre, and there were apparently the beginnings of factional behaviour in the federation at this time (meetings of groups of members outside of Party bodies etc.).

The case of Bari illustrates the important role that one or a few intellectuals can play all the more clearly because Reichlin made several errors which eventually, after 1966, lost him the support which he had earlier gained.[23] These were not related essentially to the failure of his line to produce results. While his political line was accepted, especially at the beginning, his personal relations with the cadres in Apulia were not good; and in the south, personal relations are very important. As an intellectual, he was somewhat aloof and distant. He appeared to treat the traditional Apulian cadres with disdain, preferring instead to promote younger intellectuals who had not been closely involved in Party work in the past and had few links with the rank and file. As one informant put it, he did not know how to 'work on men'. Nor did he sink deep roots in Apulia or become an 'Apulian personality'. If he did not gain a close personal following among the cadres, he had even less direct influence on the attitudes of the membership; no *rinnovamento* was undertaken while he led the Party. By the time he left Apulia in 1968, Reichlin was considered to have largely failed there. But his intellectual vigour and prestige had been enough to bring Bari and the whole of the region into Ingrao's camp in the battle of the XI Congress.

Notes

1. See S. Tarrow, *Peasant Communism in Southern Italy* (New Haven and London, 1967), p. 238.

2. See A. Blok, 'The South Italian Agro-Town', *Comparative Studies in Society and History*, II, 2 (Apr. 1969).

3. *L'azione dei comunisti per il rinnovamento democratico della Puglia* (progetto di tesi per la Conferenza Regionale del P.C.I., Taranto, marzo-aprile 1962) in Archives of the Federation of Bari of the PCI (AFB); and interview, 10 July 1973 (1).

4. G. Gramegna, *Braccianti e popolo in Puglia* (Bari, 1976), pp. 154-62.

5. *VII Congresso*, p. 255.

6. *Puglia*, 3, 28 Feb. 1963 and 4, 15 Mar. 1963; interview 25 Oct. 1973; Gramegna, *Braccianti*, p. 199.

7. *L'azione dei comunisti*, p. 18.

8. See G. Vacca (ed.), *PCI, Mezzogiorno, e intellettuali* (Bari, 1973), p. 298; interview, 10 July 1973 (3).

9. Ministero dell'Interno, *Compendio dei risultati delle elezioni comunali e provinciali dal 1946 al 1960* (Rome, 1961), p. 107; *Puglia*, 5, 6 Apr. 1963, p. 7.

10. AFB.

11. V. Parlato, '325,000 emigrati in 10 anni', *Puglia*, 1, 23 Jan. 1963.

12. For examples of contracts, see Gramegna, *Braccianti*, p. 234 n. 3; cf. Arts. 2164-9 of the Civil Code.

13. *Puglia*, 9, 31 May 1963, p. 17.

14. A. Reichlin, 'Una linea di lotta'; *Puglia*, 1, 23 Jan. 1963; 'Verso le elezioni', *Puglia*, 2, 15 Feb. 1963; 'Classi dirigenti e programmazione in Puglia', *Cronache meridionali*, XI, 5-6 (May–June 1964).

15. *Puglia*, 1, 23 Jan. 1963, p. 1.

16. See above, Chapter 5, pp. 93-5. The following account of Reichlin's position is based on 'Appunti sul centro-sinistra nel Mezzogiorno', *Cronache meridionali*, IX, 12 (Dec. 1962); reply to V. Fiore, ibid., X, 11-12 (Nov.-Dec. 1963); 'Classi dirigenti e programmazione in Puglia', ibid., XI, 5-6 (May-June 1964); 'Una linea di lotta', *Puglia*, 1, 23 Jan. 1963; 'D'accordo sulla programmazione: ma con chi e contro chi?' ibid., 3, 28 Feb. 1963.

17. *Puglia*, 1, 23 Jan. 1963, p. 4.

18. A. Reichlin in *Cronache meridionali*, X, 6-7 (June-July 1963), pp. 84 ff., quoted in Gramegna, *Braccianti*, pp. 231-2.

19. G. Matarrese, 'Il dramma del vino', and L. Visani, 'Il regime di proprietà alle origini della crisi del vino', in *Puglia*, 2, 15 Feb. 1963.

20. On the struggle for a contract for the coloni, see G. Damiani, 'Luci e ombre delle recenti lotte contadine', *Puglia*, 1, 23 Jan. 1963; Gramegna, *Braccianti*, pp. 224-30 and 238; *L'azione dei comunisti*; G. Papapietro, 'Andremo avanti così', *Puglia*, 9, 31 May 1963.

21. *Puglia*, 2, 15 Feb. 1963, p. 20; A. Novella, 'Votate per la riforma agraria', ibid., 3, 28 Feb. 1963.

22. Interview, 11 July 1973.

23. Interviews, 10 July (1 and 2), 11 July and 25 Oct. 1973.

10 THE INGRAO LEFT AND ITS DEFEAT

1. The National Bases of Support for the Ingrao Left

Before attempting to explain the pattern of support for the Ingrao left, we shall assess the extent of its success. The group's high point in the 1960s was the XI Congress of the PCI, after which a 'purge' removed many of its leading exponents from their positions of influence. Though clearly a minority in the Party, it was a significant one. While it must be stressed again that the label 'Ingraian' does not denote an organised faction or a homogeneous group, and it is therefore impossible to measure exactly its strength, some indication of its following, both in the territorial units of the Party and in the apparatus and mass organisations, can be obtained.

The left was in a clear majority in some territorial organisations.[1] It was in control of all the federations of Umbria and Apulia; the Perugia federation even took the extraordinary step of not approving the national theses. It had a strong following in Piedmont, where the Turin federation was clearly on the left. It was also dominant in parts of Tuscany, including the federations of Pisa, Livorno, Massa-Carrara and Prato. The Pisan federation voted to approve only the 'general lines' of the national theses, while that of Prato also voted another document containing the main themes debated at its congress. Several federations along the Adriatic coast, including Venice, Ravenna, Pesaro-Urbino and Ancona were also in the leftist camp. So was that of Bergamo in Lombardy. Besides these areas where it was in the majority (at the federal congresses and among the local leadership, at any rate), the Ingrao left constituted a significant minority in several other major organisations. One of these was the federation of Naples. Another was that of Rome, where the federal congress was a real contest between the two lines, and where some 'Ingraian' delegates had to be included among the federation's representatives at the national congress. There were also some leftists present in Genoa and the other Ligurian federations. In Milan the left were a fairly small minority: their amendments to the theses were rejected by a vote of 500 to 60 and they were excluded from the congressional delegation and the leadership of the federation. The left-wing minority was not always dealt with in this way, however: in Chieti, for instance, an amendment rejecting

the formula 'failure of the centre-left' was defeated by a vote of 88
to 15 but the new federal organs included members of both groups.

On the other hand, Amendola's followers dominated Emilia, a large
part of the south, especially Campania, and much of the Roman Party,
and in some of these federations the left had no support whatever.
Many other federations were 'centrist', faithful to the Party line as
represented by Longo and his closest associates, such as Berlinguer.

At the same time the section and provincial congresses leading up
to the XI Congress saw many expressions of dissent: amendments
to the theses, elections of delegates by secret ballot with open lists,
leading to the choice of a fair number of opposition delegates, and a
few abstentions or negative votes on the theses were common.
Fernando Di Giulio, in an effort to minimise the extent of such dissent,
stated in an article in *Rinascita* that the vote on the theses as a whole
was less than unanimous in only a few — less than half a dozen, he
wrote — of the federal congresses; in others, a few delegates had voted
against particular points only.[2] This may have been true when he wrote
it, but Di Giulio's total was soon made obsolete by the last federal
congresses. In a sample of 32 federations[3] there were some negative
votes or abstentions on the theses as a whole in at least nine, including
one (Perugia) where they were actually rejected. In at least four others
there were abstentions or contrary votes on parts of the theses. (In
Ancona amendments were carried.) In at least a further two federations
amendments to the theses were proposed. Therefore the federations in
which the national theses were approved without dissent of any sort
constituted little more than half of the sample. Some of the expressions
of dissent were no doubt inspired by the ideas of Ingrao and his
followers, while many others were prompted by residual Stalinist
opposition or pro-Chinese sentiments. In Pavia, for instance, 30 of the
260 delegates abstained on the section of the theses which criticised
the Chinese Communists.

Longo became so worried about the danger of factionalism that, in a
confidential circular to provincial secretaries, he recommended a return
to open voting and closed lists for the choice of delegates and federal
committees. It was probably not by accident that the congresses of the
most left-wing federations were held among the last, so that they could
not give the example to others: those of Perugia, Prato, Pesaro, Livorno
and Pisa were held in the last week (13-19 January) of the congressional
period, which had begun in mid-December.

In the party apparatus the left also had positions of strength.[4] It was
strongest in the cultural sphere, where Rossana Rossanda headed the

cultural section of the Central Committee, and where the editor of
Il Contemporaneo, the editorial secretary of *Critica marxista* and others
in editorial positions in *Rinascita, Critica marxista*, the publishing house
Editori Riuniti and the daily *l'Unità* belonged to the 'Ingraian' group.
It also enjoyed some support in the unions, particularly the *Federbrac-
cianti* (agricultural labourers' union). In the five federations we have
studied, the local Trades Council (*Camera del Lavoro*) was aligned with
the left in every case where its orientation was known. The *ingraiani*
were quite unrepresented in other mass organisations such as the
Alleanza contadini, which was pro-Amendola even in Perugia, and the
co-operatives. The youth organisation, the FGCI, which was thought to
be prevalently pro-Ingrao, at the last moment aligned itself with the
national leadership; but many of its cadres clearly sympathised with
the left.

On the basis of this information it is not possible to arrive at definite
quantitative conclusions about the strength of the left in the Party
overall. Giorgio Galli estimates that 15-20 per cent of the active Party
members were *ingraiani*;[5] it would not be feasible to estimate the left's
following among the mass membership of the Party because most of
these were not sufficiently up to date in their political information to
appreciate the terms of the discussion – their political awareness
remained at the level of common sense and folklore inherited from a
previous period. We have seen that at least 17 of the 113 federations
were controlled by the *ingraiani*, and they constituted a sizeable
minority in other large federations. Even in provinces like Milan, it is
probable that the federations' efforts to prevent the sections from
electing 'opposition' delegates meant that the small left group present
at the congress represented a larger proportion of the active membership. Both left and right often excluded the minority from the
congressional delegations elected by the sections and federations they
controlled; in any case the active members in any section (on average
some 5 per cent of the total) tend to be homogeneous, both politically
and socially. As to whether the passive, less politicised, mass membership who turned out for the section or cell congresses were more
inclined to follow the left or the right, this can only be a matter for
speculation, though the right was more able to play on Party loyalism
and tradition after Ingrao's 'undisciplined' action in criticising the theses
in the Central Committee and his outspoken comments on the USSR.
On the other hand, Amendola had also seriously offended the
sentiments of ordinary Party members with his articles on reunification.
Neither of the two leaders fully represented their point of view.

2. Causes of the Rise of the Ingrao Left

Among the causes of the rise of the Ingrao left, the most important
were the very rapid economic and social changes which were provoked
by the economic miracle of the 1950s and early 1960s. Where these
were most seriously felt, the arguments of the left received a more
attentive hearing. This was not surprising, since Ingrao's thought began
from the recognition that Italy had now become an advanced capitalist
country (see Chapter 3). The first hypothesis enunciated in Chapter 4
has been by and large confirmed by the study of the five cases: Turin,
a centre of economic growth, and Perugia, a province threatened by
marginalisation, both supported the left. Naples, the most stable of the
five, supported the right, though there was a significant left-wing
minority there. Of the two intermediate cases, one (Bari) was on the
left, and the other (Modena) was clearly on the right. Our other
hypotheses will be especially necessary to explain the behaviour of these
two federations. This conclusion based on five case studies clearly
cannot be generalised without any qualification to the whole country.
Many, but not all, of the most rapidly developing provinces supported
Ingrao (e.g. Venice and Bergamo, but not Milan), and most of the
south remained in Amendola's camp, though emigration was proceeding
apace there. Furthermore, some of the *ingraiano* federations (e.g. in
Tuscany) appear to be in areas of fairly balanced growth.

Social and economic change helped to undermine the hitherto
accepted strategy of the PCI: in Perugia and Turin there was an
increase in the importance of the working class, and a decline in that
of the middle strata (especially the *mezzadri*). This tended to lead to a
questioning of the Popular Front policy (never fully accepted in Turin)
and a renewed emphasis on the role of the working class. In Bari the
shift was more complex, for both a new industrial proletariat and new
middle strata (*coloni* and white-collar workers) were coming into being,
while the proletarian *bracciantato* was losing its former importance.
Here the Popular Front strategy had never been fully accepted, and the
left wing was able to gain a hearing by offering a more viable policy
than that of the older 'Secchian' cadres for dealing with these new
groups. Thus any rapid socio-economic change, regardless of its
direction, seemed to lead to doubts about the policy hitherto followed,
and make the local Communists receptive to the ideas of the left.

Reconsideration of policy was all the more likely because these
social and economic changes often led to defeats, or at least setbacks,
for the PCI in the areas most affected. The most spectacular of these

defeats was of course the election of the Fiat *commissione interna* in 1955, which led to a complete renewal of the leadership of the Turin federation. In Perugia the disappearance of the PCI's *mezzadro* base, the failure of its campaign for a regional plan and the loss of the provincial capital to the centre-left in 1964 created a need to find a new base of support in the working class and to reinvigorate the Party's strategy. In Bari the Party's decline was particularly noticeable in the city, where it suffered a setback in the 1959 election and where its membership continued to fall. However, the centre-left and the prosperity brought by the miracle were exercising their attraction in the countryside as well and the loss of formerly 'red' communes like Andria brought this home to the Party. In Naples, too, there had been some signs of difficulty for the PCI, particularly the decline in Party membership. But the electoral losses of 1956 were quickly recouped, and the Communists made some modest progress in the next few elections. Though socially more dynamic than Naples, Modena was more stable politically: there was never any serious threat to the Party's predominance in local politics, from the centre-left or any other source, and the general prosperity only seemed to increase its prestige. The thesis that 'defeat is always the most convincing objective criticism for the working-class movement'[6] was borne out in all these situations.

If defeat prompted rethinking of the Party's policy, it also, in some cases, led to a rapid de-Stalinisation. The term 'de-Stalinisation' must be used with care, because it is used to denote at least two different processes which were by no means always concomitant. Both also went under the name of *rinnovamento*. The first was the replacement of the older, more sectarian or ouvrierist attitude typical of the Cold War, and especially of the 'Secchian' cadres in the Party. The second involved an attempt to reform the Party's internal life, eliminating bureaucratic and authoritarian habits and promoting internal democracy, discussion of Party policy and an airing of differences of opinion. Nor is the term 'Stalinist' fairly applied to many of the cadres who followed Secchia's line and were eliminated because of their insufficient enthusiasm for the alliance policy. In Turin the defeat at the Fiat plant led to the replacement of the older leadership and *rinnovamento* was entrusted to a left-wing group who soon developed a more offensive strategy. In Modena, by contrast, the Party suffered no defeats, the process of de-Stalinisation was long and bitter, and the leadership emerged from it firmly on the right of the Party. This happened not only because of Amendola's personal influence, but also because the

traditionalist cadres found his positions on the USSR and on intra-
party democracy less repugnant than Ingrao's.

The other three federations we have studied are more complex than
these two polar cases. In Perugia *rinnovamento* took place in 1951-4.
The new leading group, who were supporters of the *via italiana* in
Togliatti's interpretation, evolved gradually, as a result of their difficult
experiences, a left-wing variant of this strategy. The case of Perugia
is closest to that of Turin. In both provinces *rinnovamento* was
almost contemporaneous with the period of most rapid economic and
social change, and hence led directly to the development of an
'Ingraian' line. In Naples the *via italiana* had been imposed by
Amendola in the mid-1940s; it was not adopted as the result of a
defeat, nor was it accompanied by much internal democratisation. Such
a situation was not conducive to left-wing dominance, though it did
allow a leftist minority to appear after 1956.

The Bari federation is a totally atypical case in this respect: like
many other southern federations, it did not undergo democratisation
(de-Stalinisation in the second sense) until after 1966; unlike most
others, it had not accepted the alliance policy, at Amendola's
prompting, before 1956. Therefore it was Reichlin's version of
rinnovamento which first reached the cadres of the federation, and they
found it more palatable than the more traditional alliance policy of
Amendola. At this level, the hypothesis that there is a correlation
between rapid social and economic change, defeats and early de-
Stalinisation partly breaks down. It does suggest, however, why most
of the south, though increasingly marginalised in the 1950s and 1960s,
did not support Ingrao. The personal influence of a few leaders was
decisive there. In Apulia the influence of Reichlin explains a good part
of the success of the left.

The second major factor explaining the rise of a left wing in
particular regions of Italy is the character of the leaderships of the
various federations. As we pointed out in Chapter 1, innovation in
policy and strategy is generally impossible if no intellectuals are
present. Even a few of them can transmit a new line to the organic
intellectuals and the mass membership of the Party. This second
hypothesis (enunciated in Chapter 4) has been confirmed even more
strikingly than the first: the most clearly right-wing federation,
Modena, was the one with the lowest proportion of intellectuals in its
membership. In the three left-wing federations, there were a certain
number of intellectuals, though not a very large concentration. In this
context the Perugian leadership is particularly interesting: it was

composed largely of minor professionals, who were nevertheless capable
of absorbing and diffusing Ingrao's ideas among the cadres and the base
of the Party. The other right-wing federation, Naples, had the highest
concentration of intellectuals and students; this fact would seem to
confirm the prediction that if there are a large number of intellectuals
in a federation it will generally support the right. It is not certain,
however, that the crucial threshold beyond which this occurs had been
reached in the Neapolitan federation. Amendola's support came chiefly
from peasant and sub-proletarian sections, while those in working-class
or middle-class districts were more to the left. It is not because of their
influence as ordinary members of the Party but because of their crucial
role in the personalistic political networks typical of Naples and the
south, that the presence of a large number of intellectuals in Naples
favoured the right. As members of a largely intellectual section (e.g.
Vomero), they do not play this linking role, and they may become a
force on the left. In Naples both the critical number of intellectuals
necessary for the formation of a left-wing faction and another group
who supported the right were present. Amendola had recruited some
members of the middle strata in his pursuit of the policy of alliances,
and many of these became convinced adherents of his policy. In a
milieu different from the south, the numerical threshold beyond
which the intellectuals exert an influence in favour of the right could
be higher.

Another hypothesis mentioned in Chapter 4 helps to account for the
different fortunes of the left in the two federations in 'red' regions,
Perugia and Modena. While in Modena there was an extensive and
solidly established Marxist subculture, in Perugia the situation was
somewhat different. There the co-operatives were much less important,
and the Party's tenure of local government was less certain, as its loss
of the provincial capital in 1964 shows. The DC and the right could
hope to regain power in Perugia, while this was quite out of the
question in Modena. Perugia was clearly on the left within the PCI,
Modena on the right. This third hypothesis, with the second, helps to
account for the difference between Bari and Modena, both of which
were in the intermediate range as far as socio-economic change is
concerned.

Besides these general factors, the interest in certain issues in the
Party helps explain the success of the left in some provinces. Where
relations with the PSI locally were very bad, as in Perugia, especially,
and Bari, this provided a powerful stimulus to leftism. In Modena, by
contrast, Socialists and Communists continued to manage local govern-

ment together in relative harmony and tranquillity. International affairs were most important in the south, where *rinnovamento* came later. Both in Bari and in Naples, this issue strengthened the left as disenchantment with the USSR's policy of 'peaceful coexistence' and concern over the consequences of the Sino-Soviet dispute for the international movement grew. In Turin and Modena these problems attracted less attention. On the other hand, only in Turin were industrial questions and the problems of the trade-union movement at the centre of concern. Internal Party democracy was a major question in Naples and Perugia, but less so in the other federations. These various issues, concern over which was unevenly felt across the country as a result of the different past histories of the various federations, nevertheless contributed to the successes of the *ingraiani*.

3. Explanations of the Defeat of the Ingrao Left at the XI Congress

Some of the causes of the Ingrao left's defeat in 1966 are simply the obverse of the reason for its success. Besides the enduring strength of the Popular Front ideology and the power wielded by the PCI leadership through the apparatus, the *ingraiani* were faced with the fact that the social and economic change which favoured them was uneven, both in extent and in nature. Thus some regions underwent profound changes in a very short space of time, while others were much less seriously affected. Secondly, these changes, being of diverse types, did not engender a homogeneous political response. While in Turin the main problems were posed by the new strength of the working class and the revival of factory militancy, in Bari the central questions were those of the *colonia* and the underdevelopment of the south. And the difficulties of creating new sources of employment to stem the rural population exodus in Perugia were different again. These variations in the pace and nature of change were at the root of many of the differences between the federations with respect to the salient issues within the Party. This heterogeneity militated against a unified left-wing line of attack on the Party's traditional policy, the *via italiana*. While one merit of Ingrao's 'new model of development' was that it allowed a synthesis of the different platforms and demands arising out of local struggles, this synthesis remained somewhat vague in nature, and did not become a central, mobilising theme for the mass membership of the PCI. And, of course, the rules of democratic centralism and Party *mores* prevented the Ingrao group from openly carrying on the intellectual and propaganda work that is necessary to create unity around a policy. Some of Ingrao's articles in *Rinascita* were quoted by ordinary militants in section and federation congresses, but they did not outline a complete programme, nor did they make absolutely clear the differences which separated him from the right and centre. The great variety of methods used by the left to press its point of view in these congresses, ranging from the rejection of the national theses to the voting of amendments to other less spectacular devices, indicates a lack of a unified direction or of a factional structure. What we have called the 'Ingrao left' continued to bear the marks of its birth as a loose coalition of a number of different currents within the PCI, and its heterogeneity weakened its appeal. It even contained within itself some elements that were quite opposed to each other — e.g. both Trotskyists and their sympathisers and pro-Chinese Communists were among his followers. The unevenness of social change, then, prevented the left from penetrating everywhere in Italy and kept it from unifying itself.

Just as important as the problem of unifying the left-wing elements from different geographical regions was that of bringing together leftists at different levels of political awareness. A study of the provincial congresses[7] shows that there were a large number of objections to the national theses' position on international affairs. Many comrades rejected the criticism of China offered there; others were opposed to the Soviet formula of 'peaceful coexistence'. While Ingrao, of the major Party leaders, was the most critical of the USSR and the most careful not to launch anathemas against the Chinese Party, his position was certainly not unequivocally pro-Chinese. Many of the critics of the Party's theses on the international situation, on the other hand, were comrades whose view of the world had been shaped during the Cold War, who did not wish to see the unity of the 'socialist camp' destroyed, and who may also have approved of the Chinese Communists' refusal to repudiate Stalin in the way that Khrushchev had. Their viewpoint reflected the persistence of the ideas of a previous period at the level of folklore and common sense. The *ingraiani* were able to give voice to these humours of the base only in part, for their position on the USSR and China was much more up to date and carefully elaborated than that of the mass of Party members.

Inertia at the lower levels of the PCI seriously hampered the penetration of Ingrao's ideas. Indeed, one of the most striking findings of this study is the sheer weight and impenetrability of the ideas each Party generation receives in its formative period, which survive like

sedimented layers for years afterwards. Many members were unreceptive
to Ingrao's arguments because they had stopped absorbing new political
ideas; they did not read political books, nor did they read the more
sophisticated PCI publications such as *Rinascita* or *Critica marxista*,
where new points of view were aired. And they never came in contact
with people who expounded new ideas. Thus their political conceptions
became more and more out of date. The constant danger of ideological
rigidity is one of the major disadvantages of the mass party, although,
as we have seen, the leadership is not always immune to this malady of
'anachronism' either. In particular, the habit of unquestioning
acceptance of the decisions of the Party leadership and the uncritical
Party loyalty which had been inculcated in members who entered in the
period 1945-54 were successfully exploited by the centre, and, to an
extent, the right, in order to place Ingrao and his ideas beyond the pale
of discussion; this was all the easier because Ingrao could be accused of
breaking discipline and endangering the unity of the Party, often
ritually referred to as its 'most precious patrimony'.

The typically Ingraian themes, such as the new model of development or direct democracy, were communicated to only the more active
minority of the PCI's members (perhaps even fewer than the 80,000
activists mentioned by Galli), and not understood by all of them. The
major ideas of Amendola and the right, on the other hand, had been
current in the Party for much longer, and had been actively taken to
the rank and file during the *rinnovamento* campaign; they had, therefore, penetrated deeper into the consciousness of Party members.
(Of course, the main ideas of the Popular Front strategy were first
made known to the mass membership of the Party in Italy by Togliatti
as early as 1944.)

Another problem for the Ingrao group analogous to that of the
different levels of political awareness in the mass membership was their
failure to establish a working relationship with the so-called 'Stalinists'
in the leadership of the PCI. The latter had many reservations about the
direction taken by the Party since 1954; they were opposed to the
concessions made to attract potential allies, and offended by doctrinal
innovations, such as the dropping of the thesis that the dictatorship
of the proletariat was necessary in Italy. Naturally, proposals such as
Amendola's 'Hypotheses on Re-Unification' provoked their deep
hostility.[8] In international affairs their prime loyalty was not so much
to the USSR as to the international Communist movement as a whole,
and they criticised advocates of the *via italiana* for neglecting internationalism. They therefore tended to stress solidarity with all

progressive forces and Communist parties, and in some cases this position took on a veiled pro-Chinese coloration, though the traditions of Party unity and discipline were too strong for these old comrades to break with the PCI on this question.[9] Secchia and many of the others in this group were not 'Stalinists'. They simply had a more traditional, pre-1935 idea of communism and class struggle, and were in many ways more faithful to the original working-class inspiration of the Communist movement than the supporters of the *via italiana*.[10] They were genuinely on the left of the Party, and agreed with the *ingraiani* on some aspects of international affairs, the centre-left and relations with the PSI. Some of them also joined the *ingraiani* in urging more internal Party democracy.[11]

Even in 1966 the traditionalists were not a negligible force in the PCI: Scoccimarro and Colombi were still members of the *Direzione*, as were Romagnoli and Sereni, who belonged to the same generation; Secchia and others were still members of the Central Committee. This orthodox group was united by the bonds of friendship and solidarity formed by their common experiences in prison and internal exile and, above all, during the Resistance. They remained in close contact with each other, so much so that one ex-member of the Central Committee wrote that a Stalinist 'factional structure' existed in the PCI up until at least 1968;[12] no doubt this 'network' continued to function even after that date. Secchia himself played a role in keeping it together. But this group was not a faction in the true sense. Most of its members recognised that they were on the defensive, as they had been ever since their defeat in 1954; therefore they seldom put forward their point of view in a vigorous or public fashion. Moreover, their attachment to Party custom prevented them from engaging in openly factional activity, however strong the temptation may have been. Even more important than their strength as a tendency in the Party's higher councils, however, was the fact that these orthodox leaders reflected the sentiments of a much larger proportion of the mass membership, and especially of the less active members, whose political outlook was still as it had been created in 1945-54.

Given this situation, a convergence of the Ingrao group and the orthodox tendency in the Party leadership would have immensely strengthened the hand of the former. It appeared objectively possible, given the many points of agreement between the two groups. In fact, informal contracts between them did take place, but no understanding could be reached. In the first place, the orthodox group was itself divided. Some of its members, like Colombi, were very hostile to Ingrao because of his breaches of Party *mores* in 'publicising debate'. They could not agree with Ingrao on the question of internal Party democracy; Scoccimarro was probably in this group as well. On the other hand, Secchia, Vidali and Roasio, who were members of the Central Committee but not of the *Direzione*, were in favour of freer debate within the Party. Secondly, the entire orthodox group had deep misgivings about Ingrao's programme. While approving his more conciliatory attitude towards China, they could not agree with his extremely critical position on the Soviet Union. Moreover, the position of the Ingrao group was a further development of Togliatti's *via italiana*; Ingrao stressed his theoretical objections to the traditional, pre-1935 conception of revolution even more than did Amendola and the right. The orthodox group were not convinced, for instance, by the proposal of an 'alternative model of development', preferring to lay emphasis on trade-unionistic objectives. It seemed to them the proposal of an alternative plan could leave the door open to class collaboration and corporatism. Furthermore, Ingrao's emphasis on winning the Catholic masses was often misinterpreted. It generated fears that he was suggesting ideological capitulation. Longo exerted his considerable personal influence on the orthodox group as well; he was preoccupied in this period with maintaining Party unity. Therefore no agreement between them and the left was concluded, though Secchia continued to defend the principle of freedom of debate both before and during the XI Congress. And this failure to establish a united front on the part of the two major left-wing groups in the Party cut Ingrao off from a large potential base of support among the rank and file, which, as it was, was tapped instead by Amendola and the right, whose real policy positions were even further from those of the orthodox group, but who were able to take advantage of emotive issues such as Party unity.

A similar misunderstanding arose between Ingrao and the FGCI. As we have seen in Chapter 3, Occhetto was elected Secretary of the FGCI in 1962. He defeated Guerzoni, the candidate closer to Ingrao. Nevertheless, in the next few years Occhetto and his group developed a line that was considerably to the left of the PCI's official position, and similar to Ingrao's on many points. The FGCI had taken advantage of the debate on reunification to hold a joint meeting with the central committees of the youth movements of the PSI and PSIUP, in which it advanced the Ingraian idea of a refoundation of the left with an anti-capitalist programme. As we have seen, it took up Ingrao's ideas on direct democracy and the new model of development, with a particular

emphasis on the role of workers' councils. The youth federation
therefore appeared a natural ally of the left in the battle engaged at the
XI Congress. It was all the more surprising, then, when it decided to
align itself loyally with the centre of the Party. Occhetto, in his speech
at the XI Congress, condemned factionalism and, furthermore, said he
agreed with Lombardi that the left should unite on an advanced
democratic programme, not a socialist one.[13] This substantial withdrawal from the positions the FGCI had elaborated in the preceding
three years was the result not only of the pressures of the leadership
of the Party but also of the divergences between Ingrao and the youth
leaders on questions such as the role of the workers' councils. Ingrao
and his group had even gone so far as to criticise the FGCI's draft theses
for their projected XVIII Congress.[14] The heterogeneity of the left
opposition again in this case prevented it from attaining its maximum
possible strength.

One further cause of the left's failure, in some parts of the 'red
regions', was the presence of an extensive network of co-operatives and
similar institutions controlled by the working-class movement, which,
as in Modena, made the Party leaders more conservative and cautious.
To these factors we would add some tactical and strategic errors
committed by Ingrao, though these were by no means decisive in the
defeat of the left. First of all, he did not clarify sufficiently his position
vis-à-vis the Catholics, and it alienated many Party members from him.
His real objective was to create a working-class bloc by separating the
Catholic workers from the DC and organising them directly, either in
the PCI or in some other left-wing party or organisation; whereas
Amendola was content to deal with these 'Catholic masses' through the
DC and maintain the lay character of the left-wing bloc. Ingrao, then,
wanted to woo the Catholics but not the DC. However, his preference
for Fanfani rather than Saragat as President of the Republic in 1964
gave the impression that he was also ready to adopt a more conciliatory
attitude towards the Christian Democrats. Second, the 'alternative
model of development' which was the central feature of his programme
remained too vague, and was not sufficiently linked to concrete
problems. It therefore failed to gain acceptance among the mass
membership, who could not really understand it; it appeared to many
an abstract, intellectualistic exercise with little relationship to the
practical, day-to-day struggle. Third, Ingrao himself did not have a
combative personality. He did not attempt to organise a real faction or
tendency around his position. He was quite sensitive to criticism.
Sometimes, his hesitation or changes of position, such as his rejection

of the version of the theses approved by the committee of the Central Committee, cost him support or credit. In a sense, he had been chosen by some of the left-wing groups in the Party as their standard-bearer, rather than seeking the role for himself.

A more profound reason than Ingrao's personal characteristics for the uncombative stance adopted by the left was the deep pessimism which suffused their analysis. Rather than seeing the social and economic changes of the previous decade mainly as the breeding-ground of fresh revolutionary forces, they believed that the economic miracle and the centre-left threatened to integrate the Italian working class and opened the way for the social-democratisation of the PCI.[15] They intuited that Italy could go the way of the North European countries, and seriously underestimated the specificity of the Italian situation. Therefore, they saw their struggle as a desperate defensive battle against the drift to the right in the Party. Their analysis was mistaken for the short term, at least, as later events were soon to prove. The right was much closer to the truth when it argued that the centre-left would fail both to implement a reform programme and to integrate the working class into bourgeois society; the nature of Italian society made such outcomes impossible. The thesis that the *ingraiani* believed they were on the defensive is corroborated by their substantial abandonment of the internal Party struggle, though not of their ideas, for a long time after the XI Congress. When, only two years later, the student movement shook Italy and initiated a period of profound social transformation in a radically progressive direction, the *ingraiani* were divided on its significance, and many, including Ingrao himself, did not appreciate fully the momentous importance of the new movement.

Notes

1. The sources for the following estimate are, besides those given in previous chapters, the reports of federal congresses which appeared in *l'Unità* from 20 Dec. 1965 to 20 Jan. 1966, and *l'Espresso*, 9-30 Jan. 1966.

2. 'Migliaia i protagonisti del dibattito nel partito', *Rinascita*, 22 Jan. 1966.

3. Those whose congresses were reported in *l'Unità*, 20 Dec. 1965 to 20 Jan. 1966, plus Turin and Modena.

4. The sources of the following information are R. Rossanda, 'Note sul PCI dagli anni '60 al XIII Congresso', *Il Manifesto*, 22 and 24 March 1972; and L. Castellina, 'Da forza di frontiera alla ritirata dell'XI Congresso', *Il Manifesto*, 16 Dec. 1965.

5. G. Galli, 'Il PCI rivisitato', *Il Mulino*, XX, no. 213 (Jan.-Feb. 1971).

6. S. Garavini, 'Gli anni '50 alla FIAT', p. 44.

7. Cf. note 2 above.

8. For a typical, though measured, reaction, see P. Secchia, 'La questione essenziale è l'unità della classe operaia', *Rinascita*, 12 Dec. 1964.

9. Giuseppe Alberganti, former secretary of the Milanese federation, was the only prominent orthodox comrade to leave the PCI. He joined an extraparliamentary group in the 1970s. Prof. Ludovico Geymonat, a prominent former PCI intellectual, stood as an independent for *Democrazia proletaria*, another left-wing group, in the 1980 administrative elections.

10. See above, Chapter 2, pp. 46-7.

11. See P. Secchia, *L'azione svolta dal partito comunista in Italia durante il fascismo 1926-1932* (Milan, 1970), p. xxvi; Secchia's speech in *XI Congresso*, pp. 425ff.; Chapter 3, pp. 70, 71.

12. R. Rossanda, 'Note sul PCI', *Il Manifesto*, 24 March 1972.

13. *XI Congresso*, pp. 114-20.

14. Rossanda, *Il Manifesto*, 22 March 1972.

15. This analysis is based on R. Rossanda, 'Note sul PCI'.

11 THE 1968 MOVEMENT AND THE *MANIFESTO* AFFAIR

1. Left and Right in the PCI after 1966

The XI Congress was a serious defeat for Ingrao and the Communist left, but it did not lead to their disappearance. While the right's point of view has always prevailed in the long run within the Party's highest leadership and determined its political course, the 'two souls' of Italian communism have continued to coexist within the same Party. As we saw in Chapter 3, the left's questioning of the Party's traditional interpretation of the Popular Front strategy on an intellectual level had been prompted by the rapid growth of Italian capitalism in the decade 1953-63. At the same time, as the federation studies have demonstrated, it was the social upheavals that the miracle brought in its train that made the rank and file of the PCI aware of the same strategy's practical inadequacies. After 1966, while the right's programme remained essentially one of reforms which would modernise Italian capitalism as the first stage in a two-stage advance to socialism, developments both in Italy and abroad reinforced the impression that such a strategy was outdated; objective reality seemed to confirm the left's arguments.

In the first place, the student movement of 1967-8 was just the sort of autonomous organisation within civil society which the Communist left, and Ingrao himself, had theorised. It was the first major social movement really independent of political parties to appear in Italy since the war. Its radical nature and goals substantiated the left's contention that the advance towards socialism could be undertaken in collaboration with such autonomous movements rather than through agreements between political parties. It also initiated a thoroughgoing process of cultural criticism, a questioning of all established roles and values, in the family, at school, on the job, in all sectors of life. This 'cultural revolution' undermined the hegemony of the Catholic Church and traditional attitudes over a large part of society and furthered the political radicalisation of millions of Italians which became evident in the elections of 1975 and 1976. This electoral 'earthquake' could be interpreted as vindicating the Communist left's view that masses of people, and especially workers, could be won directly to socialism as a

170

result of persuasion and action in civil society; they could be won from the other parties, and did not have to be approached through them. The Soviet invasion of Czechoslovakia also brought home to many that the 'socialist' countries had to be viewed more critically. Finally, the major strike wave of the 'hot autumn' of 1969 reconfirmed the strength and central role of the working class in Italy. The workers showed that they had the capacity to impose reforms through the bargaining process at the same time as they asserted their own autonomy and that of the unions from political party tutelage.

In the period after the XI Congress, the inherent limitations of the Party's traditional two-stage strategy also became even more apparent. The middle strata continued to decline as a proportion of the active population, and many Communists realised that large sectors of them were not available as potential allies of the working class or the PCI. In the south, for example, many petty bourgeois were bound to the Christian Democratic regime because they owed their positions to state subsidies and patronage. And the PCI's insistent and tireless courtship of these groups continued to bear little fruit. Many of them, far from being in competition with the large 'monopolies', depended on them for their livelihood; others, such as middlemen in commerce, were members of the parasitic groups who were responsible for the ineffi-ciencies and backwardness of Italian capitalism. In the early 1970s some of these groups appear to have given increased electoral support to the neo-fascist MSI. These facts gave rise to doubts about the possibility of a reform programme that could unite the working class and the middle strata; indeed, the strength of the parasitic groups led many to wonder if there were any margins for reformism within Italian capitalism at all[1] — the record of the centre-left was not encouraging. To many it seemed that the only reforms possible, if any, were those that would strengthen capitalism politically and economically.

On the other hand, many of the premisses of the left's position were also called into question in the period after 1966. As we noted in the last chapter, the right's prediction that the centre-left would fail to reform Italian capitalism and split the working-class movement proved correct: none of the longstanding problems of Italian society, such as the southern question or the agrarian question, was solved; many in fact grew worse, as a distorted form of development continued. The attempt to create a social-democratic rival to the PCI out of the unification of PSI and PSDI also came to naught when the unified Party won only 14.5 per cent of the popular vote in 1968 and split in 1969. The centre-left coalition itself came to a final end in 1974, after an interruption in 1972-3 when Andreotti formed a centrist government.

Moreover, capitalism entered a new economic crisis in the 1970s. While not as traumatic as that of the 1930s, it nevertheless led to a slowing down in the rate of growth of all the Western economies, an increase in unemployment, and in many, including Italy, a sudden rise in the rate of inflation, which generated serious social tensions. For the Communist right, these developments only confirmed the thesis that Italian capitalism was in need of urgent reform in order to prevent disaster, and that a coalition of political forces had to be formed to implement these reforms. The priority of the battle against inflation became one of Amendola's favourite themes. Furthermore, the economic crisis was in part, it seemed, a consequence of the strike wave of 1969-70 and the new, strengthened position of the working class in the factories, which had reduced profit margins and the rate of investment. The workers had shown, in other words, that they were strong enough to put capitalism in crisis, but not strong enough to transform it; for the right, the danger of a repetition of the débâcle of 1922 was real.

And indeed perhaps the most disquieting sign for the Communist right was the right-wing backlash to the student and worker struggles of 1968-9. The spring of 1969 saw the first episodes of neo-fascist terrorism masquerading as ultra-left violence in order to provoke a reaction in public opinion. They culminated in the bombing of the Banca Nazionale dell Agricoltura at Piazza Fontana in Milan in December of that year which killed 16 people. The split in the Unified Socialist Party was itself largely motivated by the ex-PSDI's desire to take advantage of the anticipated backlash in public opinion. The neo-fascist MSI reaped unprecedented electoral successes, particularly in the south. It had taken the head of the revolt of Reggio Calabria in 1970, organised to protest against the establishment of the regional capital at Catanzaro. In the Sicilian regional election of June 1971 the MSI advanced from 6.6 per cent to 16.3 per cent of the popular vote; in the national election of May 1972 it reached the record level of 8.7 per cent. At the same time, rumours of attempted *coups d'état* were circulating; the neo-fascist terrorists clearly enjoyed support or complicity in some sectors of the state apparatus. For the Communist right, the parallel with 1922 was again easily drawn. In the face of a fascist, authoritarian danger, the prime task of the working-class movement was to unite with other democratic forces to defend the Republican Constitution and eliminate the social causes of fascism.

The electoral advance of the PCI and the left in 1975-6 was, in this context, interpreted by the Communist right not as the long-term result of the struggles of 1968-9 and of the extension of the left's hegemony in civil society, but rather as the people's reaction to the failure of the centre-left and the economic crisis. They also pointed to the PCI's gains among the middle strata, particularly in the 1975 election, although there was no conclusive evidence concerning the class composition of the Party's gains in 1975-6.[2] The parliamentary situation after the 1976 election forced the DC to reach a form of agreement with the PCI to keep a government alive; this lent support to the right's contention that an agreement with other democratic parties was possible.

Thus left and right within the PCI, viewing the events of 1966-76 from different perspectives, drew different conclusions from them. Each chose to emphasise the factors that buttressed its argument: for example, the left did not take the danger of a *coup d'état* as seriously as the right. While the course of events on balance reinforced the position of the left, and maintained it as a viable alternative within the PCI, the right also was able to find justification for its policy in the Italian political conjuncture.

2. The PCI and the 1968 Student Movement

The year following the XI Congress was not only one of organisational setbacks for the Communist left. The renewal of collective agreements in industry in 1966, in the midst of a recession, showed that the working class was not even in a position to defend its own economic interests, much less impose reforms on the whole of society. On the political level, the centre-left coalition had already encountered major difficulties in implementing its reform programme, as the conservative sectors of the DC put up a successful resistance to change. In spite of the unification of PSI and PSDI, the right's strategy had a reasonable chance of success over the long term, once the centre-left had come to an end.

But in the next year the student movement exploded with full force in Italy. The immediate cause was the backwardness of the university system: the structure of the university was hierarchical, almost feudal; all power was in the hands of a few senior professors, the 'barons'; the content of the courses was in many cases seriously outdated. The fragile fabric of the university was subjected to intolerable strains by the increase in student numbers which began in the early 1960s. Lecture halls, residences and other facilities became overcrowded. At the same

time the lack of job opportunities for graduates generated increasing
tension within the student body. But the archaic character of the
Italian university system did not produce, as the Communist right
expected, a reformist student movement aiming at the modernisation
of higher education on advanced capitalist lines. On the contrary, the
student movement soon went beyond demands for educational reform
to question the nature of society itself and adopt revolutionary
positions. In accordance with a 'law of combined and uneven development', the very backwardness of the Italian situation called forth a
demand for total change rather than reform.

Another factor which radicalised the student movement was the
presence of a large number of cadres who had received their political
education and a background in Marxism in the youth movements of
the PCI or the PSI. Still other leaders of the student movement were
influenced by *Quaderni rossi*, the review which had grown up in Turin
on the left of the PCI in 1961. Many of these cadres first became
involved in politics in the early 1960s; in some ways the movement
of 1967-8 was the delayed result of that of 1960-2, though the crisis of
bourgeois ideology, symbolised by the movement against the war in
Vietnam, also stimulated it, as did the Chinese Cultural Revolution.
Starting from the problems of the university and the government's
reform proposals, which they found inadequate, the students soon
raised more general complaints. They criticised in the first place the
selective nature of the educational system which favoured the children
of the upper classes. This issue was felt particularly by the mass of
students from less privileged backgrounds who were the first in their
families to attend university and who feared that it might not be the
avenue of social mobility that they had expected. The movement
demanded the elimination of class barriers to access to higher education
by the extension of student aid and more generally the creation of a
more egalitarian society in which selection would not be necessary.
Similarly, the students pressed for courses that would prepare them
better for the labour market, while at the same time they requested
that their content should no longer reflect bourgeois ideology. The
movement also criticised the already existing student organisations —
the students' councils (Representative Organisms) and the national
students' association (UNURI) — because they were dominated by
student associations grouping the youth movements of the various
parties (UGI for the left, Intesa for the Catholics, FUAN for the
neo-fascists, AGI for the Liberals). The record of these organisations,
which served as training grounds for budding politicians rather than

reflecting the immediate needs of the student body, was unhappy. Therefore the student movement made direct democracy, as opposed to representative democracy and the system of delegation, one of its cardinal principles. These ideas were embodied in the theses drawn up during the occupation of the University of Pisa in February 1967, known as the *Tesi della Sapienza*.[3]

The movement soon spread to the majority of Italian universities, involving large numbers of students. They resorted to new forms of struggle, in particular the prolonged occupation of university buildings. The position of the Communist Party as a whole towards the student movement evidenced its incapacity to appreciate the novelty of the situation. Until November 1967 the PCI continued to focus its attention on the old student organisations, even though they were clearly in a crisis and not likely to survive the movement.[4] This line reflected the Party's preference for representative bodies in which it is possible to encounter members of other parties over spontaneous assemblies and other less organised expressions of civil society. Even after the demise of UNURI in mid-1967, the PCI proposed that it be replaced by a 'mass union organisation' of students. This body would confine itself to specifically university problems and would be organised on representative lines rather than based on the student assemblies.

It was only in April 1968, at the height of student agitation all over Italy, that the PCI realised that the proposal for a 'mass union organisation' had no following among the students, who had moved far beyond such conceptions. Furthermore, the approach of general elections made the Party sensitive to the need to win the votes of the large numbers of radicalised students. Therefore Luigi Longo made a gesture of recognition towards the movement, which the PCI had ignored or criticised for months. He stated that the student movement had had a positive effect in politicising many young people, and that the Party had to recognise its right to take up its own positions not only on university questions but also on 'the more general problems of the Italian revolution'.[5] This position was tactically correct, for it allowed at least a temporary *rapprochement* between the Party and the students, in contrast to the open break which occurred in France at the same time.

For Amendola, however, this tactical concession was unacceptable because it was not coherent with the Party's general strategy. In an article entitled 'The Communists and the Student Movement: Necessity of a Struggle on Two Fronts'[6] he pointed out that the movement's general political position was opposed to that of the Party; it was much farther to the left, and influenced by the line of the Chinese Communists. Therefore the PCI had to carry out a struggle against the 'extremist and anarchist positions that have appeared in the student movement'; Amendola even called for 'revolutionary vigilance' because of the possibility of 'provocateurs' in the movement.

Amendola's position, while consistent with his own preference for a parliamentary alliance with other political forces, was not tactically feasible because the PCI had lost almost all its following in the student movement and could not hope to win a struggle for leadership within it such as he suggested. Some members of the Communist left, on the other hand, went beyond Longo's indications and greeted the student movement as the first of a novel type of social movement which would be the basis of a new revolutionary strategy in the West. Rossana Rossanda's book *The Year of the Students*[7] developed this theme: the movements could create situations of 'dual power' throughout society, which would lead to a revolutionary confrontation. This scheme was different from the classic Leninist strategy for the seizure of power at the centre; hence a new, non-Leninist type of party would be necessary, one that would not 'direct' the mass movements, but would exercise 'hegemony' over them, in the Gramscian sense. These formulations seemed to verge on spontaneism; in this new strategy, which was compared to the 'long march through the institutions' theorised at the time by Rudi Deutschke in Germany, the role of the Party appeared unclear.

3. Czechoslovakia and the 'Left Turn' of the XII Congress

The events in Czechoslovakia during 1968 provided further arguments for the Communist left, who had been the most insistent on the need for a thoroughgoing critical analysis of the socialist states. The whole of the PCI greeted with favour the new course initiated in Czechoslovakia by the election of Alexander Dubček as Secretary-General of the Communist Party in January 1968. If the Czechoslovak attempt to create a liberalised Communist regime succeeded, the PCI's professions that it wished to build a democratic socialist regime would at least appear more credible to its potential allies. During the 'Prague spring' the PCI leadership made clear its support for Dubček's policies and its opposition to any interference by the Soviet Union in Czechoslovakia's internal affairs.

The Soviet invasion was therefore immediately condemned by the

Executive of the PCI, which reasserted both the right to autonomy of every Communist party and its solidarity with the course undertaken by Dubček and his comrades. The PCI leadership remained firm in this position in spite of the wide support the Soviet action enjoyed among the rank and file of the Party. (A survey carried out in 1977-8 revealed that 39 per cent of a sample of PCI members who had joined the Party by 1969 approved of the Soviet invasion.[8]) But the left wing wished to go even further than the leadership and use the episode as the occasion for a radical reassessment of the nature of the socialist states and of the PCI's relations with them. The right, on the other hand, did not wish to sharpen the polemic with the USSR in order to keep the Party united in the pursuit of the immediate objective of a broad democratic coalition.

In the aftermath of the student movement and the invasion of Czechoslovakia, the PCI held its XII Congress at Bologna in January 1969. While Ingrao himself and the majority of the former *ingraiani* had been relatively silent during the previous year, a small group of leaders of the Communist left, including Lucio Magri, Rossana Rossanda, Luigi Pintor and Aldo Natoli, came to the congress with a common critical position *vis-à-vis* the Party's official line. They voiced it clearly both in their speeches and in a motion which, in the end, was withdrawn after the reply to the debate by Berlinguer, elected Vice-Secretary-General. At this congress Berlinguer adopted some of the themes of the left, so much so that observers spoke of a 'left turn' by the PCI. In fact he appropriated some of the left's ideas only to integrate them in the Party's traditional strategy. He asserted, for example:

> In Italy there are emerging — and we want to favour their development — democratic realities and also revolutionary realities that go beyond the Communist Party. On the theoretical level, that probably means that moments of socialist consciousness among the masses arise today not only because they are brought from outside, by the party, into movements born for immediate demands, but also as the result of new forms of exploitation and oppression and of the general political climate created by the extension of the revolutionary forces in the world, by the diffusion of Marxism and, in Italy, by the climate created by all our political and ideological battles.[9]

Berlinguer proposed that the autonomy of the various mass movements be recognised. Furthermore, they were to be an integral part of the

Party's strategy for the conquest of power, as they formed part of
the 'historic bloc' the PCI was seeking to form:

> We have often said . . . that, in our conception, it is not the party
> which conquers power, but a bloc of diverse social and political
> forces, of which the party is a part, and that we must proceed, step
> by step, starting now, to construct this historic bloc, affirming
> within it the hegemony of the working class.[10]

But the 'historic bloc' which Berlinguer proposed strongly resembled
the old system of alliances. And in practice Berlinguer proposed to
insert the new mass movements into the PCI's struggle for a new
parliamentary equilibrium, and to use them eventually as a means of
bringing pressure to bear on the DC and other potential coalition
partners:

> We must . . . succeed in connecting and uniting the more radical
> tendencies to the movement of the great masses, creating a fusion
> of revolutionaries, progressives, and democrats; we must develop
> and consolidate the alliance of the working class with the masses
> of peasant smallholders, with the urban middle strata, with the
> intellectuals. Promote, that is, together, the radicalisation and the
> broadening of the struggle . . . And the experience of the last
> months shows us that it is possible to promote simultaneously
> radicalisation, the broadening of our bases and social alliances,
> unitary trade-union initiatives, and forms of rapprochement and
> even partial agreement between the most diverse democratic
> forces.[11]

He went on to warn against underrating the importance of alliances
between political forces as opposed to work with the new movements
in civil society. This theme had also been stressed by Longo in his
introductory report to the congress.[12] While Berlinguer did not aim
at the immediate entry of the PCI into the government, but rather at
a more open relationship between government and opposition in
Parliament, his long-term objective was a 'new majority' including the
Communists, which would not be a purely left-wing majority but would
include substantial sectors of the DC as well. Longo looked forward, in
his report, to the formation of such majorities at the local level after
the forthcoming series of regional, provincial and municipal elections.[13]
   On the question of Czechoslovakia, Berlinguer not only repeated the

PCI's condemnation of the Soviet invasion, but affirmed that the Soviet action could not be considered an 'accident' or an 'error', but rather was also the product of 'contradictions and objective difficulties of the socialist world'. Therefore a fuller analysis of the socialist states, both of their positive and negative aspects, was necessary:

> We understand all the fundamental democratic and liberatory value of the socialist bases of the socialist countries, of the marvellous progress they have achieved, of their victories; and, at the same time, the contradictions which derive from the way in which, historically, a socialist society was constructed in a single country, and which, today, raise the problem of institutional arrangements which limit in part freedom and democracy in a country which is nevertheless, in many ways, the most advanced in the world.[14]

At the same time, however, Berlinguer rejected any concession to anti-Sovietism, and any suggestion that the PCI should break with the USSR. And he criticised Rossanda for comparing the reality of the socialist states to an 'abstract model', accusing her of adopting a 'utopian' attitude. Berlinguer was more willing to make a substantial move towards the positions of the left on this question, since the PCI would be more acceptable to potential allies the more critical it was of the USSR. Nevertheless, he was more concerned with the unity of the Party than they, and did not want to jeopardise it by initiating a full-scale debate on the nature of the socialist states.

The XII Congress, at which Berlinguer emerged as Longo's heir apparent, did not then mark a genuine shift to the left in the PCI's perspective. The centrist group around Longo and Berlinguer did not aim at a direct passage to socialism, but rather at the eventual admission of the PCI to the governmental majority. The entry into the majority corresponded to the first stage of the Popular Front strategy. The fact that it was no longer clearly presented as part of such a general strategy made it appear, if anything, a more purely reformist line. Unlike Amendola, however, the centrist group aimed to conciliate the left within the Party, rather than confront it openly. Hence Berlinguer's references to the necessary autonomy of the mass movements and the need for fresh analysis of the socialist states. In this the centre of the Party was much more realistic; it understood that it needed to keep in touch with the internal left and the mass movements in the country. Hence also its refusal to theorise a two-stage strategy, which later led Berlinguer to attempt to present the entry of the PCI into the majority as a step towards socialism rather than the first stage of a more complex design. While politically more realistic, this position was less clear and also less credible than Amendola's.

4. The Programme of the *Manifesto* Group

The group of former *ingraiani* who had criticised the official position at the Bologna Congress were encouraged by the desire for conciliation demonstrated by Berlinguer, but not satisfied by the results as far as the PCI's line was concerned. They therefore decided to publish a monthly journal as a means of promoting their own ideas and stimulating debate around them.

The platform of the *Manifesto* group, as it was expressed in the successive numbers of the journal and eventually in the theses published in September 1970, 'For Communism',[15] represented a clearer, more coherent and less reticent statement of the positions of the Communist left of the early 1960s. The starting-point for the group, as for the Communist left, was the thesis that Western capitalist society was ripe for a Communist revolution, rather than for some sort of intermediate stage. They deduced that communism was on the agenda, not from an analysis of contradictions inherent in the capitalist economy and destined to arrest its growth, but from the irrationality, waste and, in general, the quality of capitalist development: 'The crisis arises not so much from the arresting of the mechanisms of development as from development itself' (thesis 33). They explicitly rejected the notion of a catastrophic economic crisis of capitalism (theses 21, 56), and foresaw instead a crisis that would be simultaneously political, economic, and social (thesis 63). They believed such a crisis had been precipitated by the new wave of struggles which began in the West in 1967; hence the possibility and necessity of more radical demands. If anything, it was the struggles of the working class that could interrupt economic growth (thesis 110). For Italy, the theses foresaw one of two prospects: relative stagnation on the margins of the world economy (an 'English' solution), or economic development of a 'Japanese' type in the context of increasing social tension and a defeat of the left (thesis 124).

The first contradiction of the advanced capitalist economies was identified as that between the actual level of economic development and the potential level that capitalism is incapable of reaching. Instead of satisfying human needs, it wastes resources on armaments and socially harmful or useless consumer goods. It also cannot guarantee a qualitatively adequate type of development. Work is alienating and repetitive. Consumption is a function of the productive system rather than a result of free choice. Individuals are increasingly isolated. Power is concentrated in fewer and fewer hands. Furthermore, capitalism generates 'new needs' which it is incapable of satisfying: for instance, it trains large numbers of technicians and skilled workers, but is unable to employ them in jobs where they can fully use their skills. It destroys traditional institutions, such as the family, without satisfying the new demands that arise from this social change. It breeds new diseases, and it marginalises larger and larger groups of the population, such as the old (theses 62-7). The *Manifesto* group took up many of the themes of the international 'new left' in their insistence on the problem of the quality of life under capitalism. They saw the parasitic groups within Italian society, too, as the product of capitalist development, rather than the residue of a previous era (thesis 121).

Not only did the qualitative contradictions of advanced capitalism generate a new type of class struggle; this class struggle in the metro-poles had, in the international context, a 'primary value' (thesis 52). The *Manifesto* group rejected any suggestion that revolution had to begin in the underdeveloped areas of the world, asserting instead that the two struggles had to be contemporary and co-ordinated.

However, a socialist revolution is not the inevitable outcome of the newly identified contradictions of capitalism. The alternative is barbarism (theses 76-7), made all the more likely by the increasing capacity for repression of the modern state. In keeping with its general project of revising the elements of the Marxism of the II International which had survived into the era of the Third, the group rejected the 'deterministic theory of the ineluctability of socialism'.

Italy, for the *Manifesto* group, was an advanced capitalist country, but one characterised by all the contradictions deriving from its lower level of economic development and its inherited backwardness (the southern question etc.) as well as those of advanced capitalism:

Italian capitalism thus has to face, at the same time, problems of underdevelopment and of hyper-maturity. A situation that capitalism has already known in other contexts, for example in pre-revolutionary Russia, is repeated, in the sense that Italy not only appears as the most backward country of the advanced area, but reflects within itself the extreme poles of this contradiction [thesis 104].

They admitted that the Communist right had been correct in fore-
seeing that economic development would not solve the age-old
'secondary' contradictions of Italian society, and that their own
analyses of the early 1960s had been wrong in this respect. But this
admission did not lead them to alter their basic premiss that Italy was
mature for a socialist transformation rather than an intermediate,
democratic phase.

In view of this analysis of the nature of advanced capitalism, the
Manifesto group rejected social-democratic reformism and 'frontism'
(the Popular Front strategy), on the one hand, and the classic Leninist
insurrectional perspective of 'the revolutionary break as the intervention of a conscious minority, which inserts itself in a situation of social
disruption and uses the elementary demands of the masses to seize state
power and subvert the system of property', on the other (theses 1-23).
Even if such a crisis were to occur, they argued, the mass of the people
would not follow the revolutionaries, but rather would allow the right
to regain control of the situation (thesis 22). Their argument drew on
Gramsci's thesis that a war of position — i.e. a war in civil society — is
a necessary preliminary to winning a socialist revolution in the West.
But the *Manifesto* group did not foresee a general crisis of capitalism
such as that which Gramsci had experienced in the aftermath of the
First World War, and which he assumed would recur, making necessary
a war of movement as well as one of position.

The theses argued that the new contradictions typical of advanced
capitalism demanded a new kind of struggle which would express
immediately some of the contents of a socialist society. The separation
between 'social' and 'political' demands, and between the 'economic'
and the 'political', could be overcome. This meant that the working-
class movement should struggle directly against the capitalist division
of labour, for equality, and against the separation of the state from
civil society (thesis 79). The group also proposed a new type of direct
struggle within the sphere of the social services (e.g. occupation of
empty houses by the homeless), instead of simply bringing pressure to
bear at the political level for reforms. They proposed that in this field
as well the movement's objectives should in some way prefigure the
future socialist society — for instance, in the demand for the combination of work and study (theses 144-8). In this perspective, intermediate
objectives took on a new valence:

> The first new feature is that their value is no longer reductive,
> instrumental, and disruptive (as the terrain on which various

interests united in the common struggle against the bourgeois state converge), but is also a value as prefiguration, as the progressive clarification of a perspective and as the creation of the political and organisational capacity to manage a different society. The second new feature is that the intermediate objectives are no longer useful only in moments of acute crisis: the specificity of their contents prevents their being absorbed in a reformist design and makes them permanent instruments for the construction of an alternative force [thesis 82].

. . . Traditionally, mass struggles have had a defensive character, so that only the radicalisation of a substantially economic perspective allowed them to break out of a trade-unionistic horizon and establish a connection between particular struggles and the political perspective. Corresponding to this relationship between social and political movement was the distinction between union and party, in the two forms of the transmission belt and of pure unionism. In advanced capitalism, this distinction between economic struggle and political struggle tends to disappear [thesis 83].

The struggle for these intermediate objectives, as it becomes more radical, itself generates a crisis of the capitalist system, which involves an extraconstitutional confrontation, though not necessarily a civil war (thesis 87). For this reason, the group rejected the formula 'model of development' because it did not suggest the need for a revolutionary break with capitalism.

The *Manifesto* group, then, envisaged a new type of struggle which was to be fought above all in civil society rather than within the political institutions. The mass movements in civil society were to organise themselves in councils, modelled on the Turinese workers' councils of the *Ordine Nuovo* period. These were to be organs that were

. . . political and trade-union at the same time, continually revocable: not organs of self-management, nor transitory manifestations in a phase of dual power, but organisational forms that stabilise and develop the levels of political consciousness of the masses in the midst of a specific social conflict [thesis 84].

The councils were to be formed in all sectors of civil society: factories, schools, neighbourhoods. They were instruments of struggle that would also guarantee that a future socialist state was democratic in character, by controlling the Party and government and preventing the consolidation of a political power separate from the masses (theses 96-8). In such a state the 'dictatorship of the proletariat' would be maintained so long as the construction of communism had not been completed; the 'dictatorship of the proletariat' was interpreted as the denial of equal political rights to the former exploiting classes (thesis 95). On this point the theses of the *Manifesto* group, no longer constrained by the need to conciliate potential allies in the middle classes, negated directly one of the main tenets of the *via italiana al socialismo*.

The strategy of direct struggle for socialism involved, for the *Manifesto* group, a different set of class alliances from those of the Popular Front. In the first place, they suggested that the proletariat included more than the traditional manual workforce of the factories: wage labour had spread to many other spheres. Nor could it be limited to workers in industries that were productive in the Marxian sense, since the boundary between productive and unproductive labour was difficult to establish. They were prepared to consider some, though not all, non-manual workers as part of the proletariat, thus widening its boundaries.[16] The PCI, faithful to the Popular Front strategy, had never done this; it preferred to consider white-collar workers as potential allies rather than part of the proletariat, in order not to underestimate the importance of the policy of alliances by treating them as the Socialists had treated the rural middle strata in 1918-22. For the *Manifesto* group, on the other hand, the primary task was the unification of the proletariat — 'the majority of the exploited' — rather than the formation of alliances; only those groups of wage workers who were struggling against capitalist relations of production could be considered as full-fledged proletarians — the working class is a class which constitutes itself in struggle (thesis 90).

Apart from the proletariat itself, the *Manifesto* group identified two other non-proletarian strata as 'decisive for the revolution': 'the intellectuals and technicians with functions of direction and research, and the oppressed minorities at the margins of society (women, emigrants, racial minorities, the unemployed)' (thesis 91). Their relationship to the proletariat could not be conceived in terms of a traditional alliance, but rather had to be seen as much closer. Only the technicians could criticise science and technology from a proletarian point of view and permit their alternative use; and the marginal groups represented values such as equality, community and anti-productivism that were part of the Communist ethic. Students were seen as sharing in the social role of both these groups: future scientists and technicians, they were at present marginal to capitalist society. They were, in fact, the vanguard of the stratum of researchers, technicians and intellectuals (thesis 138).

As far as class alliances were concerned, the *Manifesto*'s most notable innovation with respect to the position of the PCI was their attitude to the intermediate strata (other than technicians and proletarianised white-collar workers): the state bureaucracy, workers in the scholastic and cultural spheres, the professions, the sphere of circulation etc. These the group saw as characteristic of mature capitalism, not residues of Italy's pre-capitalist past. The objective of the left's action towards the vast majority of them had to be their neutralisation, rather than an alliance, because these strata were beneficiaries of the capitalist system, privileged in many ways, in fact largely parasitic. For the *Manifesto* group, these new 'middle strata' had to be analysed carefully in their different components and could be neutralised by 'decapitating' them – if the revolutionary movement established a relationship with their political leaders (theses 92, 164-9). Significant groups of these 'new middle strata' could however be won over to the left, but only on the basis of a very advanced programme that redefined their roles in terms of a new organisation of society – one that appealed to their ideological commitment and to the professional frustrations they felt in attempting to perform their duties, rather than to their material, corporative interests. At the same time the workers' struggle had to reduce their privileges in order to force them to make a clear choice of sides. This also was analogous to the policy followed by the PSI in 1920-2, which Togliatti had criticised because it had driven the intermediate strata into the Fascist camp.

With respect to one component of the classic 'middle strata' which was very important for Togliatti, the peasantry, the solution proposed by *Il Manifesto* was similar: they rejected any attempt to defend the peasants' immediate, corporative interests as they were constituted within contemporary capitalist society (e.g. high support prices for agricultural products), and advocated a directly socialist policy, the collective management of the land and of related activities. An intermediate, 'democratic' solution, such as the creation of an agriculture based on small peasant farming, was economically unviable (theses 158-63): the effective proletarianisation of the small peasants, forced into part-time wage labour and crushed by the weight of the monopolies, was already underway. For this reason the peasants, unlike the new middle strata, were considered available as allies, rather than simply neutralisable. Again the *Manifesto* group embraced one of the theses that Togliatti had criticised severely as one of the causes of the defeat of 1922: the 'proletarianisation' of the peasantry.

The group did not view the agrarian question as a matter of liquidating some pre-capitalist residues left by Italy's 'incomplete bourgeois revolution' because the agrarian sector was not separate from the rest of the capitalist economy, but ever more closely integrated with it. Similarly, the other major 'secondary contradiction' of Italian capitalism, the southern question, was, for the *Manifesto* group, not soluble in a 'democratic' way. The south was not a separate, underdeveloped area; nor would capitalist development eliminate the imbalance between north and south. Its underdevelopment was the product of its integration into the Italian capitalist economy, and was destined to increase with time. Hence only a radical, anti-capitalist programme was appropriate for the south: only in this way could the simmering discontent and frustration of the masses of the region be channelled in a progressive direction (theses 150-7). This analysis was consistent with the group's general thesis that Italy was both underdeveloped and hyper-mature, the advanced capitalist country whose contradictions were most explosive.

In discussing the problem of alliances, the *Manifesto* group did not consider the possibility of a coalition with, or even a neutralisation of, elements of the bourgeoisie proper. The classic version of the Popular Front strategy had, on the other hand, foreseen alliances with the anti-monopoly sectors of the bourgeoisie.

The group's conception of the Party was coherent with its proposed revolutionary strategy, based on the activity of autonomous movements in civil society. The Party was seen as

> . . . a political organisation no longer understood as a consciousness external to the movement, but as a continuous synthesis between the movement in struggle and the patrimony of theory and organisation of the class, a corrective to corporative dispersion and a guarantee of strategic unification [thesis 83].

It would also play an important role in the phase of transition to socialism, when it would be a counterweight to the councils, representing the interests of the community as a whole (thesis 98). The Party was to be a mass proletarian party; the rules of democratic centralism as it was practised by the Communist parties were considered 'historically surpassed' and 'one of the basic causes of the present-day revisionism of the Western Communist parties' (theses 99-100). The

Manifesto group clearly rejected the Leninist model of the Party, recognising that the mass movements had the right to act politically in their own right, while at the same time repudiating the spontaneist theory that the movements themselves could bring about a revolution and that the Party was not necessary.[17] This, however, left them with the task of defining the role they envisaged for the Party, a totally new one of 'synthesis' and 'hegemony' rather than 'direction' of mass struggles. The very brevity of the theses' references to the question of the Party testifies to the difficulties this problem raised for them.

For the *Manifesto*, as for the Communist left, a critique of the USSR was absolutely necessary in order to clarify the type of socialism they wished to construct. But they went considerably further, identifying China as the new 'organic point of reference of the revolutionary forces on a world scale' (thesis 46). Unlike the Maoist groups which had appeared in Italy and elsewhere since 1962, the *Manifesto* took inspiration from the democratic, egalitarian aspects of the Chinese experience rather than its neo-Stalinist features. The Chinese, unlike the Soviets, had refused to give absolute priority to the development of the productive forces, insisting that it was necessary to transform the relations of production at the same time. They had attacked hierarchy in production and sought to avoid the development of inequalities between city and country and between different regions. They had attempted to prevent the formation of a bureaucratic class. The group went so far as to accept the Chinese thesis that the rise to power of Khrushchev marked the beginning of a process of capitalist restoration in the USSR (thesis 30), but, again unlike the Maoist groups, they saw the roots of this restoration in the Stalinist period, and precisely in the priority given to the productive forces, the inequality between city and country and within the factories, and the bureaucratisation of the Party and the state (theses 25-9).[18] They noted that Mao, as early as 1956, had criticised the Soviet model of the construction of socialism. For *Il Manifesto*, China, while a 'point of reference', was not to become the directing centre of the international Communist movement in the way the USSR had been in the 1920s and 1930s (thesis 49).

The platform of the *Manifesto* group, then, was in its essentials that of the Communist left of the early 1960s, but it was more radical, more fully developed, and enriched with the contributions and lessons received from intervening events, such as the Chinese Cultural Revolu-, tion. The theme of 'intermediate demands', in the first place, was presented in a new way. Instead of constituting an 'alternative model' of economic development, involving macro-economic choices over

investments and consumption, they were instead to serve mainly as a
'prefiguration' of a future socialist society — hence they were to
attack such points as the division of labour, inequality and the
separation of state and civil society. They offered a positive solution to
the problems of society, but in a clearly socialist direction. These
intermediate demands were meant to exploit the new contradictions
which the group had identified in advanced capitalism, for instance the
alienation of work, and drew inspiration from the Cultural Revolution.
The original structural reforms of the post-war period were intended
to alter the balance of forces in the country in favour of the working
class by changing the economic and class structure of the country
and forming a system of alliances around the working class. The
intermediate objectives of the *Manifesto* group, like those of the
Communist left of the early 1960s, aimed at reinforcing the working
class in a somewhat different way, by increasing the power of the class
and its closest allies in the various sectors of civil society: factories,
schools and other institutions. As Natoli put it:

> There is no doubt that when Berlinguer links the problem of the
> strategy of reforms to the endeavour and the struggle to construct
> an historic bloc, he makes an important step towards overcoming
> a certain practice, which has become current in the Party in recent
> years, of seeing the strategy of reforms as a series of sectoral
> measures. In this way only their economic content is taken up, while
> their original inspiration is lost from view: they were originally
> a new way to carry forward the struggle for socialism in a Western
> country, by means of a process which tends to construct and
> conquer points of new power with which to disrupt the power of
> the ruling class.[19]

In developing the idea of councils, the *Manifesto* group adopted a
line that was more coherent than that of the earlier Communist left,
who had envisaged the creation of a network of autonomous institutions of a more traditional kind — local governments, trade unions etc.
These were in fact a part of the political society as well as of civil
society, because of the presence of representatives of political parties
within them. The councils were more adapted to act as expressions of
autonomous movements in civil society. Ingrao himself, at the October
1969 Central Committee meeting, criticised the *Manifesto*'s 'conciliar'
strategy;[20] this intervention pointed out the difference between
the two lines. The idea of a conciliar strategy was suggested by the

radical critique of representative democracy advanced by the student movement, and by the experience of the factory councils that were then being formed in many Italian factories. The group did not go so far as some other extraparliamentary political groups who condemned the factory councils too on the grounds that they involved a form of representation as opposed to direct democracy based on the assembly of all workers.

In the third place, the *Manifesto* group not only explicitly argued, as the Communist left had implied, that the question of alliances was secondary to the action of the working class itself, but rejected some of the traditional 'allies' among the intermediate strata and, even more important, redefined the working class and proposed some new groups as close allies: technicians and professionals, students and marginalised groups. This was a genuine innovation, though it had some points of contact with the line of the Communist left. It reflected the ideas of the international 'new left' and of French sociology (e.g. Mallet and Touraine). The proposal of alliance with the technicians and other intellectuals in production was related to the group's analysis of the new contradictions within capitalism, while the link with students and other excluded groups was based on a supposed common cultural critique of the quality of life.

With respect to the USSR, the Cultural Revolution and the invasion of Czechoslovakia had radicalised the position of the *Manifesto* group, so that they believed that a capitalist restoration was underway there. They also presented a fuller and more damning account of the roots of this degeneration in the history of the USSR. And the failure of the centre-left to solve the southern question and the other 'secondary contradictions' of Italian society had led the group to revise its judgement on these problems.

The positions of the *Manifesto*, in general, were a legitimate derivation from Eurocommunism, developed by Togliatti as the *via italiana al socialismo*, but had moved far beyond it by rejecting the alliance policy, stressing extraparliamentary as opposed to parliamentary struggle and adopting some of the themes current in the European and American left in the 1960s.

5. The Exclusion of the *Manifesto* Group

While the promoters of *Il Manifesto* had had the idea of publishing an independent review in 1968, they waited until after the XII Congress to

put it into practice.[21] When the leadership of the PCI was informed
of the initiative in April 1969, they advised against it on the grounds
that it could lead to factionalism. They were no doubt concerned that
the sharp divisions that had appeared during the debate on the theses
for the XII Congress in some federations, particularly Rome and
Naples, might be crystallised. In May, before the first number of the
journal had appeared, the PCI leadership attacked it publicly.[22] When
it did appear in late June, it was immediately criticised by Paolo
Bufalini, for the *Direzione*, in *Rinascita*, and the question was referred
to the V Commission of the Central Committee, after the Central
Committee itself had heard a report from the *Direzione* which strongly
condemned the journal. When number 4 of the journal appeared on 20
September, it led to a hardening of the Party's attitude: it contained an
article, 'Prague is Alone',[23] which severely criticised the 'normalisation'
in Czechoslovakia and called on the Western Communist parties to
support the opposition in Eastern Europe with the aim of the 'defeat
and replacement' of the ruling groups in Eastern Europe by 'a new bloc
of social forces led by the working class'. The V Commission of the
Central Committee proposed in early October that collaboration with
Il Manifesto and membership of the Party should be incompatible, but
in the full Central Committee debate of 15 October it seemed that
a compromise between the dissidents and the Party might be reached.
This would have taken the form of a modification or closure of *Il
Manifesto*, accompanied by the institution of new forms of debate
within the Party. In this debate Berlinguer rather than Ingrao was
most concerned to maintain the unity of the Party by avoiding
expulsions. Ingrao did nothing to defend the *Manifesto* group,
while the right wing were pressing for 'administrative measures'
against the dissenters.[24]

However, in the latter part of October the attitude of the PCI
leadership suddenly became much more rigid, and the *Manifesto* group
were told that they must close the journal unconditionally. Since they
refused to do so, Natoli, Pintor and Rossanda were 'struck from the
rolls' of the Party (*radiati*, a disciplinary measure less drastic than
expulsion) by the Central Committee on 25 November; the same
penalty was inflicted on Magri the following day by the Central
Control Commission, and on Massimo Caprara, the Neapolitan
deputy, a few days later.

The abrupt stiffening of the Party leadership's stance seems to have
been prompted by the direct intervention of the Soviet Party, who were
outraged by the article 'Prague is Alone'. The Soviets threatened to

support an 'orthodox' tendency within the PCI; it was rumoured that
Ambrogio Donini, the only delegate to speak in favour of the Soviet
invasion of Czechoslovakia at the XII Congress, and other members of
the pro-Soviet 'old guard' were preparing to launch their own journal,
'The Call of Lenin', unless *Il Manifesto* was closed. As Bufalini said to
one of the promoters of the journal after the *Direzione*'s communiqué
of 12 November, inviting the Central Committee to 'take the necessary
measures by the end of November': 'We have signed a blank cheque
for the Soviets, and now we must honour it.'[25] The PCI leadership was
no doubt also worried about the possible effects of an open debate on
strategy on a divided Party, in particular after the publication of an
article by Amendola, 'A Party of Government',[26] in which he proposed
that the PCI should enter the government in the near future. This
proposal was certainly to the 'right' of the current line of the Party
leadership, though it indicated the direction in which it was tending.
It was very unpopular with the rank and file, and was strongly
criticised by the *Manifesto* group.

In the federations a debate on the *Manifesto* had been initiated
by the Party leadership before the decision to exclude its editors from
the Party, but had not been carried to the section level in all parts of
the country. In Bari and Modena the *Manifesto* had had scarcely any
impact, and there was very little discussion of it. In the case of Bari this
may have been the result of a deliberate decision not to debate a subject
that could be embarrassing to the left-wing leadership of the federation;
the federal committee did not discuss the question until the exclusion
of the group was certain. In Perugia and Turin there was moderate
interest in the *Manifesto*; in particular, several active members of the
Party in Perugia sided with the new journal.

But the liveliest discussion of the *Manifesto* affair took place in the
Naples federation, where a serious dispute between the 'new left' and
the right had taken place at the 1969 federal congress.[27] The political
commission had rejected the theses proposed by the *Direzione* and
presented an alternative document to the congress; by a small majority
the congress voted to approve the official theses. The new leading
bodies of the federation were formed in such a way as to practically
exclude those who had supported the left-wing position, and this only
increased the discontent and ill feeling among the rank and file. During
the debate on the *Manifesto* affair in October and November 1969,
many sections of the Naples federation expressed support for the
journal or approved the position of the *Direzione* with a large minority
dissenting. When the decision to exclude the promoters of the journal

was taken, many Neapolitan sections sent letters of protest to the Party
leadership. On the motion to strike Caprara from the Party rolls there
were 31 votes in the federal committee against the measure, 13 abstentions and 80 in favour. Another Neapolitan deputy, Liberato Bronzuto,
also expressed his solidarity with the *Manifesto* group and was
similarly excluded from the Party. Within the province the strongest
support for the journal came from the urban sections in Naples itself
and, in particular, in Portici and Resina (Ercolano). Both working-class
and middle-class Party organisations gave it their backing, often
rejecting the arguments of the federal officials sent to hold the
meetings. The Party leadership, on the other hand, received more
support from the sections of the province.

In Rome as well a very serious split had developed at the federal
congress, where Natoli had made a particularly sharp attack on the
leaders of the federation who had consistently followed an
'Amendolian' line.[28] They had consequently arranged that his name
be cancelled from the ballot for the federal committee, along with
those of other members of the left, by a majority of delegates. He and
the others were thus not elected. (On the other hand, Natoli was re-
elected to the Central Committee at the XII Congress.) This episode
had seriously embittered relations between left and right in the
federation, so that when the federal committee met to consider
the exclusion of members of the Rome federation who had collaborated
with the journal a demonstration of Party members was held outside
federation headquarters. Many Roman sections of the Party also
disapproved of the exclusion of the *Manifesto* group.

Another federation where there was strong support for the *Manifesto* group was Bergamo, whose leading members had supported the
left within the Party for years.[29] In general, interest in the ideas of
the group was greatest in urban areas, particularly the central sections
of the cities, in the centre and in the north. In the south, on the other
hand, the ideas of the new left had very little currency. This fact can
be explained by the concentration of student and worker struggles in
the north and centre and the larger cities. The presence of a number
of intellectuals seems also to have been a necessary condition for the
penetration of the ideas of the *Manifesto* — witness the cases of Naples
and Rome, both with large numbers of intellectuals, where the debate
was particularly sharp, on the one hand, and of Modena, where there
was very little debate, on the other. A history of very sharp conflict
with a right-wing local leadership also seems to explain the strength of
support for *Il Manifesto* in Naples and Rome; where there was a left-

oriented leading group, as in Turin, Bari and Perugia, the debate was deliberately kept in a low key. The case of Bergamo, where a left-wing federal leadership was openly sympathetic to the *Manifesto*, appears to have been exceptional. The pattern of support for *Il Manifesto*, then, was different from that for the Ingrao left in 1965-6: it was strongest where there was a large concentration of intellectuals, who were open to the new ideas of the movement of 1968. These were federations where the left had been a significant minority at the XI Congress. It attracted a following in other areas involved immediately in the struggles of 1968-9, if there was a minimum number of intellectuals present. But many of the federations that had supported the left in 1966 remained relatively untouched by the ideas of the group. When *Il Manifesto* founded an organised political movement in 1970 (later to become the Party of Proletarian Unity for Communism), much of its support in the provinces was to come from groups of radical Catholics or young people new to political activity, while its leadership continued to be composed of ex-Communists.

Notes

1. See V. Parlato (ed.), *Spazio e ruolo del riformismo* (Bologna, 1974).
2. See M. Barbagli, P. Corbetta, A. Parisi and H.M.A. Schadee, *Fluidità elettorale e classi sociali in Italia: 1968-1976* (Bologna, 1979), who suggest that in Bologna the largest part of PCI gains came from the working class. This appears to be the case for Italy as a whole.
3. In *Nuovo impegno*, 6-7 (1967); cf. Movimento studentesco, *Documenti della rivolta universitaria* (Bari, 1968).
4. R. Luperini, *Il PCI e il movimento studentesco* (Milan, 1969), Ch. II.
5. *Il Contemporaneo*, 3 May 1968; cf. 'Su alcuni aspetti della campagna elettorale', *Rinascita*, 12 Apr. 1968.
6. 'I comunisti e il movimento studentesco: necessità della lotta su due fronti', *Rinascita*, 7 June 1968.
7. R. Rossanda, *L'anno degli studenti* (Bari, 1968).
8. Elaborated from table in M. Barbagli, P. Corbetta and S. Sechi, *Dentro il PCI* (Bologna, 1979), p. 26.
9. A. Cecchi (ed.), *Storia del PCI attraverso i congressi* (Rome, 1977), p. 400.
10. Ibid., p. 394.
11. Ibid., pp. 396-7.
12. Ibid., pp. 331-2.
13. Ibid., p. 347.
14. Ibid., p. 380.
15. *Il Manifesto*, II, 9 (Sept. 1970).
16. See the two documents, 'La divisione del lavoro in fabbrica', *Il Manifesto*, I, 5-6 (Oct.-Nov. 1969), and 'Tecnici e strati intermedi', ibid., III, 3-4 (Spring-Summer 1971), where the proletarianisation of white-collar work is analysed.
17. Cf. J.-P. Sartre and R. Rossanda, 'Classe e partito', *Il Manifesto*, I, 4 (Sept. 1969).

18. See among others L. Foa and A. Natoli, 'Origini della rivoluzione culturale', and Mao Tse-tung, 'Sui dieci grandi rapporti' [1956], *Il Manifesto*, II, 5 (May 1970); also R. Rossanda, 'Il marxismo di Mao Tse-tung', *Il Manifesto*, II, 7-8 (July-Aug. 1970).

19. Quoted in M. Argilli, *Un anno in sezione: Vita di base del P.C.I.* (Milan, 1970), pp. 161-2.

20. Cf. L. Magri, 'Una risposta a Ingrao', *Il Manifesto*, II, 1 (Jan. 1970); see L. Magri, 'Le origini del Manifesto — Appunti per l'introduzione al seminario di Rimini (sett. 1973) sulle Tesi' (n.p., 1973), for a general discussion of the relationship between *Il Manifesto*'s line and that of the PCI.

21. The following account is based largely on 'Sul "caso" del Manifesto', *Il Manifesto*, I, 7 (Dec. 1969).

22. *L'Unità*, 15 May 1969.

23. 'Praga è sola', *Il Manifesto*, I, 4 (1969).

24. *La questione del 'Manifesto': Democrazia e unità del PCI* (Rome, 1969).

25. *L'Espresso*, 9 Dec. 1979, p. 20.

26. *L'Unità*, 21 Aug. 1969.

27. See the account in *Il Manifesto*, I, 7 (Dec. 1969), pp. 23-4.

28. The following account is based on Argilli, *Un anno*, and *Il Manifesto*, I, 7 (Dec. 1969), pp. 22-3.

29. *Il Manifesto*, I, 7 (Dec. 1969).

12 THE HISTORIC COMPROMISE: FURTHER DEVELOPMENT OF EUROCOMMUNISM

1. The Hot Autumn and Right-wing Reaction

The *dénouement* of the *Manifesto* affair coincided with the high point of working-class struggles of the late 1960s, the 'hot autumn' of 1969.[1] After the revival of union activity in 1962, the recession of 1963-4 had weakened the unions, throwing a large number of men and women out of work. The 1966 round of renewals of the major collective agreements hence brought few gains for the workers, and the economic upturn of 1966-9 was characterised by speed-ups and overtime working. Furthermore, the inadequacy of housing and social services in the northern industrial cities became increasingly acute as immigration from the south continued. Finally, the student movement gave an example of militant action and radical criticism of existing society that the workers were to follow; it introduced many forms of struggle and practices, such as the assembly and the method of direct democracy, which the workers took up and adapted to their own purposes.

The objectives of the hot autumn were also in many respects new for the trade-union movement. While substantial wage demands were advanced, they had a strong egalitarian character for they tended to reduce differentials between white- and blue-collar workers and between categories of workers. The workers also criticised the division of labour as it existed in the factory, calling for the reorganisation of the system of qualifications and categories. And the unions, partly in an attempt to channel this militancy in a direction they could more easily control, began to adopt a more directly political role, negotiating with the government over a series of major reforms (pensions, housing, transport and health). The first initiative in this campaign was the general strike for pension reform in 1968, which brought about the new pension law of the following year. This political involvement by the unions soon led to unease within the Communist Party for they seemed to be usurping the role of the parties as mediators of interests. Above all, the unions did not take sufficient account of the interests of the other classes who were the potential allies of the working class.[2]

The right-wing reaction to the student movement and the hot autumn took many forms and proceeded on many levels at once:

neo-fascist terrorism, riots in Reggio Calabria and the MSI's electoral victories. The regional elections of June 1970 showed no gains at all for the Communists over their 1968 showing, contrary to expectations that the strike movement would have an impact at the polls. The PCI and PSIUP together lost 1.3 per cent of the popular vote, while the newly reconstituted Social Democratic Party (PSU), which had run a fiercely right-wing campaign, won an unprecedented 7 per cent. The election campaign had been accompanied by a series of rumours about a possible *coup d'état*, particularly in the event of an advance by the left. The DC was also moving to the right: after the fall of the Colombo government, Andreotti formed a centrist coalition with the Republicans, Social Democrats and Liberals, who returned to the cabinet for the first time since 1957. He was immediately forced to dissolve Parliament, but in the ensuing election (May 1972) the Communists scored only marginal gains (0.3 per cent of the popular vote) while their allies, the PSIUP, lost over half their support and disappeared from the Chamber. The centrist government survived for a year longer.

At the same time sections of the state apparatus were also reacting to the new wave of agitation. The police and judiciary were particularly zealous in repressing illegalities they believed the workers had committed during the strikes. A so-called 'Silent Majority' organised marches in the major cities, grouping right-wing Christian Democrats, Social Democrats and neo-fascists with the tacit support of many members of the police and armed forces. The attempted *coup d'état* organised by Prince Junio Valerio Borghese in December 1970 was a comic-opera affair, but the involvement of senior generals, including the head of the secret service, General Vito Miceli, in protecting or even promoting neo-fascist terrorists and plotters was much more serious. The general situation, from the point of view of the left and of the Communists in particular, was ugly.

The hot autumn had also provoked an economic recession: in 1970 hourly wage costs in manufacturing surged ahead by a record 24 per cent as a result of the new collective agreements, and this led to a halt in the growth of investment in both 1971 and 1972.[3] This increased the discontent of many members of the middle classes. The revival of economic activity in 1973-4 was cut short by the oil crisis, but it was easy for the right to blame the workers and the unions for all the difficulties of the economy.

2. The PCI Moves to the Right

These events had a primary role in determining the right turn which the PCI leadership began to execute in 1969. To speak of a 'shift to the right' in the Party's position is accurate, but in part misleading, because this suggests that the fundamental perspective of the right wing was not already shared by the leadership. In fact from 1969 on the Party leadership was engaged in a reformulation of the traditional *via italiana* to respond to the pressing dangers which it perceived and the urgent choices which the PCI's new strength forced on it. Berlinguer and his associates stressed the importance of avoiding an economic crisis which they believed could only damage the left, and the pressing necessity of unity with the other democratic forces to defend democracy and republican institutions from the fascist attack. In this process certain transformations in social and economic relations would have to be introduced (the 'structural reforms'). To these urgent priorities another aspect of the traditional, dominant right-wing interpretation of the *via italiana* was largely sacrificed: the anti-monopoly alliance. In practice, if not in theory, this concept was abandoned in the 1970s. If the Italian economy had to be saved from collapse, and the monopolies were a mainstay of the economy, then they had to be saved as well. Indeed, in early 1973 Amendola went so far as to identify the parasitic groups (mostly members of the middle strata) as the enemy of the modernisation and development of the economy, and to propose an alliance between the working class and advanced capital to eliminate them.[4] The boundaries of the alliances of the working class were therefore redrawn in such a way that it was no longer clear who was excluded from the alliance, particularly since the parasitic groups were not identified precisely in theory, and even less so in practice.

Parallel to this reformulation of the policy of class alliances — never officially announced as such — was a clarification of the PCI's strategy for attaining power at the political and parliamentary level. In the early 1950s, at the height of the Cold War, the PCI's slogan had been 'the conquest of the majority' for the PCI and PSI, which were bound by a unity of action pact. Togliatti, in the mid-1950s, had repudiated this slogan in favour of the 'democratic government of the working classes', and later this too was replaced by the formula 'a new majority'. The components of this 'new majority' were not clearly specified: it might include the DC, only a part of the DC or, just conceivably, exclude it altogether. Togliatti leaned towards the first of these three possibilities,

particularly after the creation of the centre-left coalition. At the IX
Congress (1960), for instance, he stated:

> The necessary starting point is therefore always the same: the
> break-up of the political monopoly of the DC, accompanied by a
> return of this party, or of a part of it and of its leaders, to the
> democratic terrain and by the collaboration of new democratic
> forces in the direction [of the country] .[5]

The V Conference of the PCI in January 1964 offered PCI participation
in a government with all the centre-left parties.[6] While Amendola wrote
at the same time of unifying the '48 per cent of Italians to the left of
the DC' in a single party, this did not exclude the possibility of a
governmental coalition with the Catholic Party; only Ingrao aimed at
winning over the working-class following of the DC to the left. In the
later 1960s it was assumed by many Communists that the 'new
majority' would be formed with the left-wing minority of the Christian
Democrats, which would split from the rest of the Party, though the
view dominant among the leadership was already that an agreement
should be sought with the whole DC.

By 1970 the official orientation of the PCI leaders was that any
arrangement had to be reached with both the left and the centre of the
DC; the secession of a right-wing minority from the Catholic Party was
considered at the time a price that might have to be paid for such an
accord. Berlinguer's proposal of the 'historic compromise', first
advanced, though without the name, at the XIII Congress in 1972,
made it clear that the PCI sought to collaborate with the DC as a whole.

If the 'historic compromise' was in some way equivalent to the first
stage of the two-stage strategy of the Popular Front, the PCI leadership
was careful to point out that its proposal for the immediate future, an
'emergency government' including the DC, the PCI and other democratic parties, would not be the same thing as the 'historic compromise',
but a step preceding it and not necessarily leading to it. Hence the
Popular Front strategy was 'enriched' by the addition of a third stage.
And at least in this stage even monopoly capital would not necessarily
be excluded from participating in the common task of dealing with
the emergency. Even in the second phase it would still have a role,
as no one could deny that some sectors of the DC represented the
monopolies.

The PCI leadership under Berlinguer also blurred the classic Popular
Front strategy in another quite different way. As we saw in discussing

the XII Congress, Berlinguer, unlike Amendola, chose to deal with the internal left by means of concessions (even if they were only verbal) and mediation, rather than direct conflict and political debate. Hence also his real attempt to avoid the exclusion of the *Manifesto* group. The reasons for this difference in approach between two leaders who shared a commitment to the same fundamental line were both temperamental and political. Berlinguer, as we noted, realistically did not wish to alienate important masses of radical students and workers. As Vice-Secretary then Secretary-General, he felt a greater obligation to maintain the unity of the Party, while Amendola preferred the relative freedom his position of lesser responsibility allowed him. At the same time the only group within the PCI strong enough to seriously challenge Berlinguer's leadership was the right which looked to Amendola for political guidance. Berlinguer's major rival for the succession to Longo had been Giorgio Napolitano, a former protégé of Amendola. He needed the support, active or passive, of the internal left for his own 'centrist' leadership and hence sought to avoid alienating it unduly.

For these reasons Berlinguer chose to present the strategy of the historic compromise as something more than simply a first stage of progressive democracy. It was to involve the introduction of 'elements of socialism' as well, though these 'elements', such as social security and income redistribution, proved to be scarcely radical.[7] This innovation led to further confusion in the minds of many Communists, though it was in fact only a way of presenting an essentially reformist programme. Amendola's line, on the other hand, had the merits of clarity and coherence which Berlinguer's lacked.

The policy of the historic compromise, then, is substantially a continuation of the PCI's traditional strategy, the Popular Front adapted to Italian conditions as the *via italiana*; and, more precisely, of its dominant right-wing interpretation. The thesis of continuity is reinforced by the fact that the PCI, PSI and DC had already served together in the 'tripartite' cabinet coalition of 1945-7 which Togliatti thought might be the basis for the formation of a regime of 'progressive democracy'. The PCI, from 1972 in particular, sought to stress the 'popular' nature of the DC, the fact that it represented many workers and, especially, the majority of the 'middle strata' essential in the Popular Front alliance. (The fact that it may have also, perhaps even predominantly, represented the interests of large capital was not generally emphasised.) What was different about the historic compromise was its clear acceptance of the salvation of capitalism and bourgeois democracy more or less in their existing form as the prime goal of its programme (hence the possibility of an alliance with the whole DC), and its blurring of the previously clear outlines of the two stages, the 'democratic' and the 'socialist'.

The exclusion of the *Manifesto* group strengthened the hand of the right wing within the PCI: the campaign to expel the most active supporters of the journal and remove its sympathisers from positions of responsibility continued at least until the section congresses of the autumn of 1970. But perhaps the most spectacular sign of the PCI's new rightward course was the call issued by the *Direzione* on 8 July 1970 for a 'qualified revival of production', or, as Berlinguer put it, a 'carefully qualified expansion of production'.[8] This rightward shift may have been precipitated by the worrying results of the regional and provincial elections of the previous month (see p. 196 above). Berlinguer, in an article in *l'Unità* four days later, justified this re-definition of the Party's line. He recognised that the workers' struggles had disrupted the capitalist mechanism of accumulation, and that a crisis was imminent if they continued. But the PCI was not ready to take the offensive in this manner; its tradition prepared it for defence, rather than attack: 'We cannot forget that there are forces which consciously aim at further worsening the present state of affairs, in order to use the economic difficulties and disorder as a pretext to attempt reactionary, adventurist, rightist political operations.'[9] Therefore the Party had to do what it could to stave off a recession or a period of expansion fuelled by inflation. It must promote a revival of production, 'qualified' in the sense that it had to favour the truly productive forces in the country, not those that lived on para-sitism and rent.

Berlinguer sought to link the newly identified principal enemy, the parasitic strata, to the old antagonist, the monopolies:

> [The] great monopolistic groups . . . have founded their fortunes on a distorted process of economic development, on low wages, on compromise with the most backward and parasitic classes and strata, old and new, in society. This explains how the economic development of the country is restricted and deformed by the weight of a series of very extensive unproductive sectors, positions of parasitism and rent . . .[10]

At the same time he seemed to extend an offer of collaboration to the 'truly productive forces', the dynamic and productive sectors of Italian capitalism. He added two indications of the Party's immediate political objectives: first, he demanded 'a government that governs seriously'; in order to do so it would have to accept, in Parliament, 'the positive contribution of the left-wing opposition in the determination of national policy'. In effect, he was proposing that the government begin negotiating the content of major pieces of legislation with the PCI, which would in turn ensure their passage, even in the face of right-wing defections on the government benches – a sort of *régime d'assemblée*, in contrast to the classic model of cabinet government. This would be a first step towards an eventual government coalition with the DC. In the second place, he insisted that the governments of the newly created regions and other units of local government should not be mechanical copies of the national coalition formula (which was then centre-left). He saw these local administrations, especially the regions, as testing grounds for various forms of co-operation between the PCI and the DC that might later be introduced at the national level.

During the centre-left government led by Emilio Colombo from mid-1970 to January 1972, Berlinguer's objective of a role for the PCI in policy-making was partially achieved. The Party remained in opposition, but collaborated with the government on some important legislation. In November 1970 it agreed to set a limit to debate on the government's decree-law containing a series of major deflationary measures.[11] (A decree-law, in Italian procedure, becomes ineffective if not approved by Parliament within 60 days of its issuance by the cabinet.) Some important reforms were passed by Parliament only thanks to the abstention or support of the PCI: an agrarian reform law that set maximum and minimum rents for land held by tenants and sharecroppers, and an urban planning law that set a price ceiling for land expropriated for municipal use.[12] Without PCI support these laws would have been defeated by the defection of right-wing 'snipers' from the majority. While it would be an exaggeration to speak of the *de facto* inclusion of the PCI in the majority, the Party had certainly won an increased role in legislation. In December 1971 some Communists wished to reproduce this 'extended majority' in the presidential election by voting for the Christian Democratic candidate Fanfani. But pressure from the left, both inside and outside the Party, made this impossible.[13] The PCI did, however, accept the dissolution of Parliament in 1972 one year before the end of its term as a way of postponing the referendum on divorce, scheduled for that spring, which they feared would worsen relations with the DC.

At the XIII Congress of the PCI (Milan, 13-17 March 1972) Berlinguer enunciated for the first time his proposal of an historic compromise with the DC, though he did not yet use this expression. In his report he set the entry of the Communists into the government as the immediate, urgent goal of the Party's action, and emphasised that this would involve a coalition with the DC:

> In a country like Italy, a new perspective can be realized only by collaboration between the great movements of the people [*correnti popolari*] : communist, socialist and Catholic. The unity of the left is a necessary but not sufficient condition for this collaboration.
>
> The nature of Italian society and of the Italian state, its history, the weight of the intermediate strata, the pressing nature of great social questions which are also political and ideological (the women's question, the peasant question, the Southern question), the depth of the roots of fascism and therefore the very magnitude of the problems to be solved and dealt with make collaboration of this sort necessary.[14]

While Berlinguer spoke of the movement of unspecified 'Catholic currents' towards an agreement with the Communists and Socialists, his speech made it clear that the main objective was a 'change of line and political position' by the DC as such.[15] This Party was *the* political expression of the Catholic component of the 'people's movement'. The precise timing of this proposal, which was the logical development of the Party's position since July 1970 or earlier, may have been due to the fall of the Colombo government and its replacement by Andreotti's centrist coalition. Berlinguer felt the need to take counter-measures to block what appeared to be a dangerous shift to the right:

> Even within the elected assemblies [Parliament and local government] they have had to reckon with the force of our Party. Old barriers have fallen, crude prejudices against us have been abandoned; we have begun to set on foot a process of exploration of our respective positions. What is the real question which emerged at this point? The leadership of the DC reversed itself, when it understood that a new relationship with us meant, in reality, abandoning the policy of supporting the great industrial and financial concentrations . . .[16]

The *coup d'état* in Chile in September 1973 provided Berlinguer with the opportunity to work out even more clearly and forcefully his

strategic conception and its theoretical underpinnings.[17] The analysis
he offered of the Chilean *coup* and the lessons he drew from it for the
Italian Communists bear a striking resemblance to Togliatti's analysis
of the Fascist seizure of power in 1922. Berlinguer stated clearly that
the middle strata, between the bourgeoisie and the proletariat, hold the
balance of power in any modern society: 'The problem of alliances,
therefore, is the decisive problem of any revolution and any revolutionary policy . . .'[18] On the one hand, the right could not rule on the
basis of force alone, but requires some sort of consent, a mass base,
which the intermediate strata can provide. On the other, the proletariat,
Berlinguer affirmed, is a minority of the population in Italy and almost
every other capitalist country. (In other words, he considered only the
traditional manual working class as constituting the proletariat, and
viewed white-collar workers as part of the 'intermediate strata'.)
Therefore, 'It is completely evident . . . that whether the weight of
these [intermediate] social forces is shifted to the side of the working
class or against it is decisive for the success of democratic development
and of the advance towards socialism.'[19] Along with the intermediate
classes, Berlinguer grouped a series of other social categories — women,
youth, intellectuals and much of the population of the south — just as
Dimitrov, in his report to the VII Congress of the Comintern, had
referred to women and youth as such, independent of their class
position, as allies in the anti-fascist struggle.

   The object of the alliance policy of the working class, for
Berlinguer, had to be in the first place a defensive one — to prevent
the victory of fascism and reaction. While in Togliatti's and
Dimitrov's formulations of the 1930s a possible offensive role for the
Popular Front was adumbrated, Berlinguer, preoccupied with the threat
of a *coup* or a shift to the right, put to the fore their defensive aspect:

> The central political problem in Italy has been, and remains more
> than ever, precisely that of avoiding the creation of a stable and
> organic union between the centre and the right, of a broad front of
> the clerico-fascist type . . .[20]

He clearly implied that this was what had happened in Chile. To
prevent a similar outcome in Italy, he continued, it was necessary for
the PCI to unite not only with the other forces of the left, but also with
those of the centre — i.e. with the DC. Even a mathematical majority
of 51 per cent for the left, he argued, would not be enough to
guarantee the survival of a left-wing government:

This is why we speak not of a 'left-wing alternative' but of a
'democratic alternative', and that is of the political perspective
of a collaboration and an agreement between the popular forces
of communist and socialist inspiration and the popular forces of
Catholic inspiration, as well as formations representing other
democratic tendencies.[21]

He pointed out that the DC had a mass base among the intermediate
strata, as well as some following in the working class. From these
considerations he deduced the need for an 'historic compromise' with
the Christian Democrats to deal with the threat of fascism and the
other urgent problems of Italian society.

So central was the problem of alliances to Berlinguer that he stated
once more, forcefully, that it had to take precedence over that of
reforms — reforms should not be pursued if they alienated the potential
allies. These should be won over by offering them both material advantages and a different perspective, an alternative, progressive world-view.
Berlinguer justified the PCI's dread of an economic crisis, and its policy
of shunning any kind of *politique du pire*, with the need to retain the
consent of the allied middle strata. It was necessary 'not only to avoid
a collapse of the economy but also to guarantee, even in the critical
phases of transition to new social arrangements, the efficiency of the
economic process'.[22] Again, the influence of Togliatti's thought was
clear, as well as the implied criticism of the Chilean *Unidad Popular*
government's policy.

The adoption of the policy of 'historic compromise' by Berlinguer
and the leadership of the PCI was motivated, above all, by the right-
wing threat to democracy and the conquests of the working classes
which they perceived. While the period 1970-3 was also characterised
by other trends that pointed in the opposite direction, such as the
consolidation and further growth of the trade unions, the appearance
of a militant women's movement and the passage of a series of reforms,
the mental *habitus* and traditions of the PCI leaders prompted them to
see above all the dangers, rather than the opportunities, and to assess
the situation very pessimistically. The fear of a repetition of the trauma
of 1922 dominated their thought. The DC, they reasoned, at least kept
large masses of potential supporters of a fascist or authoritarian
solution within the fold of democracy. These forces, even if they could
not be won over as allies, could at least be neutralised by a suitably
moderate policy. For this reason they considered a split in the DC not
only highly unlikely, but probably undesirable. The DC, furthermore,

had demonstrated a remarkable capacity to survive as a united party
and maintain its electoral position, so much so that the PCI may well
have decided that only by an agreement with it could it begin to
implement any transformations in Italian society.[23]

Berlinguer and the other leaders of the PCI were so frightened by
the fascist upsurge, particularly in the south, that the criticism of
'parasitism' was relegated to the background of their analysis. It is
significantly absent from Berlinguer's articles on Chile. Much of the
support garnered by the MSI in the south was assumed to come from
these middle strata, angered by reforms such as the 1971 law on
agrarian rents. But as part of the potential mass base of fascism, these
groups too had to be appeased.[24] Hence, in the last analysis, the
boundaries of the traditional policy of alliances were not so much
redrawn as blurred during the early 1970s, as references to the
'monopolies' as the enemy became less and less frequent, while
attacks on 'parasitism' were not pressed home either.

A further element which determined at least the form in which
Berlinguer articulated the policy of historic compromise was the
thought of a small group of Communist intellectuals, previously
members of the Movement of Catholic Communists, a radical Catholic
group of the Resistance period (1943-5).[25] These included Franco
Rodano and Antonio Tatò, both close to Berlinguer himself. The classic
right in the PCI, represented by Amendola, was attached to lay liberal
traditions; it was prepared to collaborate in government with the DC
in the context of a Popular Front alliance, but saw this as a compromise
between groups with radically different ideological heritages. The
Catholic Communists, on the other hand, stressed the similarities
between Marxist and Catholic ideas: both involved a critique of liberal
individualism, of 'anarchism' as Rodano often put it, and an emphasis
on discipline and social, collective goals. The slogan of 'austerity',
later coined by Berlinguer, which expressed an attack on waste,
ostentatious wealth, luxury and the values of consumer society in
general, was in this context a potential point of contact between
Christian and Marxist ideas. This identification of a possible terrain of
convergence between socialist and Christian values also helped
Berlinguer to blur the distinction between the democratic and the
socialist stages. The Communist left had also favoured a direct appeal
to the working-class and progressive elements in the Catholic camp,
but it had aimed at winning them away from the DC rather than laying
the basis for an agreement with it. Nor did it share the Catholic
Communists' near-Stalinist attitude towards party discipline and

loathing of individualism. On this terrain there was more common ground between the Catholic Communists and Amendola.

By the end of 1973 the PCI's policy had shifted to the right in many respects. Just at this time, however, the course of political events turned decisively in the left's favour, making the pessimistic analysis which lay at the base of that policy outdated.

3. The Left Gathers Strength, 1973-6

While they led to the radicalisation of a fairly numerous vanguard, the student and worker movements of 1968-9 also influenced much larger numbers somewhat differently, by breaking down traditional modes of thought and making them available and open to reformist suggestions. These people who felt the impact of the movement in a delayed and attenuated way included those who lived outside the large cities, particularly in the south, and the older age groups, who may well have been influenced by their more politicised children in school or university. This shift to the left in people's attitudes was a long-term process, as the stagnation of the left-wing vote in the elections of 1970 and 1972 demonstrates. Nevertheless, it was real, and so significant that it can be called a crisis of the hegemony of Catholicism and traditional values. The whole period which began in 1968 and ended with the formation of the Andreotti government thanks to the abstention of the Communists in 1976, was one of 'organic crisis' in Gramsci's sense, in which

> social groups break with their traditional parties; that is, the traditional parties in that given organizational form, with those particular men who constitute them, represent them and direct them are no longer recognised by their class or class fraction as their own expression.[26]

The signs of this 'organic crisis' could be seen in many spheres of social life. Religious practice declined significantly: the number of persons attending mass at least once a week fell from 40 per cent to 30 per cent. The Italian women's movement became one of the most radical in the capitalist world, and many women (and men as well) began to question the backward, pre-bourgeois nature of family relationships. 'Contestation' swept through not only the schools and universities, but also other institutions such as the judiciary, the military, the civil service and the medical profession, all characterised by hierarchy and traditionalism. The ACLI (Italian Christian Workers' Association) and the CISL union confederation loosened their ties with the DC. Young voters, in particular, oriented themselves massively towards the parties of the left, while only a quarter or fewer of them supported the DC.[27]

The mass of people who broke with the Catholic bloc were not in the main revolutionary. They wished to see reforms that would end some of the longstanding distortions of Italian society: reforms of the health system, of public transport, of housing policy, of the public administration, all of which became more pressing as urbanisation proceeded. None of these problems had been seriously tackled during the centre-left period. Disillusioned with the DC and the PSI, people were prepared to turn to the Communists as the only force which could credibly promise to implement reform measures.

The increase in the price of oil at the end of 1973 brought about the end of the economic revival which was beginning to get underway after the recession of 1971-2. From early 1974 the Italian economy entered into crisis once again, a crisis characterised by unemployment and continuing inflation (10.5 per cent in 1973, 19.5 per cent in 1974). This interruption in growth no doubt contributed to the radicalisation of many Italians, and also reduced the amount of public funds available to the DC to support its network of clienteles.

Furthermore, the mid-1970s were punctuated by a series of spectacular revelations of bribery and corruption involving above all Christian Democratic politicians. Most notable of these was the Lockheed affair, which touched the President of the Republic himself, Giovanni Leone. The Communists, on the other hand, were unsullied by these allegations, and their claim to be 'the party whose hands are clean' no doubt weighed with many voters.

The Christian Democrats were led from July 1973 until mid-1975 by Amintore Fanfani as Secretary. Fanfani pursued a losing strategy of religious traditionalism ('integralism') and anti-communism. He threw his weight into the 1974 divorce referendum on the anti-divorce side and suffered a humiliating defeat. The Party's campaign for the 1975 regional elections, moreover, relied strongly on 'law and order' and the need to stem the Communist tide. Fanfani and the DC leadership misjudged completely the mood of the electorate.

These were the major factors which contributed to the spectacular electoral advance of the PCI in 1975-6. The most important of them was the organic crisis set off by the events of 1968-9, a crisis neither

promoted nor desired by the PCI. The Party was, however, able to
reap the electoral benefits of a movement which it had at first opposed,
then sought to brake and moderate. Certainly the policy of the
historic compromise also played a role, but a limited one, in attracting
new voters to the PCI. It reassured many that the Party had accepted
the rules of the democratic game, and other positions taken up by the
PCI as a consequence of that strategy, such as the abandonment of the
demand that Italy leave NATO, also contributed to that result.

The first sign of an inversion of the tendency of 1970-3 appeared
with the partial local elections of November 1973: while the left
remained stable or scored gains, the DC suffered losses of 1.8 per cent
to 3.6 per cent, and the MSI met with even more serious setbacks
(down 2.7 per cent in the major communes).[28] This hint that public
opinion was shifting was followed by the divorce referendum, which
the PCI had done everything it could to avoid, fearing not only
defeat but above all a split between Catholics and non-Catholics that
would make the historic compromise all the more difficult to achieve.
In the event, the divorce law of 1970 was approved by a surprising 59.1
per cent of the electorate (May 1974). This result showed that the
Church and traditionalism were clearly losing ground. The Sardinian
regional election of June 1974 confirmed the shift to the left: the DC
lost 2.6 per cent of the popular vote, the MSI 3.5 per cent, while the
left as a whole gained 4.1 per cent.[29]

In the same period the PCI's organisation strengthened itself
quantitatively and qualitatively, reversing the decline which had begun
in the mid-1950s and continued until the late 1960s.[30] The Party's
membership began to rise again, increasing by 20 per cent from
1,496,000 in 1969 to 1,798,000 by 1976. Furthermore, it became
more stable, as fewer members left the PCI each year while
recruitment increased. The Party's strength also became more evenly
distributed over the country. The PCI was more successful than before
in attracting young people: the percentage of its members who were
under 25 increased from 6.4 per cent in 1966 to 11.3 per cent in 1974.
At the same time the PCI's ability to finance itself with its members'
dues and subscriptions increased, and the number of sections and nuclei
(sections with under 20 members) began to grow again in the early
1970s. Much of this organisational growth seems to have occurred
not in the areas that were the centre of the 'movement' of 1968-9,
but in the peripheral regions that were touched by it only later and in
an indirect fashion; it reflected, that is, the 'long wave' of 1968.

The renewal of cadres within the PCI meant also the entry of a

large number of students and other young militants into the corps of
Party functionaries. By 1975, 35.3 per cent of the members of the
federal committees were 30 years old or younger; by 1977, fully 42.5
per cent of them were. And by 1975, 50.9 per cent of those federal
committee members active or at school were intellectuals and
white-collar workers, and a further 14.1 per cent were students, while
only 26.2 per cent were workers. These young cadres had a new
outlook on the Party's strategy and the historic compromise: many of
them had remained with the PCI during the student movement when all
the most radical students had joined the extraparliamentary groups.
They were therefore convinced adherents of the *via italiana* in its right-
wing interpretation. Furthermore, the PCI was able to offer more
possibilities of gainful employment with the creation of the regional
governments of 1970 and, especially, the conquest of so many
municipal governments in 1975. At the same time the weight of the
'middle strata' among the ordinary membership of the Party increased,
intellectuals and white-collar workers increasing from 3.3 per cent in
1968 to 6.9 per cent in 1974, students from 0.6 per cent to 1.9 per
cent, and shopkeepers from 2.0 per cent to 3.8 per cent. While these
figures remained relatively small compared to a constant 40 to 41 per
cent of workers, these groups are capable of exercising an influence
which goes far beyond their numerical weight.

While the movement of 1968-9 radicalised Italian society as a whole,
the cadre of the Party was in this way becoming more conservative.
Berlinguer and the group around him encouraged the entry and the
rapid promotion of many of these young cadres, so that they were
called jocularly 'the sons of Berlinguer'. Some were raised to the
position of federal secretary as early as the age of 24. This change in
the composition of the corps of functionaries was both a cause and an
effect of the policy of the Party leadership.

The left-wing advance of the years 1973-6 culminated in the regional
elections of 1975, in which the PCI advanced to 32 per cent of the
popular vote while the DC fell to 35.3 per cent, and the general election
of 1976, in which the PCI scored further gains, reaching 34.4 per cent
of the popular vote, but failing to 'pass' the DC, which recovered to a
level of 38.7 per cent. These unprecedented victories placed the Party
on the threshold of power, but also presented it and its strategy with
the most difficult test it had ever had to face.

Notes

1. J. Halevy, 'Evoluzione ed effetti degli scioperi negli ultimi vent'anni', *Quaderni di Rassegna Sindacale*, no. 38 (Sept.-Oct. 1972); see E. Reyneri, 'Comportamento di classe e nuovo ciclo di lotte', in A. Accornero (ed.), *Problemi del movimento sindacale in Italia 1943-1973* (Milan, 1976); and A. Pizzorno, E. Reyneri, M. Regini and I. Regalia, *Lotte operaie e sindacato: il ciclo 1968-1972 in Italia* (Bologna, 1978).

2. P. Weitz, 'The CGIL and the PCI: From Subordination to Independent Political Force' in D.L.M. Blackmer and S. Tarrow (eds.), *Communism in Italy and France* (Princeton, NJ, 1975).

3. Table in R. Convenevole, *Processo inflazionistico e redistribuzione del reddito* (Turin, 1977), p. 189.

4. Cf. V. Parlato (ed.), *Spazio e ruolo del riformismo* (Bologna, 1974), p. 15.

5. A. Cecchi (ed.), *Storia del PCI attraverso i congressi* (Rome, 1977), p. 200.

6. V^a *Conferenza*, resolutions.

7. E. Berlinguer, *La proposta comunista* (Turin, 1975), pp. 48-50.

8. *L'Unità*, 12 July 1970; reprinted in E. Berlinguer, *La questione comunista 1969-1975*, ed. A. Tatò (hereinafter *QC*), vol. I (Rome, 1975), pp. 200-4; cf. V. Parlato, 'La virata di Berlinguer', *Il Manifesto*, II, 7-8 (July-Aug. 1970).

9. *QC*, vol. I, p. 201.

10. Ibid.

11. See *Il Manifesto*, II, 10-11 (Oct.-Nov. 1970), p. 15.

12. Law no. 11 of 1971, amended as law no. 945 of 1972, and law no. 865 of 1971. See S. Hellman, 'The PCI's Alliance Strategy and the Case of the Middle Classes' in Blackmer and Tarrow (eds.), *Communism in Italy and France*, pp. 401-2; cf. G. Di Palma, 'Risposte parlamentari alla crisi del regime: un problema di istituzionalizzazione' in L. Graziano and S. Tarrow (eds.), *La crisi italiana*, vol. 2 (Turin, 1979).

13. The daily *Il Manifesto* could legitimately claim a large share of the credit for this result.

14. *QC*, vol. II (Rome, 1975), p. 415.

15. Ibid., pp. 417, 419.

16. Ibid., p. 416.

17. *Rinascita*, 28 Sept., 5 Oct. and 12 Oct. 1973, reprinted in E. Berlinguer *et al., I comunisti italiani e il Cile* (Rome, 1973).

18. *I comunisti italiani e il Cile*, p. 30.

19. Ibid., p. 31.

20. Ibid., p. 36.

21. Ibid., pp. 36-7.

22. Ibid., p. 35.

23. For this point see S. Hellman, 'The PCI in Transition: The Origins of the Historic Compromise', paper presented at the annual meeting of the American Political Science Association, Chicago, 1976; cf. also S. Hellman, 'The Longest Campaign: Communist Party Strategy and the Elections of 1976' in H. Penniman (ed.), *Italy at the Polls: The Parliamentary Elections of 1976* (Washington, DC, 1977), pp. 166-8.

24. See the excellent treatment of this point in Hellman, 'The PCI's Alliance Strategy'.

25. See C.F. Casula, *Cattolici, comunisti e sinistra cristiana (1938-1945)* (Bologna, 1976); and F. Rodano, *Sulla politica dei comunisti* (Turin, 1975), for a contemporary Catholic Communist viewpoint.

26. A. Gramsci, *Note sul Machiavelli* (Turin, 1966), p. 50; the same passage is translated in *Prison Notebooks*, p. 210.

27. G. Sani, 'Ricambio elettorale, mutamenti sociali e preferenze politiche',

in Graziano and Tarrow (eds.), *La crisi italiana*, vol. 1, p. 312.

28. *L'Unità*, 20 Nov. 1973.

29. *Rinascita*, 21 June 1974.

30. The following analysis is based on M. Barbagli and P. Corbetta, 'Partito e movimento: aspetti del rinnovamento nel PCI', *Inchiesta*, VIII, 31 (Jan.-Feb. 1978).

THE PARTY IN THE 'GOVERNMENTAL AREA':
CRISIS OF THE HISTORIC COMPROMISE

1. The PCI's Record in the Governmental Area

The situation following the election of 20 June 1976 presented both
opportunities and risks for the PCI. On the one hand, the political
conjuncture which had occasioned the formulation of the 'historic
compromise', the right-wing backlash and the fascist offensive of
1970-3, had changed radically. The MSI had suffered a setback at the
polls and right-wing terrorism was on the wane; it had been over-
shadowed by the enterprises of the Red Brigades and other extreme
left-wing armed groups. The economic situation, though, was still
preoccupying: production and growth had not yet recovered from the
1974 downturn and inflation, running at over 16 per cent, unemployment, particularly among the young, and the balance of payments
deficit all gave cause for serious concern. Taken together, these factors
indicated to the PCI leaders that the situation was still fraught with
danger, and that a conservative, authoritarian backlash, provoked by
the continuation of ultra-left terrorism and economic difficulties, was
still possible.

The 1976 general election also showed that the many forecasts of the
demise of the DC had been unfounded. Therefore the assumption that
the PCI could achieve governmental office only through an agreement
with the DC seemed all the more plausible. But the Catholic Party
had also undergone contradictory changes in its electorate and
personnel. Its leadership had moved to the left: in July 1975 Fanfani
was replaced as Secretary by Benigno Zaccagnini, a follower of Aldo
Moro, who was supported by the left and centre of the Party.
Zaccagnini abandoned the rigid anti-Communist stance adopted by
Fanfani in the 1975 election campaign, and, relying on his personal
reputation for honesty, attempted to eliminate some of the worst
corrupt practices in the Party and improve its public image. At the
same time, however, the DC's electorate became more conservative:
in 1976 it lost a part of its working-class votes to the left, while it
gained many middle-class electors from the minor lay parties, PLI,
PRI and PSDI, and from the MSI. Several candidates representing a new
right wing within the Party, such as Massimo De Carolis in Milan and

Luigi Rossi di Montelera in Turin, were elected with large numbers of preference votes. These deputies were opposed to any form of agreement with the Communists; declaring that they represented a liberal democratic, rather than a Christian democratic, ideological tradition, they reinforced the right-wing opposition to Zaccagnini and his group.

The DC, therefore, emerged from the 1976 election as a party less 'popular' and Catholic and more 'bourgeois' than before. However, its leadership was now more open to some form of parliamentary collaboration with the PCI. In any case, the new parliamentary situation made this a necessity. A centrist majority, including the DC and the minor parties of the centre and right (PRI, PSDI and PLI), was no longer possible, and the Socialist Party made clear that it would not enter any government or parliamentary majority that did not include the Communists; it did not wish to continue to bear the opprobrium of supporting the government while the Communists reaped the benefits of being the only major opposition party. Hence the DC could not form a cabinet without the support of the Communists, or at least their abstention. Secondly, the economic emergency made the collaboration of the trade unions in containing labour costs and increasing productivity essential for the reduction of the balance of payments deficit and of inflation within a capitalist framework. In order to encourage the unions to co-operate, the government had to be willing to discuss its policy with the PCI. Finally, some important Christian Democratic leaders, in particular Moro and Andreotti, had become convinced that the Cold War discrimination against the Communists was outdated and that they had demonstrated sufficient 'democratic maturity' to participate in some way in government, where their contribution could be useful for the solution of major economic problems. At the same time, however, the DC's ability to collaborate with the PCI was limited not only by its own right wing, but also by its nature as a clientelistic party which was threatened in its interests by any serious reform programme.[1] Moreover, a large part of the Party's social base was composed precisely of the 'parasitic' and petty-bourgeois groups who would inevitably be hurt by the reforms the PCI was demanding as the price of its co-operation. These middle strata were not to be reassured by the Communists' repeated promises to take their interests into account; the PCI itself did not always realise that certain of its reform proposals were incompatible with a policy of conciliating these groups. In addition, the wishes of the American government were well known, and it brought strong pressure to bear on the DC to keep the Communists out of the Italian cabinet.[2]

The PCI approached this new situation with the proposal of a 'government of democratic unity, of national solidarity' to deal with the economic emergency. Such a government would not be a government of 'historic compromise', though it could be the prelude to one. It would have a duration of a few years, perhaps one legislature (five years). Its programme would be dictated in large part by the exceptional nature of the situation, but, in Berlinguer's conception at any rate, even in this phase it would not be simply a programme of restoration of the capitalist mechanism of accumulation. In a major pre-congressional report to the Central Committee in December 1974, which served as a framework for the Party's action in the following years, he stated that, if the Communists' emergency programme were implemented,

> the new situation that would gradually be created – in relations of production, in income distribution, in consumption and people's way of life, and in the nature of power, through social reforms, the planning of important economic sectors, and the extension of democracy – would introduce in the organisation and general functioning of society some elements which are peculiar to socialism. It would not be a question, then, of setting a socialist society as a goal for the near future, because some basic conditions, both internal and international, for it are lacking, but of implementing measures and guide-lines that are in some respects of a socialist type.[3]

The main elements of this emergency programme, however, were economic planning, a more just distribution of income, and an equitable sharing of the sacrifices necessary to deal with the crisis.[4] At this point he significantly enough felt it necessary to defend himself from the charge that this approach was too *radical*. First, he dealt with the argument that the emergency situation left no leeway for social reforms. He replied that it was impossible to separate the measures necessary to combat the emergency from the social reforms the country needed; the situation could be dealt with only by introducing profound social transformations. A policy which did separate these two types of measures, both in substance and in time, would be a policy of 'two moments' (*due tempi*) like that pursued by the centre-left governments – with the result that social reforms were put off indefinitely.[5] Second, he asked if talking about measures of a socialist type was not in contrast with the policy of alliances, and replied that other, non-proletarian groups could also support these proposals for their own reasons, simply because they saw them as necessary for overcoming the crisis of the country.[6] He repeated that the PCI did not contemplate any extension of the public sector of the economy. Both of these objections had come and were to come from the PCI right wing.

Berlinguer believed, unlike the right, that the economic crisis could be used positively by the left.[7] It was not, in his view, a classic crisis of capitalism which would result in a breakdown of the system. It had been caused by the new power of the Third World (particularly the oil-producing countries) and the socialist states on the one hand, and by the new combativity of the Western working class on the other. The monopolies could not respond to the new demand from workers by increasing production, and therefore induced an inflationary spiral. This new type of crisis, Berlinguer argued, was not simply cyclical, but economic, political and cultural. It could lead to a fascist solution, but it also held opportunities for the working-class movement: in dealing with the emergency situation created by the crisis, new, socialist values and policies could be introduced. If, for example, the oil crisis and the balance of payments deficit required sacrifices from Italians, these should fall largely on the well-to-do, who should be forced to reduce their superfluous, luxury consumption. The crisis would be solved by means of planning and redistribution of income — indeed it could be solved only in this way.

This was the origin of the slogan of 'austerity', which Berlinguer was to launch in a speech in January 1977.[8] The sacrifices necessary to avoid economic collapse had to be made in such a way as to eliminate waste, parasitism, privileges and consumeristic excesses, as well as clientelism, which drained the public purse. A profound change in people's habits was necessary. This slogan had an unenthusiastic reception among the rank and file of the Party and among its electorate, who did not appreciate its progressive, 'socialist', aspect. It was vitiated by the PCI's too acritical acceptance of the analysis of the economic crisis and the solutions proposed by more conservative bourgeois economists such as Ugo La Malfa, leader of the Republican Party, who demanded severe deflationary measures and the reduction of the state deficit in spite of the possible consequences for employment and production. This analysis was shared by both Amendola and Berlinguer; the major difference between them was Berlinguer's attempt to give a 'socialist-type' content to the policy of austerity.

A second weakness of the PCI's position was its failure to present more specific proposals in the field of economic policy. The Party spoke in general of the need for planning, austerity, income redistribution and a new model of development, but had few detailed demands to place before the other parties at the bargaining table. In September 1975 Napolitano had launched the idea of a medium-term plan (*progetto a medio termine*) for the Italian economy,[9] but nothing was done about it until October 1976 when Berlinguer proposed that one be drawn up in order to counter charges that the PCI was supporting a policy of 'two moments'. The plan, which was published in July 1977 as a text for discussion,[10] was intended to provide a justification for the sacrifices which the workers, hurt by the deflationary policies of the government, were being asked to bear, by linking them with the longer-term goals of reform and an advance towards socialism. Although it appeared after the Party had begun the experiment of parliamentary collaboration with the Christian Democrats, the proposed plan is a good indication of the PCI's more general goals in this period. Only the right wing of the Party was lukewarm to the idea of the plan; they laid so much emphasis on the need to deal with the emergency situation that they opposed demanding social reforms as a *quid pro quo* for the workers' sacrifices.

The plan itself, however, was scarcely likely to inspire the PCI's followers or spur them on to further sacrifices. It contained no trace of the old two-stage, anti-monopoly strategy; its reform measures were aimed more at creating a modern, efficient capitalist system on North European lines by penalising, if anyone, the parasitic groups, though the references to these strata were quite vague. While small, medium and co-operative industry was to be encouraged, no anti-monopolistic measures were contemplated. The state would simply negotiate with large private firms to ensure that their plans were in harmony with the interests of the collectivity: 'The multi-national enterprises can also find a place for themselves in a new industrial policy.'[11] Peasant farming was to be promoted, but the capitalist farm would have a role as well.[12]

Instead of the struggle against the monopolies, the medium-term plan set itself as a goal the affirmation of a series of values and guidelines: work, and specifically productive work, was defined as a fundamental value, and hence the elimination of unemployment was made a fundamental objective. Other values to be promoted included education and culture, liberty and equality, a more humane and sociable life, international co-operation and disarmament. Equality involved equality between men and women, between north and south, and between classes — hence the need for some measure of income redistribution.[13]

These values, a much edulcorated version of Berlinguer's 'austerity' proposals, were adopted as guidelines without any consideration of whether they could be realised under capitalism or of their relationship to the process of transition to socialism. There was little evidence either, in the detailed proposals made in the programme, of a drastic reorientation of production towards new consumption patterns and lifestyles: their thrust was mostly towards creating employment and dealing with the balance of payments deficit.

The plan, therefore, aimed to expand employment and the productive capacity of the country while at the same time reducing, rather than aggravating, the rate of inflation and the balance of payments deficit. It also refused to contemplate any solutions that would isolate Italy from the free international market (e.g. import quotas). It tried to avoid the potential contradiction between growth and the control of inflation by a series of qualitative, structural changes in the Italian economy that would increase its productivity and competitiveness. Many of these structural changes involved no more than bringing Italy up to the Northern European standard of efficiency: the elimination of tax evasion, a universal national health service, the elimination of waste in the public sector, an end to clandestine employment (*lavoro nero*) and so forth. These reforms, if implemented, would be major breakthroughs, and powerful interests would oppose them, but none of them was in principle incompatible with the persistence of the capitalist social and economic framework. It is worth noting too that the plan advocated no expansion of the public sector of the economy, a substantial reduction of the government deficit, a reduction of transfer payments to individuals and of waste in the social security system, and a temporary suspension of government hiring. These measures were justified with the argument that the DC had used the public sector in order to build up a network of clienteles; it had therefore become an area of waste and inefficiency in the national economy.

Besides specifying some of the objectives of economic planning, the PCI proposal made it clear that planning decisions would be made, in the last analysis, by the elected assemblies (national and local), and that the participation of the workers in the factories was additional and supplementary to this primary role of the organs of representative democracy.[14] Instead of co-management, as practised in West Germany and elsewhere, the PCI's plan suggested that workers' participation at the factory level could take the form of negotiated agreements with management on particular investment and production plans. It considered that it was premature to sanction by law the right to information about the state of the firm which some workers had gained in the 1976 contracts.

The medium-term plan, then, was directed at dealing with the emergency situation which the Italian economy faced in 1976-7, and particularly with unemployment and the balance of payments deficit. It gave prior importance to these problems rather than to inflation, Amendola's *bête noire*. Its claim to embody 'elements of socialism'[15] was largely spurious; this was chiefly a justification for its reform proposals, none of which involved any real break with the capitalist system. The reduction of unemployment would, it is true, strengthen the working-class movement and end the dangerous divisions between employed and unemployed, and between those employed in the primary and the secondary labour markets. And the balance of payments deficit left Italy open to foreign pressure. Similarly, the reduction of parasitism and clientelism would seriously weaken the forces opposed to socialism in Italy. In this sense the proposals of the medium-term plan could be justified as 'structural reforms'. However, they did not constitute part of a more general plan or strategy which foresaw using these conquests to press on to further gains; instead, they were meant to respond to an emergency which the Party leadership thought could lead to an economic collapse and an authoritarian backlash.

These were the PCI's policy aims in the period 1976-9. But the Party was also concerned to use the new situation in order to gain full legitimacy as a democratic party which could take part in government on the same basis as the others. This was an aim of the changes in the Party's line and ideology over the previous forty years. For this reason the PCI had indicated at the XIII Congress that it no longer favoured unilateral Italian withdrawal from NATO but rather a simultaneous dissolution of both military blocs in Europe. The PCI pursued not only legitimacy but also an agreement with the Christian Democrats for its own sake, and was prepared to sacrifice some policy demands to this goal. This was in keeping with the policy of the historic compromise, which saw the prevention of the formation of a centre-right bloc as an end in itself. These two factors often outweighed policy considerations in the PCI's negotiations with the other parties.

After the governmental crisis which followed the 1976 election, Giulio Andreotti eventually formed an all-Christian Democratic cabinet, which was supported in Parliament by the votes of the DC alone but enjoyed the abstention of the Communists, Socialists, Republicans, Social Democrats and Liberals. In return for this support, which still

fell short of entry into the governmental majority, the PCI was granted
a measure of recognition as a legitimate democratic party: it received
the speakership of the Chamber of Deputies, which went to Pietro
Ingrao, and the chairmanships of several parliamentary committees
(seven altogether in both the Chamber and the Senate). Andreotti also
included numerous reform proposals in his programme, though he had,
formally speaking, drawn it up independently rather than negotiated
its contents with the abstaining parties. He made general promises to
reduce the budget deficit, to contain the balance of payments deficit,
to lower inflation without 'punishing' production, to develop an
industrial policy and to introduce special measures to reduce youth
unemployment.[16] Many specific reforms were promised: a fair rent
law would be presented by the following October, and a university
reform bill, a new code of criminal procedure, a reform of the secret
services and the secrecy laws, and a bill permitting police unionisation
were also to be introduced. Andreotti further undertook to struggle
against tax evasion, to re-present the bill creating a national health
service which had died with dissolution, and to use the powers
delegated by Parliament to devolve administration responsibilities to
the regions. The programme was sufficient to satisfy the PCI, though
many aspects of it were vague and the Communists themselves
expressed doubts about Andreotti's desire or ability to fulfil some of
his promises.

Andreotti's governments enjoyed direct or indirect Communist
support from August 1976 to January 1979; in these two-and-a-half
years their record was decidedly mixed. The serious economic crisis of
mid- and late 1976, when the balance of payments deficit was large
and the value of the lira was in danger of collapsing on world markets,
was successfully, if temporarily, overcome: by 1979, the balance of
payments was showing a surplus on current account of 4.3 trillion lire
(US $5.3 billion) and the lira had regained lost ground *vis-à-vis* the
dollar and was notably stable on the currency markets. Similarly,
Italy's economic growth rate, compared to that of the other major
industrialised nations, was good: in 1979 it stood at 5 per cent, second
only to Japan's. However, inflation had not been tamed, but simply
stabilised for a time at a rate of some 13 to 15 per cent annually, the
government deficit was still high, and unemployment, particularly
among youth, remained an acute social problem. While a débâcle
had been avoided, the evils of inflation and unemployment persisted,
and the PCI feared that these could, over a longer period, have political
consequences similar to those of an economic crisis, dividing the masses

of the people and driving many, particularly the middle strata, to the right.

Furthermore, the crisis had been overcome by the imposition of sacrifices on the entire population, especially the working class, with very few concessions to the PCI's conception of 'austerity'. In October 1976, in the face of the serious threat to the lira, the government introduced a classic package of deflationary measures: a large number of administered prices were raised (gasoline and diesel fuel, heating oil, natural gas, tobacco, fertilisers, postal services and rail fares) and the interest rate was increased by 3 per cent. Furthermore, all increases in pay resulting from the operation of the cost-of-living escalator (*scala mobile*) for workers earning over 8 million lire annually (*c.* US $9,500) and half of the increases for those earning between 6 and 8 million were to be paid in the form of Treasury bonds for a period of 18 months. The government also abolished five statutory holidays. The PCI reacted by demanding more protection against inflation for the lowest paid, and in particular measures to differentiate the impact of the higher prices on different income groups, but it declared itself prepared to discuss the measures in Parliament in an attempt to reach an agreement on amendments. In the end it allowed them to pass with few changes.

The reforming record of the Andreotti governments was considerably worse than their performance in the field of economic management, and even less satisfactory from the point of view of the PCI. The promise of an industrial policy, with detailed plans for various sectors of the economy, resulted in the slow drafting of a three-year plan which, when it was finally presented in 1979, was judged unsatisfactory by almost all the political parties. An industrial reconversion law (no. 675), providing for subsidies to firms engaged in major restructuring, was passed in 1977, but by June 1980 none of these funds had yet reached the companies. A university reform was not passed by Parliament during the legislature. The new code of criminal procedure was not presented by the government. Another group of reforms were passed, but their effects were not those the Communists had hoped. A law creating special lists of young job-seekers was passed (law no. 285), and some 600,000 enrolled in the lists, but very few jobs or apprenticeships were found for them. A fair rent law (*equo canone*) was passed in July 1978, but, while it eliminated the jungle of frozen rents, some of them ridiculously low, it increased the total amount of rent paid by tenants and, above all, prompted landlords to withdraw their apartments from the market or seek to evade the law. These frustrated reforms were extremely damaging to the PCI, which had championed them. They had raised many hopes, only to disappoint them. At the same time the fair rent law and the 'Bucalossi law' of 1977 on the expropriation of urban land infuriated the landlords as well. In spite of a great deal of discussion, no more than the groundwork for a struggle against tax evasion was laid. Only the project for a national health service, of the major measures promised by Andreotti in August 1976, was carried through; the service actually began to operate in January 1980.

Though these reforms were part of the government's programme, which, after June 1977, was negotiated with the Communists and other parties supporting the government or abstaining, they were nevertheless the object of long debate and hard bargaining when they were presented to Parliament. Right-wing DC deputies and senators took advantage of the debates to obstruct, denature or water down these measures as much as possible, and, in a climate of assembly rule, they were often successful. One institutional reform encountered resistance from the DC as a whole: the devolution of certain powers, particularly over welfare and public assistance, to the regions, which a law of 1975 (no. 382) had delegated to the government to carry out. As many of the existing welfare institutions were important sources of patronage for the DC (many were connected with the Church), the government itself modified the recommendations of a parliamentary committee in order to limit the devolution as much as possible (July 1977). Here not only the interests of the DC's supporters, but those of the Party itself, were at stake.

In the period 1976-9 the issue of terrorism became increasingly pressing, as the left-wing Red Brigades intensified their activities. The PCI's position was not only one of firm opposition to terrorist violence; it also took the lead in demanding more vigorous action by the government to combat it. After the Moro kidnapping it took the firmest stand of any party against negotiations with the Red Brigade abductors. The Party adopted this position because it believed it could not risk the danger of being associated in any way by public opinion with terrorists who also claimed to be Marxists, and because it did not wish to let the issue divide it from the Christian Democrats. At the same time it was able to accuse the groups to its left of being 'soft' on terrorism. The PCI continued to propose reforms in the administration of justice and the organisation of the police forces to combat terrorism, but the thrust of these proposals was blunted by its acceptance of the purely repressive measures which the government introduced instead.

For instance, in 1978 the Communists opposed the abrogation of the Reale law of 1975 (no. 152), which extended the powers of the police and instituted more severe penalties for a series of crimes. (A referendum on its repeal was held in June 1978 after the Radical Party had collected over 500,000 signatures against the law.) They preferred instead to propose a series of amendments in Parliament, even though they had voted against the law in 1975. The reform of the secret services, passed by Parliament in October 1977, was to remain in many respects a dead letter because of the introduction of various forms of emergency legislation aimed at combating terrorism.

It is ironic that the PCI's support for repressive measures against terrorism has seldom been used as an argument by those right-wing pundits who doubt the sincerity of the Party's 'conversion' to Western democratic values. Most of these critics are themselves in favour of increasing the powers of the state in the fight against terrorism. Its policy in this field shows that the PCI's commitment to democratic procedures and civil liberties of the Western type is a function of, and subordinate to, its policy of alliances. (This is not to say that its democratic commitment is any less than that of the other Italian parties.)

On the other hand, the Andreotti government did allow the PCI a greater share of influence and power in some state and para-state bodies. For example, the Communists were given seats on the board of directors of the state radio and television network (RAI) as part of the reform of the network embodied in a 1975 law. Hiring of Communists by the RAI was now permitted, and even promoted. But these concessions did not imply the giving up of any decisive powers; they involved only the granting of minority votes and a small share of the patronage. They were intended more to satisfy the Communists' desire for legitimacy and induce them to continue to work together with the DC than as a sign that the government was prepared to concede them a significant share of power.

2. The Reaction of the Party and the Re-emergence of Policy Divisions

The first negative reactions to the PCI's indirect support for the Andreotti government were not slow in coming from the rank and file. The line of the historic compromise had been accepted by the majority of the Party membership, but most of them viewed it as a tactic through which the Party would eventually come to power in a left-wing coalition, or even alone. In a survey carried out in an Emilian federation in 1977-8, 67 per cent of the PCI members interviewed accepted the policy of the historic compromise, but viewed it as a tactic; another 20 per cent did not accept it at all, while only 13 per cent accepted it *and* saw it as a long-term strategy.[17] (Only these last had the same position as the Party leadership.) Given these attitudes, many members of the Party protested when the government introduced the deflationary measures of October 1976 with only a limited reaction from the PCI.

This discontent was expressed at the Central Committee meeting of 18-21 October. While some members called for tangible signs that the deflationary measures would be accompanied by reforms, Amendola defended the need for sacrifices above all: ending inflation had to be the main aim, to which all else had to be subordinated, because it divided the people and could lead to crisis, chaos and the end of democracy. He criticised the government's measures 'not only because they are contradictory and not equitable, but above all because they are insufficient'.[18] He further suggested that it was not necessary to insist that reforms and measures to promote economic growth be introduced at the same time as the anti-inflationary package. The working class, he noted, had not suffered as much from the crisis as some supposed: its real income had not fallen, there was full employment in many areas of the country, foreign labour was even being imported. The implication was that the workers could afford to make sacrifices; indeed, their wage gains over the previous several years were in part responsible for the crisis.

Amendola's position was criticised from almost all quarters – Longo, Terracini, Libertini and Minucci all pointed out that his line meant accepting a policy of 'two moments', and that the Party should, on the contrary, demand immediate measures of reform and stimuli to economic growth in return for the sacrifices that were being asked of the workers. All were particularly concerned that the Party should not appear to the masses to be supporting the existing capitalist system. Terracini was especially severe: he proposed to make the well-off pay for austerity by means of an extraordinary wealth tax. He objected to the argument, used by others in the Central Committee, that the fall of the Andreotti government would have dire consequences and only help the right. Berlinguer, in his reply, did not embrace Amendola's line outright, but the sense of his remarks, and the policy followed by the Party in practice, was more in harmony with the position of the leader of the right than with that of his critics. On the one hand Berlinguer denied that guarantees of reforms in return for sacrifices were needed from the other parties, since these guarantees could come only from the struggle of the PCI itself; and on the other he warned of overemphasising the dangers to the Party's relations with the masses that arise from the coherent pursuit of its policy of alliances and of the historic compromise.[19]

In spite of this authoritative admonition, the base of the Party became more and more alarmed as Andreotti's 'government of non-non-confidence' continued in office. In the spring of 1977 a new outbreak of student unrest, chaotic and anarchic in many of its manifestations, but with a violent fringe composed of members of 'Workers' Autonomy' (*Autonomia operaia*), provoked a complete break between the PCI and many members of the youngest generations.[20] Luciano Lama, the Communist Secretary-General of the CGIL, was shouted down by a minority of 'autonomous' students at the University of Rome. Bologna was one of the centres of the movement, and the Bolognese PCI was one of its major targets. The students considered the PCI a 'party of the regime' like the others. The PCI responded in kind, supporting the actions of the police against the students, and labelling them 'fascists' in *l'Unità*.

Another sign that the PCI was losing popular support came from the partial local elections of 17-18 April 1977. In the larger communes that voted (159,000 voters) it received only 28.8 per cent of the vote, compared with 38.3 per cent in 1976. Losses were particularly serious in the south: at Castellammare di Stabia the PCI fell from 45.8 per cent to 33 per cent.[21] Evidently many who had voted Communist had expected quick changes and reforms after the 1976 election, and were disappointed when this did not occur. The Christian Democrats had also taken advantage of their role as the opposition in many communes newly conquered by the left to capitalise on discontent with the economic situation.

These ominous signs, and the government's slowness in implementing its programme, led the PCI to demand a greater share in the formulation and monitoring of policy. At the end of June the parties which supported the government or abstained to allow its survival reached a programmatic agreement which contained many of the points in Andreotti's original programme and many others contained in the PCI's medium-term plan.[22] This new agreement was not sufficient, however, to calm the PCI's base. On 2 December 1977 the metalworkers' union called a national strike to protest against the government's economic policy. This implied criticism of the PCI itself forced the leadership to open a governmental crisis. After long negotiations the crisis was solved with the entry of the PCI into the majority for the first time since 1947. Aldo Moro, Chairman of the DC, promised the Communists that, after nine months, the question of their direct participation in the cabinet could be reopened.[23] However, there were signs that some sectors of the DC were already preparing to end the experiment of governing with the Communists before the end of the year.[24] The vote of confidence in the new government (16 March 1978) was hastened by the news of the kidnapping of Moro by the Red Brigades. Andreotti's programme on this occasion included many of the measures proposed in 1976 and 1977, but some of them were more precise in form: a three-year plan for industrial development would be drawn up, and the public sector deficit would be reduced from 29 to 24 trillion lire in 1978. The police force would be demilitarised and allowed to form a union unaffiliated with the trade-union confederations. Finally, he promised to amend the laws which the Radical Party proposed to abrogate by popular vote, thus forestalling three of the four referenda which were to be held in the following June. (In the end the amendments to the Reale law were not passed, so that the referendum on this measure took place.)

Entry into the majority did nothing to revive the PCI's declining popularity. In the local elections of 14-15 May 1978 it received 26.5 per cent of the popular vote as opposed to 35.6 per cent in 1976 in the communes with over 5,000 inhabitants (*c.* two million voters). Again, the Party's worst losses were in the south. The referenda on the Reale law and on the 1974 law on the state financing of political parties were another serious warning to the PCI: while the Party, along with the DC and all the other major parties, urged its supporters to vote against the abrogation of the two laws, and waged an extremely strident and at times frankly dishonest campaign to convince them of the dire consequences of their repeal, the share of votes for abrogation was much higher than expected (43.7 per cent against state financing and 23.3 per cent against the Reale law). Many of the PCI's most active members and some of its working-class base had grave reservations about the Party's stand on these two questions, and the referendum campaign alienated many of them.[25]

In the face of these and other negative signs, and of the government's failure to act swiftly on the programme agreed by the majority as a whole, the PCI leadership opened a government crisis by withdrawing

from the majority in January 1979. This was precisely nine months
after the formation of the government, the time Moro had set down
before the Communists' participation in the cabinet could be
reconsidered. Berlinguer cited the delays in implementing the reform
of the university, the police, pensions, agrarian contracts, the RAI-TV
and newspaper publishing, and in revising the Reale law: 'In these and
in other fields we have been confronted with exhausting procedures,
dilatory tactics, disconcerting objections to decisions that had been
already unanimously reached, back-tracking and manoeuvres of every
type.'[26] He also reproved the DC for the government's failure to
control public expenditure and combat tax evasion, and for its
tardiness in introducing an industrial reconversion plan, an energy plan
and measures to promote youth employment. Furthermore, the other
parties of the majority had not been consulted in the government's
decision to join the European Monetary System in December 1978, a
major step which made further devaluation of the lira to stimulate
exports and growth much more difficult. Nor had the PCI been
consulted about the nomination of new managing personnel to various
public bodies.

In the long crisis which ensued the other parties failed to offer the
PCI the cabinet positions which it demanded as the price of its support.
Finally, Andreotti formed a minority government which was defeated
in Parliament, and new elections were called for 3-4 June 1979. The
PCI gained little from its recent return to the opposition, falling from
34.4 per cent to 30.4 per cent of the popular vote. It lost many voters,
almost all of whom seem to have been working-class, and it failed to
gain the massive support among new voters which it had had in 1976.[27]
On the other hand, the DC failed to increase its share of the popular
vote, and the left as a whole lost only marginally, falling from 46.6
per cent to 45.8 per cent. Hence the parliamentary situation was
essentially the same as in 1976; no majority was possible without one
of the PSI or PCI. In the European elections held a week later, the
PCI declined further to 29.6 per cent of the popular vote.

These electoral results were a most convincing objective critique of
the strategy of the historic compromise. Nevertheless, the reaction
within the Party was slow. In particular, the left did not seize the
occasion to criticise Berlinguer and his line. At the Central Committee
meeting of 3-6 July Berlinguer reasserted the validity of the historic
compromise and sought to minimise the significance of the losses
suffered: it would be social-democratic, he said, to subordinate the
Party's line to electoral considerations.[28] The line itself had been

correct, the way in which it was applied had often been wrong. Many
criticisms of the Party leadership emerged during the meeting — that
it had ignored the danger signals that the PCI's links to the masses
were being weakened (Novelli), that the line had obfuscated the leaders'
view of reality (Ferrero), that a policy of 'two moments' had been
followed (Napolitano), that the slogan of austerity should be abandoned
(Terzi) — and several speakers proposed that more emphasis be put
on unity with the PSI and smaller left parties, but Ingrao's speech was
not openly critical of the line of the Secretary-General. And Berlinguer
in his reply explicitly rejected the notion of a left-wing alternative
as impracticable, repeating the need to pursue the historic compromise.
If the DC were excluded from the government, he repeated in an
interview with a German weekly, there would be a danger of a *coup
d'état*, as the Chilean experience had taught.[29]

In an important article which appeared at the end of the summer,[30]
Berlinguer reformulated the policy of historic compromise with some
new arguments in its favour. Italian capitalism was not headed for a
catastrophic crisis in the quantitative sense, but the quality of the
economic development it had generated was creating a crisis of another
type. A qualitative change in the structure of production and
consumption (e.g. with respect to energy consumption) was necessary
to deal with the current crisis of development, and around this change
the historic compromise could be realised. Berlinguer here defended
the proposal of an historic compromise with arguments typical of the
Communist left of the 1960s, and reasserted his belief that the crisis
could be used positively by the working-class movement.

Amendola, on the other hand, continued to see the economic crisis
of capitalism, understood in a more traditional way, as the central
feature of the current situation. Given the left's failure to take
advantage of the election defeat, his line was the major alternative to
Berlinguer's within the Party. In an article published in November
1979,[31] he repeated his conviction that inflation was the central
problem; it could lead to social chaos and eventually to fascism. At the
same time strikes in the public services, the high-handed methods used
by some strikers (e.g. road-blocks in city streets) and terrorism risked
alienating many Italians (especially the middle strata) from the left.
Amendola recalled that in 1919-20 the violent methods of some
unions, especially in the Emilian and Apulian countryside, had
contributed to the defeat of the left and the rise of fascism. Public
service strikes had played into the hands of the Fascists, who at least
'made the trains run on time'. The Party and the unions, he argued, had

to take a much clearer and more vigorous stand against all forms of violent struggle. They should favour an increase in productivity and the limitation of the *scala mobile*, the two most effective steps to fighting inflation. He pointed out that the workers had not suffered a reduction in real income and that many of the unemployed were young graduates who refused to accept manual work. Hence the working class was able to bear the sacrifices necessary to defeat inflation. He also expressed his opposition to 'levelling' wage demands, to absenteeism in the factories and to government subsidies to keep failing industries alive. The enemy, he said, was the 'party of inflation', composed of those businessmen who wanted public subsidies, or who stood to gain by the depreciation of their debts to financial institutions, who were supported by other forces which, with their 'corporative demands', fuelled the inflationary spiral.[32]

Amendola's line was more defensive than Berlinguer's, though in practice the two positions were quite close. Amendola accused Berlinguer and the trade-union leadership of insufficient vigour and energy in implementing a policy on whose basic lines both sides agreed: Berlinguer too was above all concerned about the danger of a crisis which could lead to an authoritarian backlash, and supported the government's anti-inflationary measures and the struggle against terrorism. He wished, however, to give a more 'advanced' ideological justification of the Party's action. And, for Amendola, he was too tolerant of the internal left. The old leader's reference to the Leninist and Gramscian role of the Party as a hegemonic force with respect to the various corporative interests and his call to put an end to ambiguous unanimity within the Party showed that he favoured a stronger line *vis-à-vis* any dissidents.

By the end of 1979, in spite of the objective conditions, in particular the electoral defeat and the failure of the hopes of 1976-9, the line of the PCI had not changed. The Party was still prepared for governmental collaboration with the DC, though determined to insist on better conditions than had been offered during the previous legislature. The internal left had not given battle, and it did not consider it had the force within the Party to win. The only possible alternative to Berlinguer's line seemed to be that offered by the right. A coalition between the left and some elements of the right (e.g. Napolitano) could conceivably form around a platform which laid greater stress on the contents of a reform programme as opposed to political alliances, and which emphasised the need for left-wing unity. But the likelihood of such an alternative seemed remote. The internal left, weakened by the battles of the 1960s, could not overcome the obstacles posed by democratic centralism, the weight of the ideology of the Popular Front and the more conservative outlook of the cadres recruited in the 1970s. The PCI was likely to continue to pursue the historic compromise, the latest version of the Popular Front strategy first formulated in 1935.

Notes

1. See A.S. Zuckerman, *The Politics of Faction: Christian Democratic Rule in Italy* (New Haven and London, 1979).
2. G. Hodgson, 'The US Response' in P. Filo della Torre, E. Mortimer and J. Story (eds.), *Eurocommunism: Myth or Reality?* (Harmondsworth, 1979).
3. E. Berlinguer, *La proposta comunista* (Turin, 1975), pp. 49-50.
4. Ibid., p. 48.
5. Ibid., pp. 50, 65.
6. Ibid., pp. 50-1.
7. Ibid., p. 8.
8. Reprinted in E. Berlinguer, *Austerità occasione per trasformare l'Italia* (Rome, 1977).
9. *Rinascita*, 26 Sept. 1975.
10. *Proposta di progetto a medio termine*, introduced by G. Napolitano (Rome, 1977).
11. Ibid., p. 73.
12. Ibid., p. 63.
13. Ibid., pp. 26-42.
14. Ibid., pp. 98-100.
15. Ibid., p. 19.
16. *L'Unità*, 5 Aug. 1976; complete text in *Il Popolo*, 5 Aug. 1976.
17. M. Barbagli and P. Corbetta, 'Una tattica e due strategie' in M. Barbagli, P. Corbetta and S. Sechi, *Dentro il PCI* (Bologna, 1979), pp. 46-7.
18. *L'Unità*, 20 Oct. 1976.
19. Ibid., 22 Oct. 1976.
20. See 'La Nostra Assemblea' in *Le radici di una rivolta* (Milan, 1977), on the Rome student movement; and S. Sechi, *La pelle di zigrino* (Bologna, 1980), on Bologna.
21. *L'Unità*, 19 Apr. 1977.
22. See text in ibid., 30 June 1977.
23. *La Repubblica*, 13 Jan. 1980.
24. *L'Unità*, 15 Mar. 1978; Andreotti's programme is in ibid., 17 Mar. 1978.
25. See F. Bertinotti, 'Anche a Torino il voto parla di noi', *Rinascita*, 23 June 1978; and R. Mannheimer, 'Un'analisi territoriale del calo comunista', *Il Mulino*, no. 265 (Sept.-Oct. 1979), pp. 705-7.
26. *L'Unità*, 27 Jan. 1979.
27. P. Corbetta, 'Novità e incertezze nel voto del 3 giugno: analisi dei flussi elettorali', *Il Mulino*, no. 265 (Sept.-Oct. 1979).
28. *L'Unità*, 4 July 1979.
29. *Stern*, 16 Aug. 1979, p. 133.
30. 'Il compromesso nella fase attuale', *Rinascita*, 24 Aug. 1979.
31. 'Interrogativi sul "caso" Fiat', ibid., 9 Nov. 1979.
32. 'I sacrifici per salvare l'Italia', ibid., 7 Dec. 1979: Amendola's reply to the criticisms of his first article.

CONCLUSION

The PCI's experience in the 'governmental area' from 1976 to 1979 demonstrated clearly the limits of Berlinguer's version of Euro-communism. While Italy was the birthplace of this strategy, and the importance of the middle strata made the *via italiana* and the historic compromise appear particularly appropriate approaches to the national situation, it was precisely the weight and nature of these strata and of their political representatives which made Italy the least promising testing ground for a reformist programme such as the PCI envisaged.

In spite of these objective circumstances, and the electoral defeat of June 1979 which resulted from them, the PCI leadership shows few signs of revising the fundamentals of its strategy; nor does the Communist left, though still present, seem likely to offer a serious challenge to it. This weakness of the left can be attributed in the first place to the background and attitudes of the new generation of cadres, and the increase in the number of intellectuals and other members of the middle classes in the Party: evidently the critical mass necessary to make these a conservatising force (cf. Chapters 4 and 10) has been reached. Thus the hypothesis advanced in Chapter 4, Section 4, has been confirmed by developments in the Party since 1966. Further evidence for this conclusion is provided by the fact that the Turin federation, with the largest concentration of working-class cadres, has demonstrated its disquiet over the historic compromise more openly than the other four studied in Chapters 5 to 9.

Moreover, the economic crisis of the 1970s has certainly induced social changes, but they have not been as spectacular and disruptive as those of 1953-63. The challenges the last decade has posed the PCI have originated more from ideological changes. The crisis of hegemony which began in 1968 developed into a crisis of politics as such: new social forces, such as the women's movement, questioned the relevance of the traditional political parties to their problems. The Communist left was less able to offer a credible response to these new problems than it had been in the early 1960s; even the *Manifesto* group failed to fully appreciate their novelty.

By the beginning of the 1980s the Communist left appeared doomed to remain a permanent minority within the PCI. The very economic growth which had favoured its rise had eventually brought about a partial integration of the Party into the political system. But the Ingrao left had provided a valuable contribution to the development of a revolutionary strategy for the Western working class.

BIBLIOGRAPHY

1. Documents, Statistics and Government Sources

Officials of the five federations studied kindly gave me access to materials in the federations' archives. The following lists published materials only.

Camera dei Deputati, Segretariato generale *Annuario parlamentare 1963-1964*, vol. I (Rome, 1963)

Communist Party of Canada *The Road to Socialism in Canada: the Program of the Communist Party of Canada* [adopted 27-29 Nov. 1971] (Toronto, 1972)

Communist Party of Greece ['Exterior'] *The Ninth Congress of the Communist Party of Greece* (n.p. [1973])

Confcoop *Annuario generale della cooperazione italiana*, 2nd edn (Editrice cooperativa, Rome, 1965)

ISTAT (Istituto centrale di statistica) 1^O *censimento generale dell' agricoltura*, vol. II (Rome, 1962)

—— 2^O *censimento generale dell'agricoltura*, vol. II (Rome, 1970)

—— 9° *censimento generale della popolazione*, 1951, vol. I (Rome, 1956)

—— 10° *censimento generale della popolazione*, 1961 (Rome, 1964-8)

—— 11° *censimento generale della popolazione*, 1971, vol. II (Rome, 1974)

Ministero dell'Interno *Compendio dei risultati delle elezioni comunali e provinciali dal 1946 al 1960* (Istituto Poligrafico dello Stato, Rome, 1961)

—— *Compendio dei risultati delle elezioni politiche dal 1848 al 1958* (Istituto Poligrafico dello Stato, Rome, 1963)

—— *Elezione della Camera dei Deputati del 28 aprile 1963* (Istituto Poligrafico dello Stato, Rome, 1964)

Movimento studentesco *Document della rivolta universitaria*, (Laterza, Bari, 1968)

Parti communiste français (PCF) *Manifeste du parti communiste français – Pour une démocratie avancée, pour une France socialiste!* [adopted 5-6 Dec. 1968] (Editions sociales, Paris, 1969)

232

Partito comunista italiano (PCI) V^a *Conferenza nazionale – Atti e risoluzioni* (Editori Riuniti, Rome, 1964)

—— *Conferenze regionali del P.C.I. 1959* (Editori Riuniti, Rome, 1959)

—— *VII Congresso del Partito comunista italiano*, 1951 (Edizioni di Cultura Sociale, Rome, 1954)

—— *VIII Congresso del Partito comunista italiano – Atti e risoluzioni*, 1956 (Editori Riuniti, Rome, 1957)

—— *XI Congresso del Partito comunista italiano – Atti e risoluzioni*, 1966 (Editori Riuniti, Rome, 1966)

—— *Proposta di progetto a medio termine*, introduced by G. Napolitano (Editori Riuniti, Rome, 1977)

—— *La questione del 'Manifesto': Democrazia e unità del PCI* (Editori Riuniti, Rome, 1969)

—— Comitato regionale umbro *Il piano regionale umbro di sviluppo economico (Note informative e osservazioni)* (Perugia, n.d. [1963])

—— Federazione napoletana *Rapporto di attività del Comitato federale*, X Congresso, 1962 (Naples, 1962)

—— —— *Rapporto di attività del Comitato federale*, XI Congresso, 1966 (Naples, 1965)

—— —— *Risoluzione politica e nuovi organismi dirigenti*, XI Congresso (Naples, 1966)

—— —— *Risoluzioni e nuovi organismi dirigenti*, X Congresso, 1962 (Naples, n.d.)

—— Federazione di Perugia *Per l'Unità del Movimento democratico*, Assemblea degli eletti e dei dirigenti di Partito, 21 Feb. 1965 (Perugia, n.d. [1965])

—— Federazione torinese *Atti dell'assemblea dei comunisti della Fiat* (Turin, 1961)

—— —— *L'VIII Congresso (27-30 Maggio 1954) – Resconto* (Turin, 1954)

—— —— *Per il progresso di Torino e della Provincia, per una nuova politica nazionale di sviluppo economico – Atti del Convegno Economico della Federazione Torinese del P.C.I.*, 1957 (Turin, 1957)

—— Federazioni dell'Emilia e Romagna *Per il rinnovamento democratico e socialista dell'Emilia-Romagna e dell'Italia, Conferenza regionale del P.C.I.*, Bologna, 27-29 giugno 1959 (Bologna, 1959)

—— Istituto Gramsci *Tendenze del capitalismo italiano (Atti del convegno di Roma 23-25 marzo 1962)* (2 vols., Editori Riuniti, Rome, 1962)

——— Sezione centrale di organizzazione *Dati sulla organizzazione del partito* (Rome, 1968)
——— ——— *La forza del P.C.I. per la pace, la democrazia, il socialismo* (Rome, 1967)
——— ——— *Organizzazione del Partito comunista italiano* (Rome, 1961)
——— Sezione lavoro di massa *I lavoratori e il progresso tecnico: Atti del convegno tenuto all'Istituto Gramsci*, 29-30 giugno e 1 luglio 1956 (Editori Riuniti, Rome, 1956)
——— Ufficio di Segreteria *Forza e attività del Partito (Dati statistici)* (Rome [1955])

2. Periodicals

(a)   PCI National Periodicals

La città futura, Rome, 1964-6; bi-monthly; FGCI
Il Contemporaneo, Rome, 1958-; monthly, cultural
Critica marxista, Rome, 1963- ; bi-monthly; theoretical journal
Cronache meridionali, Naples, 1954-64; monthly; southern affairs
Nuova generazione, Rome, 1957-77; weekly; FGCI
Politica ed economia, Rome, new series 1970- ; bi-monthly; economic affairs
Rinascita, Rome, 1944- ; monthly to 1962, then weekly
L'Unità, main offices in Rome and Milan, but the local pages were also consulted for Modena, Naples and Turin; daily from 1943

(b)   PCI Local Periodicals

Battaglia operaia, Perugia, 1965
Piemonte cronache, Turin, 1962-
Puglia, Bari, 1963-

(c)   Other Periodicals

L'Astrolabio, Rome; independent left weekly
Avanti!, Rome; PSI official daily
Corriere della Sera, Milan; independent daily
L'Espresso, Rome; radical/socialist weekly
Il Manifesto, Rome; extraparliamentary left monthly, then daily
Mondo operaio, Rome; PSI monthly
Note e rassegne, Modena; independent left quarterly
Nuovo impegno, Pisa; Marxist–Leninist quarterly

Il Popolo, Rome; DC official daily
Quaderni di Rassegna Sindacale, Rome; CGIL bi-monthly
Ragionamenti, Milan; independent left monthly
La Repubblica, Rome; radical/socialist daily
Stern, Hamburg; popular weekly

3. Books and Selected Articles

(a)   General

Accornero, A. (ed.) *Problemi del movimento sindacale in Italia 1943-1973*, Annali Feltrinelli, XVI (1974-5) (Feltrinelli, Milan, 1976)

Allum, P.A. *L'Italia tra crisi e emergenza* (Guida, Naples, 1979)

——— 'The Italian Elections of 1963', *Political Studies*, XIII, 3 (Oct. 1965)

——— *Italy – Republic without Government?* (Weidenfeld & Nicolson, London, 1973)

Amyot, G. 'What is Eurocommunism?', *Canadian Dimension*, vol. 13, no. 4 (Nov.-Dec. 1978)

Anderson, P. 'Origins of the Present Crisis', *New Left Review*, 23 and 25 (Jan.-Feb. and May-June 1964)

Barbagli, M., Corbetta, P., Parisi, A. and Schadee, H.M.A. *Fluidità elettorale e classi sociali in Italia: 1968-1976* (Il Mulino, Bologna, 1979)

Blackmer, D.L.M. and Tarrow, S. (eds.) *Communism in Italy and France* (Princeton University Press, Princeton, NJ, 1975)

Borkenau, F. *International Communism* (Faber & Faber, London, 1938)

Cammett, J.M. 'Two Recent Polemics on the Character of the Italian Risorgimento', *Science and Society*, XXVII, 3 (Fall 1963)

Capecelatro, E.M. and Carlo, A. *Contro la questione meridionale* (Samonà e Savelli, Rome, 1972)

Convenevole, R. *Processo inflazionistico e redistribuzione del reddito* (Einaudi, Turin, 1977)

Corbetta, P. 'Novità e incertezze nel voto del 3 giugno: analisi dei flussi elettorali', *Il Mulino*, no. 265 (Sept.-Oct. 1979)

De Felice, F. *Fascismo, democrazia, Fronte popolare* (De Donato, Bari, 1973)

De Masi, D. and Fevola, G. *I lavoratori nell'industria italiana* (2 vols., Franco Angeli, Milan, 1974)

Ferrari, P. and Maisl, H. *Les groupes communistes aux assemblées*

parlementaires italiennes (1958–1963) et françaises (1962-1967)
(PUF, Paris, 1969)
Filo della Torre, P., Mortimer, E. and Story, J. (eds.) *Eurocommunism: Myth or Reality?* (Penguin, Harmondsworth, 1979)
Flechtheim, O.K. *Die KPD in der Weimarer Republik* (Europäische Verlagsanstalt, Frankfurt/Main, 1969)
Gramsci, A. *La costruzione del Partito comunista 1923-1926*, Opere, vol. 12 (Einaudi, Turin, 1971)
—— *Note sul Machiavelli sulla politica e sullo stato moderno*, Quaderni del carcere, vol. 4 (Einaudi, Turin, 1966)
—— *Quaderni del carcere*, ed. Valentino Gerratana (4 vols., Einaudi, Turin, 1975)
—— *Selections from the Prison Notebooks*, eds. Q. Hoare and G. Nowell Smith (Lawrence & Wishart, London, 1971)
Harding, N. *Lenin's Political Thought*, vol. 1 (Macmillan, London, 1977)
Hayek, F. *Storia dell'Internazionale comunista* (Editori Riuniti, Rome, 1969)
History of the Communist Party (Bolsheviks) of the Soviet Union (International Publishers, New York, 1938)
Hobsbawm, E. *Primitive Rebels* (Manchester University Press, Manchester, 1959)
—— *Revolutionaries* (Weidenfeld & Nicolson, London, 1973)
L'Internazionale comunista e il fascismo (CUEM, Milan, 1971)
Kautsky, K. *La via al potere*, 1909 (Laterza, Rome and Bari, 1969)
Lenin, V.I. *British Labour and British Imperialism* (Lawrence & Wishart, London, 1969)
—— *Imperialism, the Highest Stage of Capitalism*, 1917 (Peking, 1970)
—— *La rivoluzione proletaria e il rinnegato Kautsky*, 1918 (Edizioni in Lingue estere, Moscow, 1949)
Lockwood, D. 'The New Working Class', *Archives Européennes de Sociologie*, vol. 1, no. 2 (1960)
Lyttelton, A. *The Seizure of Power* (Weidenfeld & Nicolson, London, 1973)
Mallet, S. *La nouvelle classe ouvrière*, 1962 (Seuil, Paris, 1969)
Marcuse, H. *One-Dimensional Man* (Beacon Press, Boston, 1965)
Marcuse, H., Moore, B. Jr and Wolff, R.P. *A Critique of Pure Tolerance* (Beacon Press, Boston, 1965)
Meynaud, J. *Rapport sur la classe dirigeante italienne* (Etudes de science politique, Lausanne, 1964)

Michels, R. *Political Parties*, 1915 (Dover, New York, 1959)
—— *Il proletariato e la borghesia nel movimento socialista italiano*
(F.lli Bocca, Turin, 1908)
Mills, C.W. *The Power Elite* (Oxford University Press, New York, 1956)
Nairn, T. 'The English Working Class', *New Left Review*, 24 (Mar.-Apr.
1964)
'La Nostra Assemblea' (ed.) *Le radici di una rivolta* (Feltrinelli, Milan,
1977)
Parkin, F. *Class Inequality and Political Order*, 1971 (Paladin, London,
1972)
Parlato, V. (ed.) *Spazio e ruolo del riformismo* (Il Mulino, Bologna,
1974)
Passigli, S. 'Political Finance: Italy', *Journal of Politics*, vol. 25, no. 4
(Nov. 1963)
Penniman, H. (ed.) *Italy at the Polls: The Parliamentary Elections of
1976* (American Enterprise Institute, Washington, DC, 1977)
Pizzorno, A. (director) *Lotte operaie e sindacato in Italia: 1968-1972*
(Il Mulino, Bologna, 1974-8). The following volumes in this series
were consulted: Dolci, L. and Reyneri, E. *Magneti Marelli e Ercole
Marelli* (1974); Luppi, L. and Reyneri, E. *Autobianchi e Innocenti*
(1974); Regalia, I. and Regini, M. *Sit-Siemens e GTE* (1975); Regini,
M. and Santi, E. *Candy e Ignis* (1974); Pizzorno, A., Reyneri, E.,
Regini, M. and Regalia, I. *Lotte operaie e sindacato: il ciclo 1968-
1972 in Italia* (1978)
Poulantzas, N. 'On Social Classes', *New Left Review*, 78 (Mar.-Apr.
1973)
—— *Pouvoir politique et classes sociales* (Maspéro, Paris, 1968)
Procacci, G. *Le elezioni del 1874 e l'opposizione meridionale*
(Feltrinelli, Milan, 1956)
Przeworski, A. and Sprague, J. 'A History of Western European
Socialism', paper presented at the Annual Meeting of the American
Political Science Association, Washington, DC, Sept. 1977
Sartori, G. *Il Parlamento italiano* (ESI, Naples, 1963)
Seton-Watson, C. *L'Italia dal liberalismo al fascismo 1870-1925* (2
vols., Laterza, Bari, 1973)
Sivini, G. (ed.) *Partiti e partecipazione politica in Italia* (Giuffrè, Milan,
1969)
Stalin, J.V. *The Essential Stalin*, ed. B. Franklin (Doubleday, Garden
City, NJ, 1972)
—— *The Foundations of Leninism*, 1924 (Foreign Languages Press,
Peking, 1970)

Sylos Labini, P. *Saggio sulle classi sociali* (Laterza, Rome-Bari, 1975)

Tasca, A. *The Rise of Italian Fascism* (Fertig, New York, 1967)

Touraine, A. *Le mouvement de mai ou le Communisme utopique* (Seuil, Paris, 1968)

Zuckerman, A.S. *The Politics of Faction: Christian Democratic Rule in Italy* (Yale University Press, New Haven and London, 1979)

(b)   The PCI

Amendola, G. *Gli anni della Repubblica* (Editori Riuniti, Rome, 1976)

—— *Il rinnovamento del PCI*, interviewed by R. Nicolai (Editori Riuniti, Rome, 1978)

—— *Un'isola* (Rizzoli, Milan, 1980)

—— *Una scelta di vita* (Rizzoli, Milan, 1976)

Asor Rosa, A. *Scrittori e popolo* (Samonà e Savelli, Rome, 1964)

Badaloni, N. *Il marxismo come storicismo* (Feltrinelli, Milan, 1962)

Barbagli, M. and Corbetta, P. 'Partito e movimento: aspetti del rinnovamento nel PCI', *Inchiesta*, VIII, 31 (Jan.-Feb. 1978)

Barbagli, M., Corbetta, P. and Sechi, S. *Dentro il PCI* (Il Mulino, Bologna, 1979)

Berlinguer, E. *Austerità occasione per trasformare l'Italia* (Editori Riuniti, Rome, 1977)

—— *La proposta comunista: Relazione al Comitato centrale e alla Commissione centrale di controllo del Partito comunista italiano in preparazione del XIV Congresso* (Einaudi, Turin, 1975)

—— *La 'questione comunista' 1969-1975*, ed. A. Tatò (2 vols., Editori Riuniti, Rome, 1975)

—— *et al., I comunisti italiani e il Cile*, ed. R. Mechini (Editori Riuniti, Rome, 1973)

Blackmer, D.L.M. *Unity in Diversity* (MIT Press, Cambridge, Mass., and London, 1968)

Bocca, G. *Palmiro Togliatti* (Laterza, Rome-Bari, 1973)

Bonazzi, G. 'Problemi politici e condizione umana dei funzionari del PCI', *Tempi moderni*, 22 (July-Sept. 1965)

Cammett, J.M. *Antonio Gramsci and the Origins of Italian Communism* (Stanford University Press, Stanford, 1967)

Cassano, F. (ed.) *Marxismo e filosofia in Italia 1958-1971* (De Donato, Bari, 1973)

Casula, C.F. *Cattolici, comunisti e sinistra cristiana (1938-1945)* (Il Mulino, Bologna, 1976)

Cecchi, A. (ed.) *Storia del PCI attraverso i congressi* (Newton Compton, Rome, 1977)

Classe, consigli, partito (*Il Manifesto*, quaderno no. 2) (Alfani, Rome, 1974)

Colletti, L. 'Antonio Gramsci and the Italian Revolution', *New Left Review*, 65 (Jan.-Feb. 1971)

De Clementi, A. *Amadeo Bordiga* (Einaudi, Turin, 1971)

Galli, G. 'Il PCI rivisitato', *Il Mulino*, XX, 213 (Jan.-Feb. 1971)

Grifone, P. *Il capitale finanziario in Italia* (Einaudi, Rome, 1945)

Hellman, S. 'The PCI in Transition: The Origins of the Historic Compromise', paper presented at the Annual Meeting of the American Political Science Association, Chicago, 1976

Lanchester, F. 'La dirigenza di Partito: Il caso del PCI', *Il Politico*, XLI, 4 (Dec. 1976)

Luperini, R. *Gli intellettuali di sinistra e l'ideologia della ricostruzione nel dopoguerra* (Edizioni di Ideologie, Rome, 1971)

———— *Il PCI e il movimento studentesco* (Jaca Book, Milan, 1969)

Magri, L. 'Le origini del Manifesto – Appunti per l'introduzione al Seminario di Rimini (sett. 1973) sulle Tesi' (n.p. [1973])

Maitan, L. *Il movimento operaio in una fase critica* (Samonà e Savelli, Rome, 1966)

Mannheimer, R. 'Un'analisi territoriale del calo comunista', *Il Mulino*, XXVIII, 265 (Sept.-Oct. 1979)

Rodano, F. *Sulla politica dei comunisti* (Boringhieri, Turin, 1975)

Rossanda, R. *L'anno degli studenti* (De Donato, Bari, 1968)

Secchia, P. *L'azione svolta dal partito comunista in Italia durante il fascismo 1926-1932*, Annali Feltrinelli 1969 (Feltrinelli, Milan, 1970)

Sechi, S. *La pelle di zigrino* (Cappelli, Bologna, 1980)

Sereni, E. *La questione agraria nella rinascita nazionale italiana* (Einaudi, Rome, 1946)

Tarrow, S. *Peasant Communism in Southern Italy* (Yale University Press, New Haven and London, 1967)

———— 'The Political Economy of Stagnation: Communism in Southern Italy, 1960-70', *Journal of Politics*, 34, 1 (Feb. 1972)

Togliatti, P. 'A proposito del fascismo', *L'Internazionale comunista*, Aug. 1928

———— *La politica di Salerno* (Editori Riuniti, Rome, 1969)

———— *Problemi del movimento operaio internazionale* (Editori Riuniti, Rome, 1964). Reprinted as *Sul movimento operaio internazionale*, ed. F. Ferri (Editori Riuniti, Rome, 1972))

———— *Rinnovare l'Italia (Rapporto al V Congresso Nazionale del PCI)*, supplement to *Rinascita*, I, 4 (1945)

Vacca, G. (ed.) *PCI, Mezzogiorno, e intellettuali* (De Donato, Bari, 1973)

Weber, H. (ed.) *Parti communiste italien: aux sources de l'euro-communisme* (Christian Bourgeois, Paris, 1977)

(c)   Local Studies

Allum, P.A. 'Comportamento elettorale e ceti sociali a Napoli', *Nord e Sud*, n.s., X, 45 (106) (Sept. 1963)

———— *Politics and Society in Post-War Naples* (Cambridge University Press, Cambridge, 1973)

Amyot, G. 'La ripresa e la battaglia contro il neo-capitalismo (1955-1966)' in F. De Felice *et al., I comunisti a Torino 1919-1972* (Editori Riuniti, Rome, 1974)

Argilli, M. *Un anno in sezione: Vita di base del P.C.I.* (Edizioni della Libreria, Milan, 1970)

Blok, A. 'The South Italian Agro-Town', *Comparative Studies in Society and History*, II, 2 (Apr. 1969)

Cacciapuoti, S. *Storia di un operaio napoletano* (Editori Riuniti, Rome, 1972)

Casali, L. *et al., Movimento operaio e fascismo nell'Emilia-Romagna 1919-1923* (Editori Riuniti, Rome, 1973)

———— and Pacor, M. *Lotte sociali e guerriglia in pianura* (Editori Riuniti, Rome, 1972)

Cesarini Sforza, M. *Modena M Modena P* (Editori Riuniti, Rome, 1955)

D'Alema, G. *I comunisti modenesi per un nuovo indirizzo della politica italiana (rapporto tenuto all '8° Congresso Provinciale della Federazione Modenese del P.C.I., 25-28 Marzo, 1954)* ('La Verità' editrice, Modena, 1954)

D'Amico, V. 'La nuova situazione impone più iniziativa politica', Rome, Istituto Studi Comunisti, Frattocchie, ott. 1954- genn. 1955 (mimeo)

De Marco, C. 'La costituzione della confederazione generale del lavoro e la scissione di "Montesanto" (1943-44)', *Giovane critica*, 27 (summer 1971)

Garavini, S. and Pugno, E. *Gli anni duri alla Fiat* (Einaudi, Turin, 1974)

Gianotti, R. *Lotte e organizzazione di classe alla Fiat 1948-1970* (De Donato, Bari, 1970)

Gramegna, G. *Braccianti e popolo in Puglia* (De Donato, Bari, 1976)

Lanzardo, L. *Classe operaia e partito comunista alla Fiat: La strategia della collaborazione: 1945-1949* (Einaudi, Turin, 1971)

Macciocchi, M.A. *Lettere dall'interno del P.C.I. a Louis Althusser* (Feltrinelli, Milan, 1969)

Silverman, S. *Three Bells of Civilization* (Columbia University Press, New York and London, 1975)

APPENDIX: KEY TO INTERVIEWEES

Interviews are referred to in the Notes by date. Below the interviewees are identified. Unless otherwise indicated, the position given is that held at the time of the interview. Only fairly formal, lengthy interviews are recorded here.

Naples

6 Dec. 1971 Former member of the editorial board of *Cronache meridionali*
7 Dec. 1971 Former federal secretary
8 Dec. 1971 Employee of Chamber of Commerce, former PCI activist
17 Dec. 1971 Former federal secretary
12 Jan. 1972 Former trade-union functionary, member of extra-parliamentary group; former section secretary, member of extra-parliamentary group (joint interview)
Allum interview (1963) Federal secretary

Perugia

3 Nov. 1971 Senator, former federal secretary
4 Nov. 1971 (1) Deputy; (2) former federal functionary, now in extraparliamentary group; former PCI member, now in extraparliamentary group (joint interview); (3) regional secretary
5 Nov. 1971 Lawyer, local councillor
6 Nov. 1971 Regional president
7 Nov. 1971 Former secretary, *Associazione Italia-Cina*, and former PCI member

Turin

7 July 1972 Former secretary, Chamber of Labour
6 Oct. 1972 Federal secretary; regional secretary; university professor, long-time activist (joint interview)

7 Oct. 1972   Deputy, former regional secretary
8 Oct. 1972   Former deputy

Modena

8 Jan. 1972   Former federal secretary
1 Mar. 1972   Three *mezzadri*, PCI members of long standing (joint
  interview)
2 Mar. 1972   Federal functionary
4 Mar. 1972   President, Federcoop

Bari

10 July 1973   (1) University professor, PCI activist; (2) former
  secretary, FGCI; (3) university professor, PCI activist
11 July 1973   Lawyer, PCI activist of long standing
12 July 1973   Regional councillor
14 July 1973   University researcher, FGCI activist
24 Oct. 1973   University professor, PCI activist
25 Oct. 1973   Federal secretary
26 Oct. 1973   Former federal secretary
27 Oct. 1973   Secondary-school teacher, PCI activist of long standing

INDEX